BLOOMSBURY CURRICULUM BASICS

Teaching Primary Science

By Peter Riley

B L O O M S B U R Y

LONDON · OXFORD · NEW YORK · NEW DELHI · SYDNEY

Bloomsbury Education
An imprint of Bloomsbury Publishing Plc

50 Bedford Square, London, WC1B 3DP, UK
1385 Broadway, New York, NY 10018, USA
29 Earlsfort Terrace, Dublin 2, Ireland

www.bloomsbury.com

Bloomsbury is a registered trademark of Bloomsbury Publishing Plc

First published 2015

British Library Cataloguing-in-Publication Data
A catalogue record for this book is available from the British Library.

ISBN:
PB 9781472920652
ePub 9781472920676
ePDF 9781472920669

Library of Congress Cataloging-in-Publication Data
A catalog record for this book is available from the Library of Congress.

10 9 8 7 6

Typeset by Newgen Knowledge Works (P) Ltd., Chennai, India
Printed and bound in Great Britain by CPI Group (UK) Ltd, Croydon CR0 4YY

MIX
Paper from
responsible sources
FSC
www.fsc.org   FSC® C013604

To view more of our titles please visit www.bloomsbury.com

To Mr Richard Wright, staff and children of Settle Church of England Primary School North Yorkshire.

Online resources accompany this book at: www.bloomsbury.com/BCB-Teaching-Science

Please type the URL into your web browser and follow the instructions to access the resources. If you experience any problems, please contact Bloomsbury at: companionwebsite@bloomsbury.com

Other titles in the Bloomsbury Curriculum Basics series:

Teaching Primary History by Matthew Howorth

Teaching Primary Spanish by Amanda Barton and Angela McLachlan

Teaching Primary French by Amanda Barton and Angela McLachlan

Teaching Primary Computing by Martin Burrett

Table of Contents

Introduction

How has the curriculum changed?

The National Curriculum for science was first introduced into the United Kingdom in 1988. It was divided into four sections: Sc1 Scientific enquiry, Sc2 Life and living processes, Sc3 Materials and their properties and Sc4 Physical processes. The subject was examined at the end of Year 2 and Year 6 and children were allocated levels of attainment. Later the QCA produced units for each of the major topics in Sc2, Sc3 Sc4 and provided suggestions for Sc1. These units became widely used and have formed the basis of teaching strategies and resource banks to the present day.

In 2014 a new science curriculum was introduced. The original four sections became Working scientifically, Biology, Chemistry and Physics. By then science was no longer examined at Year 2 and Year 6 and in the new curriculum the levels had been abandoned with the children now having to demonstrate mastery in the various areas of the subject.

The content of the science curriculum is divided into three age groups – Key Stage 1, Lower Key Stage 2 and Upper Key Stage 2. Dividing up the curriculum in this way provides a basis for setting up a more flexible approach.

As schools still retain many valuable resources and teaching strategies which are relevant in the new curriculum, this book begins by looking at the changes. These should be viewed with an eye to keeping what is relevant in your school to build your new curriculum.

In the online resources that accompany this book (see page iii for how to access) there is a table comparing the QCA programmes of study (units) with those in the new curriculum. The topics in the right hand column are the ones that form the new curriculum but you may find much from some of the QCA units you have used to adapt when building your new science curriculum.

In addition to this, there is also a table that shows the statements in Scientific enquiry (Sc1) compared with the skills to be acquired in the Working scientifically section of the new curriculum.

In the new curriculum, working scientifically is not to be taught as a separate topic but integrated in the study of biology, chemistry and physics. The following table shows how these skills build up as the children move through their primary science education.

KS1 Planning	Lower KS2 Planning	Upper KS2 Planning
Asking simple questions and recognising that they can be answered in different ways	Asking relevant questions and using different types of scientific enquiry to answer them Setting up practical enquiries, comparative and fair tests	Planning different types of scientific enquiries to answer questions, including recognising and controlling variables where necessary
KS1 Obtaining and presenting evidence Performing simple tests Observing closely using simple equipment Gathering and recording data to help in answering questions	**Lower KS2 Obtaining and presenting evidence** Making systematic and careful observations, and where appropriate, taking accurate measurements using standard units, using a range of equipment, including thermometers and data loggers Gathering, recording, classifying and presenting data in a variety of ways to help in answering questions Recording findings using simple scientific language, drawings, labelled diagrams, keys, bar charts and tables Reporting on findings from enquiries, including oral explanations, displays of presentations of results and conclusions	**Upper KS2 Obtaining and presenting evidence** Taking measurements, using a range of scientific equipment, with increasing accuracy and precision, taking repeat readings where appropriate Recording data and results of increasing complexity using scientific diagrams and labels, classification keys, tables, scatter graphs, bar and line graphs Reporting and presenting findings from enquiries, including conclusions, causal relationships and explanations of and degree of trust in results, in oral and written forms such as displays
KS1 Considering evidence and evaluating Using their observations and ideas to suggest answers to questions Identifying and classifying	**Lower KS2 Considering evidence and evaluating** Using results to draw simple conclusions, make predictions for new values, suggest improvements and raise further questions Identifying differences, similarities or changes related to simple scientific ideas and processes Using straightforward scientific evidence to answer questions or support their findings	**Upper KS2 Considering evidence and evaluating** Using test results to make predictions to set up further comparative and fair tests Identifying scientific evidence that has been used to support or refute ideas or arguments.

For convenience, in the curriculum, the programmes of study for science are set out year by year (and the structure of this book mirrors that) but schools are only required to teach the relevant programme of study by the end of the key stage. This means that within each key stage schools can introduce content earlier or later than set out in the programme of study to match the aptitude and abilities of the children or to fit in with a themed approach to curriculum planning.

Also schools can introduce content from a higher key stage into a lower key stage if appropriate. An example of this could be a school where there was a strong development of studying electricity, say in making models in Year 2. This could still continue by introducing elements of the electricity content from Lower Key Stage 2.

Scientific enquiry in the new curriculum

Although the words 'scientific enquiry' do not appear as a section heading of the curriculum, as in Sc1 greater emphasis is made in considering five lines of enquiry. In the past, fair testing was considered as the main example of scientific enquiry, even though other kinds were also being made. In the new curriculum five lines of scientific enquiry are set out. They are:

- **Identifying and classifying**: Identify and group leaves according to shape, and objects according to their material properties.
- **Observing over time:** Observe growth of flowers and vegetables they have planted, and record weather features.
- **Fair testing:** Effect of water/light/warmth on plant growth, effect of water/warmth on seed germination, effect of soap on cleaning a material, effect of temperature on liquid flow, comparing drainage of different soils.
- **Pattern seeking:** Distribution of plants such as daisies or dandelions in a lawn, leg length/stride length, foot size/weight, size or parachute speed of descent, temperature and wind direction, temperature/cloud cover, length of stem/leaves.
- **Researching using secondary sources:** Having learnt that some animals are herbivores and some are carnivores, using sources to find more. Finding cloud types and using them in weather reports.

Note that lines of enquiry can be linked together. For example, a number of different soils could be grouped according to whether they were clay soils or sandy soils (identifying and classifying) They could then be compared to see how they drain a certain amount of water (fair testing). The results may show that the sandier the soil the more quickly it drains the water (pattern seeking).

Glossary of terms in practical science

Anomaly: a result which does not fit in with a tend or pattern that may be due to some error in carrying out the investigation.
Comparative test: an investigation involving a comparison perhaps about how particular features differ between two different plants of animals.
Conclude: a statement based on the data collected describing what the investigation showed.
Control: a test in which all the factors except one are kept the same while one factor such as temperature is varied.
Data: the information collected during an investgation.
Dependent variable: in a controlled experiment the variable is the thing that changes as a result of varying a particular factor.
Experiment: the practical part of an investigation.
Factor: something which may affect a process. For example, light is a factor in plants producing food. Factors are sometimes called variables. (see dependent and independent variables)
Fair test: a test in which all the factors are controlled except one.
Hypothesis: an idea based on previous knowledge which is used to set up an investingaton.
Independent variable: the variable that is altered in a fair test.
Prediction: a guess as to what will be the outcome of an experiment based on knowledge of the subject being studied.

Revising or planning a new scheme of work

The new scheme of science work in your school should meet these requirements.

- Understand the world through biology, chemistry and physics.
- Recognise the power of rational explanation.
- Understand the nature, processes and methods of science.
- Be aware of the uses and implications of science now and in the future.

As a start to setting up your school science curriculum you may like to consider the following ideas to help you focus on the requirements above.

Understand the nature, processes and methods of science and be aware of the uses and implications of science now and in the future – these are the fundamental features of scientific literacy which everyone should possess. Briefly these are:

- They understand the way that scientists work.
- They have a wide knowledge of the areas of science.
- They are able to understand a scientific topic in adult life and use it as a basis for making rational decisions.

You may also like to consider how a scientist works in order for the children to become scientifically literate. Briefly these are:

- Observant, curious, imaginative, creative.
- Disciplined, analyst of data, can construct rational explanations and draw conclusions.
- Sceptical of their work and that of others.

Using the two guides above you could also consider how the children can develop their science skills as they progress through the primary science curriculum. Briefly these are:

- Key Stage 1: 'The budding scientist' – exploring by mainly first hand experience with some research. Record and review their work in a variety of ways.
- Lower Key Stage 2: 'The blossoming scientist' – exploring, talking about, testing and developing ideas. Awareness of the function of things, their relationships and interactions. Increased use of writing about science.
- Upper Key Stage 2: 'The maturing scientist' – going deeper and wider still into the three sciences. Asking own questions, analysing functions, relationships and interactions. More thorough investigation with emphasis of trust in results and the consideration of more abstract ideas.

How to use this book

This book follows the structure of the National Curriculum. It is divided into three parts: Key Stage 1, Lower Key Stage 2 and Upper Key stage 2. Each part contains two years and each year is divided into the four or five main areas of study found in the curriculum.

Each area of study follows the same format. It includes:

What does the curriculum say?

The statutory requirements from the National Curriculum. The extracts are from DfE, *The National Curriculum in England: Key stages 1 and 2 framework documents* (September 2013), pp 144–175. The full document can be found here: www.gov.uk/government/publications/national-curriculum-in-england-primary-curriculum

What do I need to know?

Everything you need to know to teach the area of study including background information, as well as:

- **Vocabulary:** key words are explained
- **Progression:** section suggesting either how the topic can be used to form a foundation to the area of study which can be further developed over the years in the primary scheme of work or how it links to a previous topic and goes on to support work in a future topic
- **Technical tips:** where preparations involve constructing apparatus or rehearsing practical demonstrations. Prior to this, check your school policies on practical work in science and select activities for which you are confident to take responsibility. The ASE book *Be Safe*, fourth edition (see www.ase.org.uk/home/) provides information for health and safety in school science and technology for teachers of 3–12 year olds.
- **Useful websites:** links for sites that include resources for the lesson plans or further research.

Lesson plans

Each area of study includes three lesson plans, following the format:

- Working scientifically skills (specifying those the lesson addresses)
- Scientific enquiry type (specifying those the lesson addresses)
- You will need
- Preparation
- Getting started
- Class activities
- Plenary

Further lesson ideas and activities

The three lessons are followed by a list of ideas and activities section which builds on the three lessons to help you to complete the construction of your science scheme for the area of study.

Cross curricular links

Finally, the area of study ends with suggestions for how the previous content can be linked to other areas of the curriculum.

Part 1:
Key Stage 1 (Years 1–2)

What does the curriculum say?

The principal focus of science teaching in Key Stage 1 is to enable pupils to experience and observe phenomena, looking more closely at the natural and humanly-constructed world around them. They should be encouraged to be curious and ask questions about what they notice. They should be helped to develop their understanding of scientific ideas by using different types of scientific enquiry to answer their own questions, including observing changes over a period of time, noticing patterns, grouping and classifying things, carrying out simple comparative tests, and finding things out using secondary sources of information. They should begin to use simple scientific language to talk about what they have found out and communicate their ideas to a range of audiences in a variety of ways. Most of the learning about science should be done through the use of first-hand practical experiences, but there should also be some use of appropriate secondary sources, such as books, photographs and videos. 'Working scientifically' is described separately in the programme of study, but must always be taught through and clearly related to the teaching of substantive science content in the programme of study. Throughout the notes and guidance, examples show how scientific methods and skills might be linked to specific elements of the content. Pupils should read and spell scientific vocabulary at a level consistent with their increasing word reading and spelling knowledge at Key Stage 1.

Year 1: Plants

What does the curriculum say?

- *Identify and name a variety of common wild and garden plants, including deciduous and evergreen trees.*
- *Identify and describe the basic structure of a variety of common flowering plants, including trees.*

What do I need to know?

Plants are found in most places on the planet. They are divided into groups: algae, mosses and liverworts, ferns and horsetails, conifers, flowering plants, fungi and lichen. The main focus of the work on plants in is on flowering plants although conifers must also be studied. When looking for common wild plants, children may also find mosses and ferns. Mosses form mats or cushions on walls and stones, and ferns can be recognised by their large feather-like leaves. Algae form green slime on damp walls and lichens (an association of a type of alga with a fungus) form grey or orange crusty structures on walls. Fungi in the form of bracket fungi on trees and toadstools may also be seen.

Some wild plants in flower throughout the year are:
January: Shepherd's Purse, Snowdrop
February: Shepherd's Purse, Chickweed, Snowdrop
March: Lesser Celandine, Daffodil
April: Primrose, Cowslip, Bluebell
May: Buttercup, Herb Robert, Red and White Clovers
June: Wood Sorrel, Anemone, Stitchwort
July: Pansy, Bramble, Meadow Sweet
August: Poppy, Thistles, Convolvulus
September: Speedwell, Foxglove
October: Wild Pansy, Ivy, White Clover
November: Chickweed, Daisy, Ivy
December: Shepherd's Purse, Daisy

See the Useful websites box for links to flowering plant images.

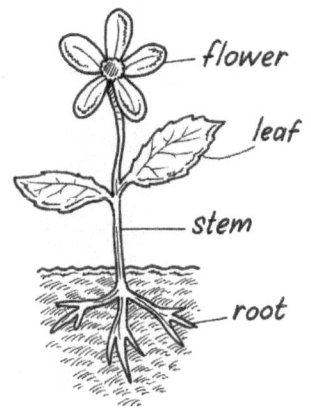

Vocabulary

Moss: a plant growing close to ground or rocks with tiny leaves.
Fern: a plant with large leaves that look like feathers.
Conifer: a plant that has woody cones.
Evergreen: a tree that has green leaves all through the year.
Deciduous: a tree that loses its leaves in the autumn and grows new ones in the spring.
Root: a part which holds the plant in the ground and takes up water from the soil.
Stem: a part which supports the leaves and flowers and takes water to them.
Leaf: a part that makes food for the plant.
Flower: a part that makes seeds.
Blossom: the groups of flowers on a tree.
Petals: the large colourful parts of flowers that attract insects.
Fruit: a part that develops from the flower that contains the seeds.
Seed: a capsule from which a new plant grows.
Bulb: a round shape made of leaves from which a flower may grow.
Trunk: the woody stem of a tree.
Branches: parts which grow out of the stem that carry more leaves and flowers.

Progression

This is the first area of study about plants in the National Curriculum. The children will have studied plants in their foundation course in reception and you should revise this in the first lesson to let them see how their earlier work is relevant to the work they are about to do. In this area of study the children should build up a foundation in plant study (botany) by learning about plant structure and use their knowledge to identify a wide range of plants. They should also briefly study where the plants grow to give them a notion of the concept of habitat for later work.

Useful websites

Lesson 1: https://gobotany.newenglandwild.org/simple/
Lesson 2: www.mbgnet.net/bioplants/parts.html
Lesson 3: www.kidsgardening.org/node/96821 www.thompson-morgan.com/
top-10-easy-to-grow-flowers peterdriley.com/growing-plants

Lesson 1 Plants outside

Working scientifically skills: Observing
Scientific enquiry type: Identifying, classifying and grouping

You will need: a photograph of the school grounds or a park, a camera, a clipboard and at least one teaching assistant/helper.
Preparation: You will need access to the school grounds or a park. Make a preliminary visit and identify as many different kinds of plants as you can. The list should aim to include: moss growing on a wall or between pavement stones; ferns growing in a shady area; a lawn area with daisies, dandelions and clover in it; longer unmown grass where the grasses have produced their flower heads (there may be plants with colourful flowers growing in this region, which you should identify); at least two different kinds of deciduous tree and one evergreen tree, preferably a conifer.

Getting started

Show the children the photograph of the general area you will visit and ask if they recognise it. Look for an answer about it being the local park or school grounds. Ask the children what plants they can see in the picture and then ask how many different kinds they think they will find.

Class activities

- Take the children to the outside area following the school policies for outdoor work.
- Take the children to one of the plants you identified on your preliminary visit and tell the children its name. Ask them to comment on the plant's appearance.
- Let one helper note down the plant and the children's comments on the clipboard and let the other helper take a picture of the plant.
- Repeat steps 2 and 3 with all the other plants on your list then return to the classroom.

Plenary

Remind the children about the number of different plants they had predicted and ask the helper to add up the plants on the clipboard list. Ask the children to name a plant they particularly liked and give reasons for their answer.

At a later time, when the photographs have been loaded on to the computer, display them in turn on the whiteboard and ask the children to identify each plant.

Lesson 2 The parts of a plant

Working scientifically skills: Observing closely, using simple equipment; identifying and classifying
Scientific enquiry type: Identifying, classifying and grouping

You will need: a large potted plant that can be easily raised out of its pot to show the roots, a set of potted plants (enough for one between every two children) which each show leaves, stem and flower, magnifying glasses, paper, pencils and coloured pencils.
Preparation: The potted plants could be a mixture of three or four kinds and feature some with hairy leaves and stems (geraniums) and some with smooth leaves and stems (thyme).

Getting started
Ask the children what they know about plants. Look for answers that they are green, they have flowers and they grow from seeds.

Tell the children that we have parts of our body like arms and legs. Ask them what body parts plants have. Look for answers that they have leaves, stems, flowers and roots (you may not get them all).

Show the children the large plant and point out the flowers, stem and leaves. Raise it out of the pot to show the roots. Write the four parts on the board and define them from the vocabulary.

Class activities
- Issue the paper, pencils and a plant between two children. Ask them to examine their plant and then draw it and colour it in.
- Ask the children to label their plant. To do this they should write the appropriate word from the board next to the feature it relates to then draw a label line between the two.
- Let two pairs of children share their plants and ask them to identify similarities and differences.
- Let the children swap plants until they have seen and compared all the different kinds.
- Ask the children to say how they would put the plants into groups. Gather the plants and group them following their suggestions.

Plenary
Review how the plants were grouped. Say that scientists sometimes use equipment to help them in their observations and introduce the magnifying glasses. Let the children examine the plants with them and discover that the plants can be put into a hairy group and smooth group.

Technical tip

To use a magnifying glass, place it about 8 cm from your eye and about 15 cm from the object you are looking at. Move the glass to and fro to see a magnified view of the object.

Lesson 3 From seed to plant

Working scientifically skills: Observing; gathering and recoding data to help in answering questions
Scientific enquiry type: Observing over time

You will need: a soaked broad bean seed from a health food store (no pesticides) and a plant pot with compost for each pair of children, spoons, broad bean seeds, a warm safe place to store the plant pot such as a windowsill, access to a camera, pictures of a broad bean plant in flower and pictures or a specimen of a broad bean pod showing the seeds.

Getting started
Ask the children to name the parts of a plant. Then say that plants make seeds and ask where they might be made. Look for an answer about the flower. Show the children a picture of a broad bean plant in flower and then a picture showing the broad bean pod and say that it forms from the flower. Show the children the soaked broad bean seeds and say that they form inside the pod.

Class activities
- Tell the children that in time the seeds would fall into soil and ask them what might happen to them. List the ideas on the board and look for one about the seed growing into another plant. Ask the children how they might make an investigation to see what happens when a bean seed goes into the soil.
- Let the children fill their plant pot with compost using a spoon. Ask the children to decide how deep the seed should be planted and steer them towards deciding on a depth of about 2 cm.
- Let the children make a hole, put in their seed and cover it up. Let them make a label for their plant pot and stick it on. They should place it on the windowsill and leave it for a few days. (You may need to check that the compost remains damp during this time.)
- Ask the children how they will find out if the seed has changed. Look for an answer about digging carefully. Ask them what they might expect to find. Look for an answer about it turning into a plant with a root and a stem and leaves. Let the children carefully dig out their seeds onto a paper towel and photograph or draw what they see. (The seed coat should have split and the root should be starting to grow). They should record the number of days since the seed was sown.
- Let the children replant their seed and leave for a few more days then repeat step 4. This can be repeated several times (each time noting the day since sowing) until the plant has produced a stem with leaves.

Plenary
Review the growth of the plant from a seed, noting the days when root, stem and leaf appear. If it is spring or summer you could repot the plants and let them produce flower buds, flowers and pods.

Further lesson ideas and activities

1. If you are teaching lesson 2 in the autumn you may like to extend it by considering the leaves of deciduous trees. Put a selection of leaves from the following trees in clear plastic bags: oak, sycamore, birch and beech. (Note that horse chestnut and ash are large compound leaves and are not suitable for studies on basic leaf structure.) Issue the bags to pairs of children and let them arrange the leaves into groups according to their shape. Let the children draw and colour one of each type of leaf, then match each of their drawings to four labelled pictures of the leaves that you have displayed from a book or the internet. You could assess the children's work for accuracy in drawing the shape and the distribution of colours.

2. Lesson 3 takes a few weeks to complete. You could speed up the children's appreciation of the changes by planting some seeds yourself: one week, two weeks and three weeks before you plan to do the lesson. Use the introduction from lesson 3, then tell them you planted a seed last week and you wonder what might have happened. You can use this approach with the other seeds you planted so that the children can see the change quickly. Tell the children that scientists repeat experiments to check the results to make sure the conclusions are correct. You could then introduce the second part of lesson 3 as a way for the children to check your experiment.

3. After making sure the children are familiar with the basic structure of a plant and how the structures form as the plant grows from the seed, you can introduce the bulb as another structure from which some plants grow. You should show the children an onion and ask them to describe its shape then introduce the word 'bulb'. Carefully cut one in half vertically and point out the following parts. The thick disk at the bottom is a flat stem. Below it small roots grow out and above it are the bases of leaves that have swollen up with stored food (the food we eat). You could show how an onion bulb can grow by filling a wide necked plastic bottle with water to the brim then placing the bulb, stem side down, into the water. Over the following days, roots will grow from the stem and leaves will start to grow out of the top. The children could compare this growth with the growth of the plant from the seed.

Cross curricular links

- Lesson 1 can be used as an introduction to plant study in any school based ecological project linked to conservation and sustainability.
- Lesson 3 can be linked with school based topics on healthy eating. It provides a knowledge of basic plant structure which can be extended by looking at the vegetables we eat – perhaps by visiting a supermarket to look at the vegetables and the plant parts they come from.
- Lesson 3 and the bulb activity can be linked to any general seasonal studies about spring as this is the time when plants develop from seeds and bulbs.
- Within the science curriculum the work in this section can be used with the seasonal changes in a later section in Year 1. It can also be used in support of the section on herbivores in 'Animals, including humans' in Year 1 and forms the foundation for plant work in Year 2.

Year 1: Animals, including humans

What does the curriculum say?

- *Identify and name a variety of common animals including fish, amphibians, reptiles, birds and mammals.*
- *Identify and name a variety of common animals that are carnivores, herbivores and omnivores.*
- *Describe and compare the structure of a variety of common animals (fish, amphibians, reptiles, birds and mammals, including pets).*
- *Identify, name, draw and label the basic parts of the human body and say which part of the body is associated with each sense.*

What do I need to know?

Animals can be divided into two groups: vertebrates and invertebrates. Vertebrates are often referred to as animals with backbones and have an inside skeleton of bone or cartilage (as in sharks). These are the animals considered in this area of the curriculum. Invertebrates do not have an inside skeleton of bone and include animal groups such as insects, spiders, worms and molluscs. You may wish to introduce invertebrates in your study of seasons in Year 1, and they will form part of habitat studies in Year 2.

The vertebrate group is divided into five large groups called classes: fish, amphibians, reptiles, birds and mammals. Fish possess scales and fins and lay eggs in water. Examples are goldfish and fish commonly kept in tropical fish tanks such as angelfish and tetras. Amphibians have a slimy skin and most have four limbs and lay eggs in water. Examples are the frog and toad (note, a toad is exceptional in having a dry warty skin) and the newt. Reptiles have dry scaly skin and lay soft-shelled eggs on land. Many have four legs such as the lizard, crocodile and tortoise while snakes such as the grass snake and the adder (the UK's only poisonous snake) do not have legs. Birds have two wings and feathers and they lay hard-shelled eggs in nests. Starlings, house sparrows and blackbirds are common examples found in school grounds. Mammals have fur and suckle their young with milk. There are three subgroups: egg-laying mammals (the platypus), pouched mammals (kangaroo), and placental mammals whose young develop entirely in the womb (cattle, mice, humans).

Interesting fact

A blue whale weighing 190 tonnes and measuring 27.6 m is the largest animal that has ever lived.

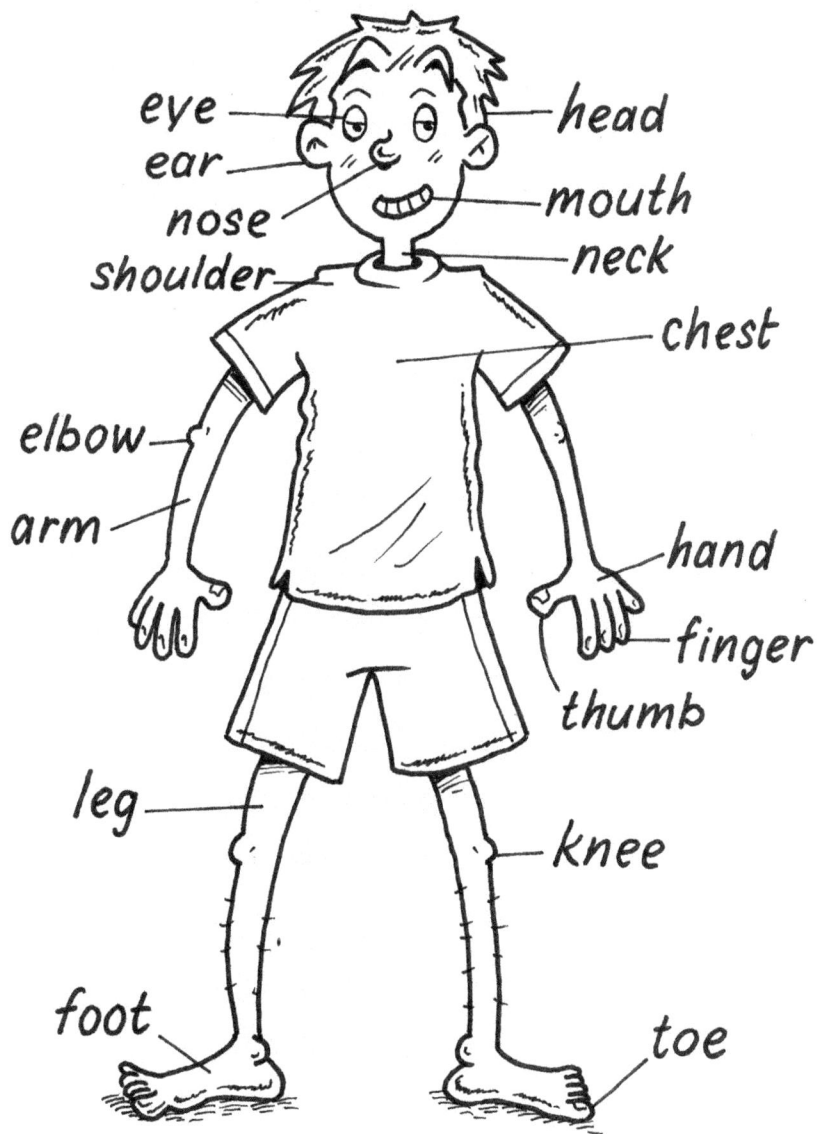

eye

ear

nose

shoulder

head

mouth

neck

chest

elbow

arm

hand

finger

thumb

leg

knee

foot

toe

Vocabulary

Fish: animals covered in scales and that have fins.
Amphibians: animals with non-scaly skin. Most types have four legs and have a tadpole stage in the life cycle.
Reptiles: animals with a scaly skin. Most have four legs but a large group are limbless.
Birds: animals with feathers and the front pair of limbs developed into wings. All possess a beak.
Mammals: animals that have hairy skin. For most the hair is tightly packed to form fur.
Carnivores: animals that eat other animals for food.
Herbivores: animals that eat plants for food.
Omnivores: animals that eat animals and plants for food.

Progression

This is the first area of study about animals in the National Curriculum. It introduces the vertebrate group to which humans belong and the study of human biology is begun in this topic and continued through all the other years. The work on general vertebrates forms a foundation for studying habitats in Years 2, 4, 5 and 6 and evolution and inheritance in Year 6.

Technical tip

All references to photographs should be found on the internet and displayed on the whiteboard or taken from a book and displayed using a visualiser.

Useful websites

Lesson 2

Shark: peterdriley.com/all-about-sharks
Rabbit: sciencenordic.com/how-wild-rabbit-was-domesticated
A bear eating a fish: fwallpapers.com/view/bear-eating-fish
A bear eating berries: www.flickr.com/photos/cvhainesphotos/10008833516
Goldfish: www.practicalfishkeeping.co.uk/content.php?sid=5679

Lesson 1 Arranging animals into groups

Working scientifically skills: Observing; using their observations and ideas to suggest answers to questions
Scientific enquiry type: Identifying, classifying and grouping

You will need: the following plastic model animals: a shark, any other plastic fish, a plastic frog, a crocodile, a snake, a duck, a chicken, an eagle or other plastic bird, a lion, a tiger, a goat, a horse, and two or three model dinosaurs which clearly have a scaly skin. The children will also need magnifying glasses.

Getting started
Show the children your collection of model animals. Hold up each one in turn and ask the children to name them. Tell the children that there are millions of different animals in the world. In order to study them, scientists put them into groups and this is what we will do with these models.

Class activities
- Tell the children that in order to put them into groups, scientists look at the bodies of the animals and see how they are different from each other and how they are similar. Say that we are going to look and see how the animals are different from each other. Pick up a fish and ask them to compare it with a goat and establish that the fish has fins. Look for fins on the birds, the crocodile and the frog. Conclude that animals with fins could be put into one group and called the fish group. Look through the collection and place all the fish together in one group.
- Repeat with the birds, establishing that they have feathers and wings which separate them from the other animals.
- Gather the frog, crocodile, snake, lion, tiger, goat and horse together and ask how they could be separated into groups. Hold up the goat and ask which animals have similar features. Look for an answer about fur then group the lion, tiger, goat and horse together and say that animals in this group are called mammals.
- Pass the plastic frog and the crocodile around the class and ask the children to say how they are different. They may mention body shapes but look for an answer about the crocodile being covered in scales and the frog's skin being smooth. Say that animals that live on land and have scales are called reptiles and animals that are found in water and on land and have a smooth skin are called amphibians. Pass around the snake and ask the children to decide if it is a reptile or an amphibian.
- Let the children divide a piece of paper into five sections and head them: fish, amphibian, reptile, bird and mammal. Ask them to draw an example of each type of animal from the collection and write its name.

Plenary
Pass round the dinosaurs and ask the children to decide which group they belong to. When all the dinosaurs have been examined, ask the children to put their hand up if they think they belong to any of the groups: fish, amphibians, reptiles, birds or mammals. Explain that the presence of scales places them in the reptile group. Now ask the children to look at themselves and decide which group they belong to. Repeat the grouping and explain they belong to the mammal group because they have hair. You may like to let them confirm this by using magnifying glasses to look at the hairs on their skin.

Lesson 2 Looking more closely at animals

Working scientifically skills: Observing closely; identifying and classifying; gathering and recording data to help in answering questions
Scientific enquiry type: Identifying, classifying and grouping

You will need: photographs of a shark, a rabbit, a bear eating a fish, a bear eating berries and a goldfish; if possible a tank containing goldfish or a video of goldfish swimming.

Getting started
Remind the children of the five groups of animals they learnt about last lesson. Ask them to give at least one example of each and say why it belongs to a particular group. Say that we are going to look in more detail at each of the animal groups but before we do that we are going to look at how animals feed.

Class activities
- Show the children the picture of the shark. Ask them to tell you what they know about it. Look for an answer about what it eats. They may say people, but steer them towards seals and say that it is an animal that eats other animals and we call such animals carnivores. Ask the children if they can think of any other animals that might be carnivores and look for answers about crocodiles and lions.
- Show the children a picture of a rabbit and ask what group it belongs to and why. Ask about the rabbit's food and look for an answer about leaves and grass. Say that the rabbit eats food from plants not animals. Animals that feed in this way are called herbivores. Challenge the children to think of more animals that are herbivores and look for answers about sheep, cattle, goats, and guinea pigs.
- Show the children two pictures of a bear: one eating a fish and one eating berries. Ask the children to identify the animal and say to which animal group it belongs. Point out that the animal eats both plants and animals and is called an omnivore. Ask the children to think of another animal that is an omnivore. This might prove difficult. If so, suggest a pig and ask them to think about the food they eat. The children should then understand that pigs are omnivores too.
- Say that once scientists have grouped the animals according to their structures and the way they feed, they try to describe them and to find out more. Let the children look at the goldfish in the tank and ask them to describe them and their actions (or show them the video of goldfish swimming). Look for answers regarding the fish having colours, scales, fins on the back and underneath, some fins in pairs, a tail fin, large eyes, a mouth, gill slits which open and close as the fish breathes. Tell the children that goldfish feed on plants, worms and water shrimps and ask them what kind of feeder they are. Look for the answer 'omnivore.'
- Let the children draw and write about goldfish. They can sit by the tank to make their drawings or draw from pictures of goldfish on the whiteboard. Assess their work on how accurately they have drawn the fish shape, positioning of fins, eyes and gills, spelling of labels, and positioning of label lines. In their writing, look for descriptions of fish swimming, having moving bodies and fins, having opening and closing mouths and gill slits, and being omnivores.

Plenary
Review all the work that has been done in class and create a display of their work on goldfish.

Lesson 3 Looking at ourselves

Working scientifically skills: Observing closely; gathering and recording data to help in answering questions
Scientific enquiry type: Comparative test

You will need: a roll of wallpaper about 1.5 m long (use the back), cardboard models of facial features (about equal size to those of a six year old): a nose, two eyes, two ears, and a mouth with a tongue hanging out; pots (a set for each group if you decide to split up the class) labelled A–F, covered in muslin and containing one each of: lemon pieces, apple pieces, crushed garlic, vinegar, curry powder, and talcum powder.

Getting started
Ask for a volunteer to lie on the blank piece of wallpaper and ask other children to draw around the outline of the volunteer's body. The arms should be slightly away from the sides of the body and the fingers and thumbs should be spread so that they can be drawn around. When the outline is complete secure it to the wall and say it is ready for labelling.

Class activities
- Ask volunteers to label the hair, head, neck, shoulder, chest, ribs, arm, elbow, wrist, hand, finger, thumb, hips, leg, knee, foot and toes.
- Let each child then make a drawing of themselves and label it using the large labelled picture to help them.
- Tell the children that you want to add more detail to the head and ask for suggestions. As they are suggested, get volunteers to stick on two cardboard ears, two cardboard eyes, a cardboard nose and a mouth with a tongue sticking out.
- Tell the children that these new parts of the head allow us to sense things. Say our eyes can sense light coming from things around us. Take the children to the class window and ask them how far they can see. Say our ears sense the sounds around us. Ask the children to be silent and listen for sounds around them. Ask them to tell you what they heard.
- Ask the children to sit back in their places and put out their tongues. Tell them that their tongues sense the tastes in food and that there are five different tastes: sweet (sugar), savoury (meaty), salty, sour (vinegar, lemon juice), and bitter (coffee). Ask the children to put in their tongues and smile or frown if they like a particular taste. List the five tastes again. Count up the responses and put them in a table. Discuss the results such as most people like sweet and savoury foods but dislike bitter tasting foods.
- Allow the children to sniff the pots and tell you what they think each one contains. These should be noted down. (Run this part in groups as long as you have an adult to supervise each group.)
- Tell the children that there is another part of the body which gives us the sense of touch. Ask for its name and look for the answer 'skin'.

Plenary
Return to the life size drawing and review the parts of the body, getting the children to touch each part as you mention them. Briefly discuss the senses then read out the results of the smell test (and the touch test, if conducted) to find out who were the best detectives.

Further lesson ideas and activities

1. In early spring, arrange for frogs and frogspawn to be brought into the classroom. Let the children look at the frogs and point out their smooth slimy skin and lack of scales, features which place them in the amphibian group. Release the frogs after they have been observed but keep the frogspawn and let the children observe it over the coming weeks as the eggs hatch and the tadpoles grow. Point out that all amphibians have a tadpole stage early in their lives. You will need to consult resources on the care of tadpoles if you plan to keep them for several weeks. The tadpoles should be placed in an appropriate habitat after their time in the classroom.

2. Show the children pictures of crocodiles, lizards, snakes, turtles and tortoises. Ask the children what one thing they all have in common. Look for an answer about scales and ask how they might be divided up into more groups (crocodiles are large, lizards are small, snakes have no legs, tortoises and turtles have a shell). Challenge the children to use secondary sources to find out what reptiles eat. They should conclude that most are carnivores, though tortoises are herbivores.

3. Show the children pictures of a house sparrow, a robin and a blackbird and ask for a description of each. In the descriptions, point out feathers as a feature of all birds but also point out scales on their legs. Explain how an accurate description of the bird's plumage is used to identify birds. Tell the children that the sparrow eats seeds, the robin eats insects and the blackbird eats insects and berries. Ask them to say which feeding group each bird belongs to.

4. Ask the children to observe their pets, take photographs of them, make labelled drawings of them and describe their food and their habits, in order to make a book called 'My pets'. Arrange the books as a display on a table.

5. Make up four drawstring gym bags (feely bags) with an orange, a plastic toy, a piece of wood, a metal spoon, a dry cloth, a piece of aluminium foil, a piece of plastic sheet, and a piece of screwed up paper in each. Give each bag to an adult and let the children take turns at feeling the items and saying what they think each item is. Let the adults record the results.

Cross curricular links

- This topic can be linked with geography work on animals in different countries or continents.
- The parts of the body section can be use with topics on health.
- The section on taste and smell can be used with topics of food and cooking.

Year 1: Everyday materials

What does the curriculum say?

- *Distinguish between an object and the material from which it is made.*
- *Identify and name a variety of everyday materials, including wood, plastic, glass, metal, water and rock.*
- *Describe the simple physical properties of a variety of everyday materials.*
- *Compare and group together a variety of everyday materials on the basis of their simple physical properties.*

What do I need to know?

The word material is commonly used to mean a fabric for clothing or for soft furnishings but in science it is used for anything that has matter. One simple way to see if something contains matter is to weigh it.

The property of a material is a feature that it possesses such as smoothness, roughness, having a shiny or dull surface, being flexible, stretchy or rigid, hard or soft, transparent, opaque or translucent, magnetic, non magnetic, waterproof or absorbent. A material can have any combination of several of these properties such as being soft, opaque, dull, flexible and absorbent. These are the properties of a piece of wool. You may also like to mention colour now as this becomes an important property when sorting out rocks in Year 3.

Sometimes the property of a material depends on the object it makes. For example, a block of wood is rigid but a strip of wood is bendy; a block of metal is rigid, a metal wire is flexible and, if it is made into a coil, it is springy; a plastic block is rigid but a plastic sponge is squashy. The treatment of a material can affect its properties too. For example, a piece of rough sawn wood has a rough surface but wood that has been shaved and polished has a smooth surface. You need to be mindful of these changes in properties if a child asks why a metal bar does not bend but a metal wire does.

> ### Interesting fact
>
> Glass is made from molten sand.

Vocabulary

Absorbent: having the ability to take up a liquid such as water.
Bendy: can be bent up and down.
Flexible: can be bent in any direction and folded up.
Foil: a very thin, bendy sheet of metal.
Material: something made of matter (not a vacuum). It can be a solid, a liquid or a gas.
Opaque: does not let light pass through it.
Prediction: a description of what will happen based on what information has been gathered.
Translucent: lets some light pass through but scatters it in all directions so nothing can be seen through it
Transparent: lets light pass through it so that things can be seen through it. (Note that some light is absorbed because transparent objects cast shadows.)
Waterproof: having the ability to stop water passing through it.

Progression

This topic provides an introduction to the study of materials. This is further developed in Year 2 before more specific areas of materials studies are made in Key Stage 2: rock and magnetic materials are studied in Year 3; the three states of matter and the reversible changes between them are studied in Year 4; and the processing of materials and investigating irreversible changes are studied in Year 5.

Useful websites

Lesson 1: www.bbc.co.uk/schools/scienceclips/ages/5_6/sorting_using_mate_fs.shtml
Lesson 3: www.bbc.co.uk/education/clips/zm2jmp3

Lesson 1 Objects, materials and properties

Working scientifically skills: Observing
Scientific enquiry type: Comparative test

You will need: a dull coloured woollen pullover, an item of clothing with plastic buttons, torches, a wooden spoon, a glass bottle, a rock, paper, metal foil, and a brick.

Getting started

Tell the children that they are going to study materials. Say that most people think the word material just means something made from cloth but that this is incorrect. Say that a material has a number of features called properties which help you to identify the material. Show them a pullover and point out its properties: rough surface, stretchy, soft. Say that these properties are not just found on wool and ask the children to feel their own clothes to see if they have the same properties as wool. The materials may not be as stretchy or soft and may be quite smooth. Say it is time to look at materials in a bit more detail.

Class activities

- Show the children the plastic buttons on the item of clothing and let them feel them. They may also be wearing clothes with plastic buttons which they can feel. Tell them that the button is probably made of plastic and ask them about its properties. They should reply that it is hard, smooth and not stretchy.
- Ask the children to feel their shoes and tell them that they are probably made of leather or plastic. Ask them about the properties. They should reply that the material is bendy and smooth but not stretchy. Give the children torches. Ask them to shine the light on their shoes and describe the shoe material. You should be aiming at an answer about the shoes being shiny but some shoes may need a quick wipe to achieve this. Let the children shine their lights on the pullover and note that it does not shine. Point out that the surface is dull. Let them shine the light on their buttons (shiny) and sleeves (not shiny) to discover two more properties.
- Take a moment with the children to consider the relationship between an object, the material it is made from and the properties of the material. Review the pullover: the material is wool, the properties of the material are soft, rough, stretchy, and dull. Reinforce this with another object, the button: the material is plastic, the properties of the material are hard, not stretchy, smooth and shiny.
- Show the children the following objects: a wooden spoon, a glass bottle, a rock, paper, metal foil, and a brick. For each object, ask the children to identify the object, identify the material and describe its properties. In their descriptions of properties, look for the addition of 'see-through' (transparent) for glass and 'bendy' for paper and metal foil. Point out that the brick has the same name as the material.
- Tell the children that when scientists collect information (data) they record it in tables. Ask them to construct a table with the headings: Object, Material, Properties of the material.

Plenary

Review what the children have learnt about materials. Explain that, if you can see through a material, it lets light through and is called 'transparent.' If you cannot see through a material, it does not let light through and is called 'opaque' (see Further lesson ideas and activities 1).

Lesson 2 Investigating a property

Working scientifically skills: Asking simple questions and recognising that they can be answered in different ways; observing closely, using simple equipment; performing simple tests; using their observations and ideas to suggest answers to questions
Scientific enquiry type: Fair test

You will need: a watering can (hidden until needed), a tray, a doll in a raincoat and a collection of different types of material: cotton sheet, wool sheet, plastic sheet, cardboard, paper, metal foil, and tissue paper. Each group will need a 5 cm square of each of the materials in your collection, a teaspoon, a beaker of water and a stopwatch. Helpers will be needed to work with the groups.

Getting started
Place the doll upright in the tray. Ask the children to pay attention. Produce the watering can quickly and water the doll. Ask them if they think that the doll has got wet and look for an answer about the material of the coat being waterproof. Say that this is another property of materials and that they are going to investigate it.

Class activities
- Show the children the collection of materials and ask how they could test to see if they were waterproof. Encourage a wide range of suggestions that might include wrapping the doll in each material in turn and watering it. Take the answers and say that scientists always look for the simplest way of investigating. Encourage the children to make a plan in which same sized pieces of material are placed on a surface and a teaspoonful of water is placed on each. The materials are left for a minute. Then the material is removed and the surface is checked for wetness.
- Go through the plan again with the children and say that they are going to carry out the investigation. Issue the squares of the different materials, Make sure one child in each group can use a stopwatch. Say that before they can begin they must construct a table and give them the column headings: Material and Waterproof. Let the helpers work with the children to construct their tables and write down the names of the materials. They may look at and handle each material as they write it down. Tell them that, if they find the water does not go through, they put a tick in the waterproof column. But, if the water goes through, they put a cross (see Further lesson ideas and activities 2).
- Issue the beakers of water and teaspoons and let the children carry out their investigations and fill in their tables.

Plenary
Say that when different groups of scientists have carried out the same investigation, they get together and present their results. This is what the children will do now. Make a table on the board with one column for the materials and one column for each group. Ask a spokesperson from each group to read out their results and fill them in on the table. Finish by comparing the results and look for agreement. Where there is disagreement discuss the technique the group used to explain the anomaly. If children have made predictions, ask them how they compared with the results. Say that the results of the investigation can be used as evidence of a material being waterproof or not.

Lesson 3 Materials, properties and uses

Working scientifically skills: Observing; using their observations and ideas to suggest answers to questions
Scientific enquiry type: Identifying, classifying and grouping

You will need: a wooden spoon, a metal spoon, a hiking boot with a cloth upper and a rubber sole and a bicycle; an additional collection of objects for each group including: metal objects (coin, paper clip, kitchen foil), plastic objects (plate, building block, shopping bag) and wooden objects (spoon, chess piece, a ruler).

Getting started
Remind the children about the difference between an object and the material it is made from. Show the class a wooden spoon and a metal spoon and ask the children what they are made of and how they can tell. As the children differentiate between them, tell them that they are using the properties of the materials to separate them into groups.

Class activities
- Give the children the mixed up collection of objects and ask them to sort them out into groups according to the material they are made from.
- Check the results with the class then pass round the hiking boot and ask what group it could be put into. The children should realise that is made from several materials and, with the exception of the metal components, could not be put into any of the other groups or even into one group. Steer the children towards the idea that an object may be made from several materials, each one being used because of a particular property it possesses. The boot has a rubber sole which is hard and does not wear easily, the fabric top is flexible for comfort and also waterproof. Metal fasteners give strength and support for the laces, which in turn are flexible so they can be knotted. (see Further lesson ideas and activities 3).
- Walk around the room and touch various things. Ask the children what material each thing is made from. On the board, ask a helper to write down the name of the thing and the material. For example, door: wood; window: glass; seat top: plastic; chair leg: metal; eraser: rubber. If the classroom has a sink, turn on the tap, let the children identify the liquid and say that this too is a material. Ask where this material is found and look for answers such as in drinks, in soups, in lakes, rivers and the sea.
- Discuss with the children the useful properties of the metal table leg (strong, hard, does not squash), the window glass (transparent, hard, strong) and the rubber in the eraser (soft, breaks up to remove pencil marks without damaging paper).
- Challenge the children to say what might happen if the wrong material was used to make an object (e.g. wooden trousers, a metal toothbrush). Let the children make their own suggestions and say why they are unsuitable.

Plenary
Ask the children to name as many different materials as they can. Call out a property and ask the children to suggest a material that possesses it. Let the children write a few sentences or make a drawing with labels and a caption about their work on materials in the last three lessons (plus any extra activities).

Further lesson ideas and activities

1. You may wish to also identify translucent material and show the children tissue paper or a piece of frosted glass.
2. You may wish to introduce the idea of making predictions before the investigation is carried out. Say that scientists often do this and say it is a kind of guess but the scientist uses what he or she knows to help in making the guess. For example, someone may already know that tissue paper soaks up water.
3. For an extra dramatic effect, you may like to wheel a bicycle into the classroom and ask the children about the materials it is made from. They are a metal frame (does not squash and is hard wearing), rubber tyres (hard wearing and squashy to give a comfortable ride), and a saddle (flexible material for comfort). Point out oil on the chain which is a liquid that makes the metal pieces move easily over each other.

Cross curricular links

- In craft and design work, you may like the children to make a model or sculpture from a collection of materials and objects. When it is complete they could explain how they used the properties of the materials. Explanations will focus mainly on optical properties such as dull, shiny, smooth, rough, transparent, translucent and opaque.
- In geography work, the children could find out about where natural materials come from.
- In history they could look at the materials used in the Stone Age, Egypt, Roman times and costumes worn in Tudor times.

Year 1: Seasons

What does the curriculum say?

- *Observe changes across the four seasons.*
- *Observe and describe weather associated with the season and how day length varies.*

What do I need to know?

The Earth is one of eight major planets moving in orbit around the Sun. It spins on its axis once a day. Due to a collision with another large object during the formation of the Solar system the Earth's axis is tilted at 23° to the vertical. The direction of tilt remains the same all the way round the Earth's orbit. This means that sometimes part of the Earth is tilted towards the Sun and sometimes it is tilted away. Sun beams contain light and heat. When a part of the Earth is tilted towards the Sun, each beam of sunlight is concentrated on a smaller area which causes it to be warmer. This results in summer weather. When the same part is tilted away from the Sun, the beam of light spreads out over a larger area and is less concentrated so its heat to any one point is lower. This results in winter weather.

The heat reaching the Earth's surface is transferred to the air causing convection currents and winds. Water evaporates from the surfaces of the seas and exists in the air as a gas called water vapour. This can cool on dust in the air and form huge groups of droplets (clouds). There are many types of clouds. The most common are stratus clouds which form a low continuous layer, cumulus clouds which have gaps between them and cirrus clouds which are higher than most other clouds and look like feathers or mare's tails.

Tell the children that they must never look directly at the Sun, even in their weather studies, as this can seriously harm their eyes.

In the autumn focus the children's attention on the lowering of the temperature, increased rainfall and increase in strong winds (autumn gales). Note how it becomes increasingly darker towards the end of the school day. Throughout winter the children could record the number of frosty mornings or days when it rains all day. In spring the children can observe the gradual rising of the temperature and record the rain in heavy showers.

Interesting fact

The Earth's atmosphere is about 1,280 km (800 miles) thick. The weather takes place in the lowest part of the atmosphere which extends from the ground to up to 17 km (11 miles).

Vocabulary

Axis: an imaginary line running through the centre of the Earth from the North to the South Pole.

Herbaceous plant: a plant which does not make wood to support its stem. All non woody flowering plants are herbaceous plants.

Horizon: the line between the land or sea and the sky.

Orbit: the path of a planet such as the Earth around the Sun.

Temperature: the hotness or coldness of a substance such as air, water or a solid.

Thermometer: a scientific instrument that measures temperature.

Compass: a scientific instrument which can be used to show directions. It has a needle which points north and south.

Shadow: a dark area on the unlit side of an object. It is caused by the object stopping light rays passing through it.

Progression

This area of study forms foundation work in many areas further up the school particularly the study of habitats. The weather recording activities do not have to be restricted to this year but can be carried on through the years if a school weather station is set up. The study of clouds and rain contributes to knowledge about the water cycle in Year 4.

Technical tips

Lesson 1: You can make a simple rain gauge by cutting the top off a plastic drinks bottle, turning the top part upside down and placing it inside the bottom part to make a funnel. The collected water can be measured using a scale drawn onto the rain gauge (or a measuring cylinder if you prefer). Readings should be taken at regular intervals and the rain gauge should be emptied after each reading.

Lesson 2: Rather than measuring their own shadows, you may prefer to let the children measure the length of the shadow of an object that is always set up in the same place, e.g. a cone. They could then use the measurements in maths lessons.

Useful websites

Lesson 1: For making a rain gauge: peterdriley.com/how-to-make-a-rain-gauge-for-measuring-rainfall
Lessons 2 and 3: For seasonal changes in Britain: peterdriley.com/seasonal

Lesson 1 The weather

Working scientifically skills: Observing closely, using simple equipment; gathering and recording data to help in answering questions
Scientific enquiry type: Observing over time; pattern seeking

You will need: a globe, some cling film, a thermometer, a cardboard box with holes in it, a rain gauge and a compass.

Getting started
Show the children a globe and say that this is the planet we live on. Point out the land and oceans. Say that this model of the Earth is not entirely complete. Take some cling film and wrap it around the globe. Say that this represents the air or atmosphere. Explain that the atmosphere is responsible for our weather and in this lesson they are going to find out more about it.

Class activities
- Say that the first thing people often ask about the weather is how cold or how warm it is. Show the children a thermometer and tell them that this measures the heat of things and at the moment it is measuring the temperature of the air. Read the temperature and say that the part of the thermometer that is measuring the temperature is the swollen part at the bottom called the bulb. Take the children outside to see if the air temperature is the same as inside. This outside temperature is the one they will use when studying the weather (see Further lesson ideas and activities 1).
- While you are outside ask the children to look up into the sky but not at the Sun as this can damage their eyes. Point out any clouds and how much of the sky they cover. A simple description could be that, if they cover half to all of the sky, it is cloudy; less than half, it is patchy cloud; and no cloud means the sky is clear (see Further lesson ideas and activities 2).
- Ask the children what happens when there are lots of dark clouds and look for an answer about rain. Take the watering can and pour some water into a tray. Ask the children how they could measure how much rain falls in a shower. Look for an answer about putting out a bottle and see how much water collects in it. Show the children the rain gauge, pointing out the scale then put it in the tray and water it to show how the water collects inside (see Further lesson ideas and activities 3).
- Tell the children that the air often moves and ask them what we call moving air. Look for an answer about wind. Ask how you can tell if a wind is gentle or if it is strong. Look for the answer that a gentle wind just blows things a little but a strong wind blows things a lot. Say that scientists have worked out a way of measuring the strength of the wind and show them a copy of the wind scale on the next page. Look outside with the children and estimate the movement of the air (see Further lesson ideas and activities 4).

Plenary
Review the children's work on measuring temperature, identifying simple cloud types, recording rainfall and estimating wind speed. With the children, decide on how the class will record the weather every day, e.g. once at midday by taking out the thermometer in a box, looking at the sky (but not the Sun), and looking at the effect of the wind on the surroundings (and the direction of the wind if compass work has been done). The rain gauge should also be read each day then emptied. The class should build up a display of weather records for a week, perhaps twice a month (see Further lesson ideas and activities 5).

Wind scale

What is seen	Type of wind
Nothing moving	No wind, calm
Leaves rustling	Light breeze
Leaves and twigs always moving	Gentle breeze
Dust blown about, small branches waving	Moderate breeze
Trees with leaves swaying about	Fresh breeze
Large branches swaying	Strong breeze
Whole trees swaying	Moderate gale
Twigs breaking off	Fresh gale
Buildings damaged	Strong gale
Trees blown over	Whole gale

Lesson 2 How day length varies

Working scientifically skills: Observing closely; using simple equipment; gathering and recording data to help in answering questions
Scientific enquiry type: Observing over time; pattern seeking

You will need: a globe, a little plastic figure (with adhesive putty on the bottom), a large yellow ball, and a large torch. Each pair of children will need a tape measure.

Getting started
Hold up the globe and slowly spin it round anticlockwise from looking at the top. Take a little plastic figure (to represent anyone in the class) and stick it on the globe, on your country, facing the direction you are turning. Turn the globe slowly to show how the person travels round. Say that this is what our planet is doing right now and we are going to find out how things change for this person as they make their trip.

Class activities
- Ask a child to pick up the ball (to represent the Sun) and stand about 2 m (6 feet) away in front of the class. Move the globe round so that sometimes the figure faces the ball and sometimes faces away from it. Ask the children when it is day and night for that person and look for the answers that day is when the figure is facing the Sun and night is when the figure is facing away from the Sun.
- Ask the child to swap the ball for the torch and shine it at the globe. Point out the position where the light just starts to shine on the person and say that this is sunrise. Draw a line to represent the horizon on the board and draw the Sun to the left just above it.
- Move the person round until the torchlight is shining directly down on it and draw the position of the Sun in the centre high in the sky above the horizon. Say that this is midday. Move the person round again until the Sun is shining on their back and draw the Sun low on the right above the horizon and say that it is sunset.
- Ask the children what happens when you shine a light on an object and shine the torch on a doll. Let the children point out the doll's shadow. Ask how they think the shadow will change if the torch is low like sunrise and sunset or high like the Sun at midday. Check their predictions by shining the torch in different places.
- Let the children go outside and measure their shadows. Get them to do this first thing in the morning, at midday and last thing in the afternoon to further check their predictions (see Further lesson ideas and activities 6). Remind the children never to look directly at the Sun.

Plenary
Review the turning of the Earth and its orbit around the Sun. Say that the Sun is higher in the sky in summer than in winter and ask the children to predict when their shadows would be shortest (summer). Ask how they could check their shadow length through the year and look for an answer about measuring it at midday once a month. Let the children carry out their plan and display their results.

Lesson 3 Recording seasonal changes

Working scientifically skills: Observing closely; gathering and recording data to help in answering questions; using their observations and ideas to suggest answers to questions
Scientific enquiry type: Observing over time; pattern seeking

You will need: a globe, a large yellow ball, access to the school grounds or a park where there are trees, bushes, herbaceous plants, a wild area of grass and helpers with clipboards.

Getting started
Remind the children that there are four seasons in a year: winter, spring, summer and autumn. Ask them what the season is now. Remind the children how the Earth moves around the Sun using the globe and yellow ball and point out how the amount of heat reaching the hemisphere changes as the Earth moves in its orbit. Ask how this change in the seasons affects the clothes we wear. Look for answers about summer and winter clothes, clothes for wet and dry, warm and cold weather. Say that the movement of the Earth makes us change our clothes but in this lesson we are going to look at how it affects plants and animals.

Class activities
- Take the children into the school grounds or a park so that they can listen for the birds, look for flying insects, and look at trees and bushes to record whether they are growing leaves, are in full leaf, are shedding leaves or have lost their leaves. The children should also look for herbaceous plants in leaf, in flower, dying back or with only brown stalks remaining. They should look at an unmown area of grass to see if it is short and brown, is growing, has long stalks with flower heads, is dying back, or is yellow and dead.
- With helpers, record the children's observations under the headings: Birds (any seen, heard); Insects flying and settling on plants (butterflies, bees, flies, beetles, e.g. ladybirds); Trees and bushes (buds opening, green leaves, brown leaves, no leaves, no flowers, flowers, fruits, berries); Herbaceous pants (soil bare, plants growing up, e.g. snowdrops, plants in leaf, plants in flower, plants forming fruits and seeds).
- With the children, select areas of the habitat to photograph. They could show a large number of trees or herbaceous plants, or photograph individual flowers and fruits. Any animals on plants or on the ground could be photographed too.
- Back in the classroom the photographs can be displayed and discussed. Some photographs could be printed off to form part of a display featuring the children's drawings and writing about the expedition.

Plenary
Look at the display with the children. Show them the globe and the yellow ball representing the Sun. Ask them where the planet will go next and encourage them to predict the changes in the weather, the changes in their clothes and the changes in the plants and animals (see Further lesson ideas and activities 7).

This lesson could be repeated each season.

Further lesson ideas and activities

1. When taking the air temperature regularly, put the thermometer in a box with holes in it (to keep it in the shade) and leave it outside for half an hour before taking the temperature.
2. When possible point out three types of cloud: layer cloud or stratus which forms a roll across the sky (model with a roll of cotton wool); heaped clouds called cumulus (model by tearing the cotton wool layer into smaller pieces); and cirrus or feather clouds (model by pulling off a little of the smaller piece of cotton wool and stretching it into a wisp).
3. When setting up the rain gauge outside make sure it is away from overhanging trees or roofs. You may wish to empty it once a week, rather than daily, and compare weeks for rain.
4. As the children become more confident at measuring wind speed, show them a compass and point out the eight main points. Say that wind direction is found by facing the wind and noting the direction it is blowing from.
5. As the data builds up, compare weeks and months to see how there is a gradual change as the seasons progress. If wind direction is being measured, this could be compared with temperature and rainfall to look for a link between them.
6. Place the yellow ball in the centre of a table in front of the class. Put the globe on the table to the left of the yellow ball as seen from the class. Point the axis towards the ball and say that this represents the Earth when it is summer in the Northern Hemisphere. Keep the axis pointing in the same direction and move the globe between the ball and the class. Say this represents autumn. Keep the axis pointing in the same direction and move it to the right and say this represents winter. Keep the axis pointing in the same direction and move the globe so the ball is between it and the class and say this represents spring.

    Follow this demonstration by telling the children that the seasons change because of the amount of light the hemisphere receives. Shine the torch from the side onto the Northern Hemisphere with the axis pointing towards the torch and note the brightly lit area is a small distance across. Say that the Sun's rays also carry heat and this warms up the area and makes the summer season. Now move the globe with its axis pointing away from the torch and let the children see the larger, more dimly lit area and say that the Sun's rays of heat spread out so the land and sea is cooler and it becomes winter. Point out that spring and autumn are in between seasons.
7. Some children may like to make a nature diary through the seasons recording the weather and changes in plant and animal life.

Cross curricular links

The weather can be used as a stimulus for creative writing. It can be considered in geography when other countries are being studied. It can be considered in technology when clothes are being designed or materials are being tested.

Year 2: Living things and their habitats

What does the curriculum say?

- *Explore and compare the differences between things that are living, dead, and things that have never been alive.*
- *Identify that most living things live in habitats to which they are suited and describe how different habitats provide for the basic needs of different kinds of animals and plants, and how they depend on each other.*
- *Identify and name a variety of plants and animals in their habitats, including microhabitats.*
- *Describe how animals obtain their food from plants and other animals, using the idea of a simple food chain, and identify and name different sources of food.*

What do I need to know?

A living thing has all the features of life such as breathing and moving. A dead thing has ceased to exhibit these features. Wood, for example, is something which is dead compared to sandstone rock that has never been alive. Metal is also another material which has never been alive while bone comes from a dead body.

A habitat is a place where plants and animals live. The habitat usually takes its name from a particular feature which it forms such as a woodland habitat or a feature in which it develops such as a desert habitat. In a habitat are a certain set of conditions, mainly climatic such as temperature, rainfall and light which determine the types of plants that can grow there. This in turn affects the animals which can live on the plants (herbivores) and the carnivores that live on them.

Within a habitat there are smaller habitats called microhabitats. These have small microclimates which differ from those in the larger habitat. For example, the space under stones and logs has damper air and allows animals such as woodlice, which lose their body moisture easily in dry air, to survive there. Conditions in lower sheltered branches of trees and bushes create microclimates where animals can move around without falling off. Microhabitats can be even smaller such as the underside of a leaf which is the home to greenfly (aphids).

The word 'suited' is used to describe how a living thing is adapted to its habitat. In later years the children will learn to use the word 'adapted' instead of suited and the features it has that suit it to its habitat are called 'adaptations.' Adaptations may involve the whole body such as the spindle shape of fish being an adaptation that allows the fish to move quickly through water. They may also involve a small part of the body such as the pointed beak of a robin which allows it to probe into cracks in bark to find insects.

Food contains nutrients and energy that living things need. Plants take in some of the energy in sunlight and use it with water from the soil and carbon dioxide from the air and minerals in the soil to make food.

Animals cannot make food in this way. The way food passes from one living thing to another through feeding is called a food chain. A simple food chain with two links is grass → rabbit. It can be extended to three links by adding a predator of the rabbit making grass plant → rabbit → fox. Food chains usually start with the food-making organ of the plant – the leaf – but seeds and fruits can also be eaten. There is a huge range of herbivores (animals that feed on plants) such leaf beetles, deer and antelopes and they form food for an equally huge range of carnivores such as frogs, wolves and lions.

grass   rabbit   fox
               herbivore   carnivore

Interesting fact

During the sixteenth century, when ships were returning from all over the world with plants, animals and minerals, wealthy people began to set up cabinets of curiosities (sometimes whole rooms) to house these collections and entertain their friends. The curiosities often stimulated thought and scientific investigation.

Vocabulary

Burrow: a hole in the ground where certain animals shelter and sleep.
Cacti: plants with spikes instead of leaves and skins covered in wax to prevent them losing water in their desert habitats.
Caterpillar: a stage in the life cycle of many insects between the egg and chrysalis (pupa) stages.
Food chain: a way of showing how a plant and some animals can be linked together by the way they feed.
Habitat: a place where a plant or an animal lives.
Microhabitat: a small part of a larger habitat which is the home for some animals and plants.
Minerals: substances in the soil that plants need for good health.

Progression

This topic builds on the children's work on plants and animals in Year 1 and shows how they survive together in habitats. It builds on the work on the environment in seasonal changes in Year 1 by more tightly focusing on the habitat concept, which is revisited in Years 4, 5 and 6 and used in the development of ideas about evolution in Year 6.

Technical tips

Lesson 2: Collect woodlice from under logs and stones. Keep them under stones that are slightly damp. Return them to their habitat straight after the lesson.

Lesson 3: Make sure the soil in the wormery is damp but not wet. Put small amounts of food on the surface after the worms have gone into the soil. If you are keeping the wormery for a week or more, check to see that the food is not going mouldy.

Useful websites

Bitesize Habitats: www.bbc.co.uk/education/topics/zxq6pv4

Lesson 1 Surviving in a habitat

Working scientifically skills: Observing
Scientific enquiry type: Identifying, classifying and grouping

You will need: photographs of: woodland, a squirrel, a wood mouse, a rabbit, a log, a bone, a rock, ivy growing up a tree trunk, a rabbit nibbling grass by its burrow, a chaffinch perched on a branch showing toes and a robin; a rock with moss growing on it and a piece of ivy showing the small roots growing out of the stem. Each group will need four pipe cleaners and a twig.

Getting started

Review the children's knowledge of plants and animals from Year 1 then say that they are going to study where plants and animals live. This place is known as a 'habitat'. Show the picture of the woodland and say that this is a woodland habitat. Ask them to identify the living plants they can see. Show the picture of the squirrel, wood mouse and rabbit and ask if they are alive. Follow these with the picture of a log and then a bone; look for answers that they were once part of a living thing but are now dead. Show the picture of the rock and look for an answer that it has never been alive (see Further lesson ideas and activities 1).

Class activities

- Ask the children what plants need in order to live; look for answers about water, light, warmth and minerals (if work on Year 2 Plants has been carried out already). Ask how the plant takes up water, then ask how roots are suited to picking up water from the soil. Look for answers about a root having lots of branches that spread out to pick up water and hairs to get between the soil grains. Ask how the plant is suited to catching light to make food; look for answers about leaves having large flat surfaces to catch the light.
- Show the rock with the moss on it and explain how the moss is suited to growing on the rock because its little plants group together to grip the rock. Show the photograph of the ivy and say that it is suited to finding light by having roots on its stem that hold onto the trunks of trees so the ivy can climb up them. Let the children look at the specimen of ivy stem and point out the roots.
- Ask the children what animals need to stay alive and look for answers about food and shelter. Show the children a picture of the rabbit and ask about its food and shelter. Look for an answer about grass and a burrow. Say that the rabbit is suited to eating grass because it has sharp front teeth (get the children to point to their front teeth) for nibbling grass and it is suited to burrowing because it has sharp claws for digging.
- Show the picture of the chaffinch and say that it shelters by perching in trees. It has feet with three toes forwards and one backwards for gripping twigs. Give the children four pipe cleaners and ask them to make model chaffinch feet (they do this by twisting the pipe cleaners together and splaying out the toes) and see if they can grip a twig (see Further lesson ideas and activities 2).

Plenary

Review the children's ideas about a habitat; the differences between items that are living, that are dead and that have never lived; the needs of plants and animals and how they are suited to getting what they need to survive.

Lesson 2 Habitats and microhabitats

Working scientifically skills: Observing closely; using simple equipment
Scientific enquiry type: Identifying, classifying and grouping; comparative tests

You will need: photographs of woodland, desert with cacti, a selection of desert animals including a rattlesnake, a tortoise, a fennec fox, a camel, a roadrunner, and a scorpion; a tray with some large stones and woodlice. Each pair should have a clear plastic pot and a magnifying glass. You will also need access to the school grounds or a park, a bush or tree with low branches, and a white sheet.

Getting started
Remind the children that a habitat is a place where a plant or an animal lives. Show the picture of the woodland and ask what lives there. Look for an answer about the trees, the rabbit, the squirrel and the chaffinch. Ask about plants growing up trees and look for ivy. Tell the children that there are many different types of habitat and show the children a picture of a desert. Point out the cacti. Say that some deserts do not have cacti and show a selection of animals that live in deserts across the world (see Further lesson ideas and activities 3). Tell the children that in each habitat there are smaller habitats called microhabitats.

Class activities
- Show the children the tray of stones. Explain that stones can be found in many habitats. Ask the children if they think anything lives under stones.
- Gather the children around the stones and slowly remove each one until a wood louse is revealed and someone has noticed it. Continue removing stones until all the woodlice are revealed. You may like to place them in separate clear plastic pots so pairs of children could examine them with a magnifying glass. Let the children draw their woodlouse and colour it in.
- Ask the children how the woodlouse is suited for a life under stones and look for answers about having flattened bodies so they can squeeze under them and being stone coloured so that predators cannot see them.
- Take the children outside and look for stones and logs. Let the children turn them over and record anything living there. There may be woodlice, beetles, spiders, slugs and earthworms.
- Take the children to a bush or low tree branch and say that a branch is a microhabitat. Ask how the children could find out what was living on the branch. Steer the children towards the idea of shaking the branch and of putting down a white sheet first so that any fallen animals can be seen more easily. Set up the investigation and let the children record the animals that fall onto the sheet. They may find caterpillars, spiders, beetles, flies and maybe snails. After the investigation has been carried out, place the animals at the base of the bush or tree for them to return to their habitat.

Plenary
Ask the children about the different habitats around the world and to define a microhabitat. Ask them to say how a woodlouse is suited to its microhabitat and to report on the animals found under logs, stones and on a branch.

Lesson 3 Life in a habitat

Working scientifically skills: Observing closely; performing simple tests; gathering and recording data to help answer questions
Scientific enquiry type: Observing over time; comparative test

You will need: a tall plastic bottle, a bucket of damp garden soil (loam), a trowel, a piece of muslin, an elastic band, lettuce leaves, cabbage, potato and carrot peelings, an apple, brown paper, sticky tape, a camera, a picture of a wood mouse and a picture of a tawny owl.

Getting started
Remind the children about animals needing food in their habitat and mention the rabbit eating grass. Say that, when one living thing feeds on another, they form a link in a food chain. Show how the link could be written down by writing 'grass → rabbit' on the whiteboard. Ask the children what might feed on rabbits and look for 'fox' as an answer. Say that this forms the second link in the food chain and add '→ fox' to the whiteboard: grass → rabbit → fox.

Class activities
- Say that when scientists study food chains they look closely at an animal in its habitat to see what it eats. Ask the children to think of an animal they have met in their habitat studies that they could investigate and encourage them to suggest earthworms.
- Ask the children about the earthworm's habitat. Construct an earthworm habitat with the children by filling a tall plastic bottle with damp soil. Place six earthworms in the bottle and seal the top with muslin and the elastic band. Secure brown paper around the bottle with sticky tape to keep out light so the earthworms can move through all parts of the soil.
- Leave the earthworms to settle in their new habitat and return to the topic of food chains in a wood. Show the children some grass seed. Say that this is eaten by wood mice and show a photograph of a wood mouse. Tell the children that owls eat wood mice and show a picture of a tawny owl. Construct the food chain on the whiteboard: grass seed → wood mouse → tawny owl.
- Remind the children about the work they did on herbivores, carnivores and omnivores in Year 1 and point out that, in the two food chains on the board, the rabbit and wood mouse are herbivores and the fox and tawny owl are carnivores.
- Return to the wormery and remove the paper to see if the earthworms have burrowed down. Show the children the selection of food you have collected and ask if it could be used to see what earthworms eat. Look for an answer about putting small amounts of each on the soil surface and looking to see what is eaten. Set up the investigation, photograph the food on top of the soil, replace the paper and muslin top and leave for two days.
- Examine the food again and compare with the photograph. You may wish to photograph again and leave for a further two days, and so on.

Plenary
Ask the children what a cow eats, where our milk comes from and challenge them to make a food chain that includes a human being. Look for 'grass → cow → human'. Challenge the children to construct other food chains with humans in such as corn → chicken → human or apple → human (see Further lesson ideas and activities 4).

Review the data collected at the wormery, describe the food eaten by the earthworms and establish that they are herbivores.

Further lesson ideas and activities

1. For lesson 1, make a curiosity box out of a shoe box and put in a pine cone, a shell, a log, a pebble, a crystal, a fossil, a container of sand, a broad bean seed, a brown dead leaf, a metal nail, a small pot plant, a piece of glass, a slug in a pot (be sure to return it to its habitat when the activity is over). Ask the children to group them into 'alive', 'dead' and 'never alive'.

2. For lesson 1, show a picture of a chaffinch and robin. Point out that the chaffinch feeds on seeds and the robin feeds by finding insects in cracks in bark. Put some cress seeds in a bowl and place an empty bowl next to it. Ask a volunteer to use a blunt pair of forceps (like the chaffinch's beak) to transfer as many seeds to the empty bowl as they can in a minute then record the result. Then ask the volunteer to repeat the challenge with a pair of pointed forceps (like the robin's beak) and conclude that the chaffinch's beak is better suited for picking up seeds.

3. Prepare photos of different habitats and the plants and animals that live in them. For example, the savannah grassland of Africa with elephants, zebras, lions, cheetahs, gazelles and gnus; tropical forest in South America with tree frogs, tapirs, parrots, jaguars, hummingbirds and howler monkeys; a pond with reeds, irises, water lilies, frogs, newts, carp, moorhens, herons, water beetles, pond snails and mallard ducks; a rocky shore with seaweed, barnacles and mussels on rocks and rock pool life.

4. Making food chains involving humans will lead to seeing humans feeding as herbivores and carnivores, even in one meal (e.g. fish and chips) and you should remind the children that humans are omnivores. You may like to point out that in local habitats blackbirds feed on earthworms and berries and squirrels eat acorns but also bird's eggs. Both are omnivores.

Cross curricular links

The study on a habitats can be used in any work on seasonal change and linked to ongoing weather studies. It can be used as a basis for conservation activities in school and with geography when studying habitats in different parts of the world.

Year 2: Plants

What does the curriculum say?

- *Observe and describe how seeds and bulbs grow into mature plants.*
- *Find out and describe how plants need water, light and a suitable temperature to grow and stay healthy.*

What do I need to know?

Most plants grow from seeds. Seeds are made in flowers after pollination and fertilisation. A seed has a tough outer coat enclosing a tiny plant with a store of food. The plant removes water from the seeds when they are made to reduce their weight. This helps them to be carried away and distributed over a wide area which in turn increases the chances of survival of the new generation of plants.

Seeds may remain dormant for a few weeks or even years before they germinate. In this process, the seed takes in water through a tiny hole in its coat then the coat splits and the root grows out which has lots of tiny root hairs near its tip. These greatly increase the water absorbing surface of the root and the water is used to stimulate growth of the shoot and further growth of the root. The shoot then bursts through the seed coat and grows up towards the light where its leaves make food. Note that seeds do not need light in order to germinate so can be buried in the soil. They should not be buried too deep and seed packets have instructions about planting the seeds. If a seed is planted too deeply the germinating plant may use up all the food stored in the seed before it reaches the light and can spread out its leaves to catch the light.

Some plants, such as the onion, grow from bulbs. At the base of the bulb is a tough disc which is flattened stem. In the centre is a bud from which a flower will grow. Around it are the bases of leaves attached to the stem. They are full of food that the long thin leaves above the soil made in the previous year. When the bulb starts to grow a flower and new leaves, it uses the food stored here. Between some of the leaf bases are side buds. These are capable of growing into separate bulbs as seen in chives and garlic.

Interesting fact

Cacti can store water inside their bodies and have a waxy skin to keep it in. They can survive without water for two months in deserts. Some cacti are known to have survived for two years without water.

Vocabulary

Bud: a growth on the stem which contains a side shoot with leaves, a leaf, or a flower. These structures come out when the bud bursts open.

Bulb: a round shape made of leaves with a flat stem at the bottom with small roots. Inside the leaves is a bud from which a side shoot, a leaf or a flower may grow. The bulb may also contain side buds from which other bulbs can grow.

Germination: the process of a seed breaking open to release a root and then a shoot.

Greenhouse: a structure in which plants are kept warm. Heat rays from the Sun pass through the glass, are absorbed by the walls and floor and reflected back to the glass but they are too weak to escape so they warm the air.

Seed: a capsule which contains a tiny plant and a store of food for it to use as it germinates.

Temperature: a measure of how hot or cold something is.

Thermometer: an instrument for measuring temperature using units called degrees Celsius (°C).

Probe: an instrument which can be used to measure the temperature and other physical features such as humidity, moisture content of the soil, acidity of substances.

Tuber: a swollen part of a plant, such as a root or stem, in which food is stored.

Progression

This area of study about plants follows on from the plant studies in Year 1. It gives you the opportunity of revising knowledge of plant structure while looking at the factors that affect plant growth and how they are controlled. This forms the basis for further investigations on plant growth in Year 3, and a closer look at plant structure and function related to water transport and reproduction.

Technical tip

Plant growth experiments take time. You may like to set up plant growth before the lessons to show the children the changes and to encourage interest and let them confirm your results by growing their own plants (see ideas for lessons and activities). But the lessons here also focus on the children designing experiments, thinking about factors that affect them, and on recording changes over time. The three lessons are designed to be done consecutively but you may like to set them up at the same time, perhaps one third of the class doing each one and all reporting back for a grand plenary.

Useful websites

For applying the scientific method to growing plants: peterdriley.com/growing-plants
www.saps.org.uk/primary/teaching-resources/639-growing-seeds-in-a-plastic-bag

Lesson 1 Plants and water

Working scientifically skills: Observing; gathering and recording data to help in answering questions
Scientific enquiry type: Observing over time; comparative and fair tests

You will need: for each group, two dishes of dry sand, a pot of 20 seeds (for example, cress or mustard) and access to a small watering can.

Getting started
Show the children some broad bean seeds and ask them what they need to grow into plants. The children may remember from last year that seeds need water to grow.

Ask how they could show that seeds need water in order to grow into plants. You may get an answer about having two seeds and watering only one. Develop this into using a number of seeds just in case one seed was unhealthy or the plant inside had died.

Class activities
- Show the children two dishes of dry sand and a pot of cress seeds. Ask how the seeds should be placed on the sand. Look for an answer about putting the same number of seeds in each dish.
- Give out the dishes and seed pots and let the children label the dishes and divide the seeds between the two dishes.
- Discuss how the two sets of seeds should be treated and produce a watering can to water just one set of seeds.
- Let the children water just one set of their seeds.
- Discuss where the seeds could be left. Put one of your trays on a windowsill and another in the cupboard. Ask if this is suitable and look for an answer that it is not. Ask for an explanation and look for an answer about all the other conditions around the plant should be the same otherwise one of the other conditions could also be affecting the growth of the plants. Agree that all the dishes should be placed in the same conditions such as a shady windowsill or on a table where they will be undisturbed.
- Discuss how changes in the seeds could be recorded and arrange for some children to draw the seeds every two days and some children to photograph them.

Plenary
The plenary may take place up to two weeks later. The children should conclude that the seeds need water in order to grow into plants. You may like to extend this basic observation by looking at seeds as they sprout and say that the seeds need water in order for the plant to burst out. This sprouting process is called germination (see Further lesson ideas and activities 1).

Lesson 2 Plants and light

Working scientifically skills: Observing; gathering and recording data to help in answering questions
Scientific enquiry type: Observing over time; comparative and fair tests

You will need: for each group: two yoghurt/plant pots each containing a pea plant only about 2 cm tall, access to a sunny windowsill, a box and a watering can.

Getting started
Remind the children about how scientists design experiments: they think of something they want to find out, they work out a way to test their idea, they record their results and use them to try to find an answer.

Show the children two plants in their pots. Ask how you could find out if plants need light in order to grow. Look for an answer about putting one in the dark and keeping one in the light. Ask the children how they should look after the plants and record how they grow. Look for an answer about giving them the same amount of water. Ask why this should be so and look for an answer about knowing that water is needed for the plant growth so giving them the same amount stops any difference in water affecting their growth.

Class activities
- Give two plants to each group and let them label the pots with their names. Let the children record the heights of the plants and draw and photograph them. All data must be dated.
- Take your two plants and put one on a warm sunny windowsill and the other in a cool shady cupboard. Ask the children if this is a suitable plan and look for an answer that it is not. Look for an explanation about there being a difference in warmth or temperature. Ask for any evidence of warmth affecting plant growth and look for an answer about the use of greenhouses to grow plants more quickly. If the answer is not given remind the children that scientists like to keep all the conditions the same except for the one they are investigating.
- Ask how the plants could be kept at the same temperature. Look for an answer about putting the plant in the dark in a box on the windowsill so it will be at the same temperature as the one in the light.
- Let the children place their plants on the windowsill and in the boxes and leave them there for three days. (If it is particularly warm water all the plants daily after school.)
- After three days let the children measure, draw and photograph their plants.
- Let the children measure, draw and photograph their plants every three days for up to three weeks.

Plenary
Ask the children to look through all their data and describe orally or in writing how each of their plants has changed. Remind the children of how scientists like to have lots of data to use in answering their questions so pool their descriptions on the board. They should find that the plant in the dark has a long thin stem with pale leaves and the plant in the light has a shorter firmer stem with darker green leaves.

Lesson 3 Plants and warmth

Working scientifically skills: Observing; gathering and recording data to help in answering questions
Scientific enquiry type: Observing over time; comparative and fair tests

You will need: a thermometer on a sunny windowsill with its bulb inside an upside down, transparent plastic cup and a second thermometer without a cup to show how the temperature inside the plastic cup is higher (alternatively you could use a temperature probe); each group of children will need two yoghurt pots of germinated cress seedlings, a transparent plastic cup to place upside down over the seedlings to make a greenhouse.

Getting started
Show the children a thermometer and ask them what it is used for. Look for an answer about measuring temperature or how warm or cold things are. Ask the children if they think that warmth affects the way plants grow and look for an answer that warmth does help plants grow. Ask for an explanation and look for an answer about plants growing in the warmth of spring and summer but not in the cold of winter. Some children may say that greenhouses provide warmth for growing plants quickly.

Class activities
- Tell the children that they are going to use a mini greenhouse and show them the upturned cup on the windowsill. Ask them to look at the two thermometers to see the temperature difference. (Or, if using the probe, show the air temperature just above the windowsill and inside the plastic cup.)
- Give each group two pots and let them label them with their names.
- Let the children record the heights of the plants. All data must be dated.
- Give out the transparent plastic cups and let the children place them upside down over one of their pots of seeds.
- Let the children place their two pots on the sunny windowsill.
- Let the children measure the heights of the plants in the two pots every two days. All data must be dated.

Plenary
Let each group present their results to the class. You could record the data in a table with the column headings 'Greenhouse plants taller' and 'Outside plants taller'. You should find that the first column has the largest number of ticks.

Further lesson ideas and activities

1. After the children have seen that seeds need water in order to grow into plants and have been introduced to the term 'germination', ask them how they can be sure that plants need water after germination. Look for an answer about stopping watering the plants. Let the children stop watering some of the plants to test their idea. They should discover that the plants wilt and die if they do not receive water.

2. In year 1, the non statutory guidance states that the pupils should become familiar with plant structures including bulbs. On page 7 of this book (Year 1 Plants, Further lesson ideas and activities), point 3 provides an opportunity to introduce the bulb and perform an experiment on it. If this was not covered, then the activity on page 7 should be covered now. If the activity was covered then you may like to test the children's knowledge on the structure of the bulb and how it grows, and challenge them to devise an experiment to investigate the effect of temperature on the growth of the bulb. You may need to steer them into planting six or ten small onions in plant pots or seed trays, then placing each batch at a different temperature – for example, a cold shady place outside, a cool place inside and a warm place inside. They should check the soil and keep it damp, and record the emergence of the bulbs shoots. If they have investigated plants and warmth in lesson 3 of this chapter (see page 37), they could use their results as the basis of a prediction that warmer bulbs will grow faster. Alternatively they may like to apply the mini-greenhouse technique to growing onion bulbs by setting up five onions without greenhouses and five onions each in its own mini greenhouse.

3. Potatoes are stem tubers. Their skin is bark and their eyes are buds. Ask the children to compare a small potato with a similar sized pebble. Ask how they are similar and different. Ask if they are both alive and look for an answer about the potato being alive but the pebble has never been alive. Ask how they might show that the potato is alive and look for an answer that over time it might start to grow. Put the potatoes and pebbles in a box and leave for two or three weeks then look for the buds (the eyes) sprouting into potato plants.

Cross curricular links

- The content of all the lessons can be linked to seasonal change which was studied in Year 1 and may be being studied again in the context of habitat studies. The children could speculate on how changes in temperature, water and light may affect plant growth.
- The potato and pebble activity can be used with Living things and their habitats in Year 2 as a comparison between something that is alive and something that has never been alive.
- The knowledge gained from the three lessons can be applied in the school garden, perhaps using cloches to speed up plant growth when the children are growing their own food.

Year 2: Animals, including humans

What does the curriculum say?

- *Notice that animals, including humans, have offspring which grow into adults.*
- *Find out about and describe the basic needs of animals, including humans, for survival (water, food and air).*
- *Describe the importance for humans of exercise, eating the right amounts of different types of food, and hygiene.*

What do I need to know?

The human life cycle can be divided into many stages but the ones you might wish to discuss with the children are babies, infants (1–3) which includes the toddler stage, childhood 3–12, teenager 13–17 (note that late childhood and the teenager years are the time of adolescence, although you do not have to discuss these changes at this level), and adult (18 onwards). You may like to divide the adult stage into young adult (18 to 45), middle age (45–70) and old age (70+). It is important to point out that an adult's physical features and capabilities change as they age so it may help to use the three adult stages suggested here.

The first living things were micro-organisms. In order to survive they had to take in a substance which gave them energy (food) and possess water in which chemicals could process the food and keep the microbe alive. To process food, a chemical is needed to help in the release of the energy. In most living things on Earth today, that chemical is oxygen, which is in either the air or water. Air, water and food, therefore, are fundamental requirements for life. Although the emphasis in this topic is growth, reproduction is hinted at and, because the mechanisms of an organ to keep processing energy gradually wear out over a life span, breeding is the strategy that ensures a species stays in existence as long as it is adapted to its habitat.

In the food studies, foods for energy include carbohydrates and fats. When introducing the concept of energy foods, you may prefer to emphasise carbohydrates, rather than saying anything about fats and health, as this will be dealt with in Year 3. You should handle personal diets with sensitivity as some children, due to economic circumstances, may not have access to a very wide range of foods.

Interesting facts

The life span of an adult housefly is 15–30 days, an elephant has a life span of about 60–80 years. The longest-living animal ever found was a quahog clam (*Arctica islandica*) living on the seabed near Iceland. The clam was discovered to be 507 years old!

Vocabulary

Carbohydrate: a food made up of carbon, hydrogen and oxygen which provides a store of quickly released energy, e.g. pasta, bread, potatoes, rice.

Extinct: when all the members of a type (species) of living thing have died out.

Fat: a food made of carbon and hydrogen which is stored in the body and releases energy slowly.

Life cycle: the stages in the development of a plant or animal over its lifetime.

Life span: the length of time that a plant or animal lives.

Minerals: in food studies, minerals supply substances to provide structure (e.g. calcium for bones) and enable the chemical processes (e.g. iron in red blood cells picks up oxygen).

Protein: a food which provides material for growth, e.g. meat, fish, and pulses.

Vitamins: substances which help in many body processes such as preventing infection and digestive disorders, and bone building.

Progression

This topic builds on work in Year 1 where vertebrates were introduced. Here studies on the body structure, growth, diet and exercise form the foundation for work in Year 3 where diet and muscles and skeletons are studied in more detail.

Technical tip

People put food into groups such as meat, vegetables and fruit but here we start to put them into groups according to how they affect the body. In Year 3 food groups are considered in more detail but here they are simply grouped: food for growth (proteins); food for energy (carbohydrates and fats); food for keeping well (vitamins and minerals).

Lesson 1 Life cycles

Working scientifically skills: Observing closely; using simple equipment; gathering and recording data
Scientific enquiry type: Pattern seeking

You will need: photographs of yourself as a baby, toddler, 7 year old, 12 year old, 16 year old, 20 year old; photographs of your parents or grandparents from age 40, 50 and onwards showing change in faces, hair, posture etc. You will also need the outline of eight bodies drawn on blank wallpaper with the heights 50 cm (baby), 75 cm (1 yr), 85 cm (2 yr), 95 cm (3 yr), 100 cm (4 yr), 110 cm (5 yr), 115 cm (6 yr), 125 cm (7 yr), a children's height chart wall sticker.

Getting started
Show the children a photograph of yourself as a baby and ask them who in school they think it might be. Show each of your other photographs in turn asking again who it might be until the children recognise you. Ask the children to select your picture which matches them (at age 6–7). Tell the children that you have some pictures of people who are older than you and show them the pictures of your parents or grandparents. Ask the children to describe how adults change as they get older.

Class activities
- Remind the children how in Year 1 they drew an outline around a body. Say that you have made body outlines to show how a person (give them the fictitious name of Wally Paper) grows in the early stages of the life cycle. Show each outline in turn and ask the children to comment on how they would expect Wally to behave, e.g. how he would move, the noises he would make, what things he can do such as crawling, standing up, talking or feeding himself at each stage.
- Show the children a height chart wall sticker and ask if anyone has been measured with them at home. Stick it to the wall and let the children measure their height if they wish. Ask how Wally's height could be found and look for an answer about putting each of his bodies against the wall sticker.
- Let a few children take turns at measuring each of Wally's bodies and point out any discrepancies. This exercise can be used to highlight the importance of accuracy in measuring. Let the children complete a table of heights on the board.
- Explain how the data in a table is sometimes made into a graph to show more clearly any changes taking place. Instruct the children in the making of a bar graph and let them construct one called 'The growth of Wally Paper.'

Plenary
Review the changes in a person through their life cycle. Start with how a baby behaves and the ages at which an infant stands, walks, talks, and gets teeth. Talk about the children at their age and what they can do such as ride bicycles and tie shoe laces. Follow this up with brief accounts of the other life stages and be sure to handle the later stages of the life cycle with sensitivity (see Further lesson ideas and activities 1).

Lesson 2 Animal survival

Working scientifically skills: Observing closely
Scientific enquiry type: Pattern seeking

You will need: photographs of pets as babies, growing up and as adults, for example, kittens, young cat, adult cat; puppies, young dog, adult dog.

Getting started

Tell the following story and ask the following questions. A group of herbivorous mammals were grazing on a river bank when a great wave came along and swept them away. They thrashed about under the water and tried to get to the surface. Ask why and look for an answer about air and establish that land animals need air to survive. Continue by saying that the mammals got to the surface and bobbed about and eventually were washed up on the shore of an island. They got to their feet and looked around. The island looked like it was made of rock and sand. Ask about whether the animals would be able to live there and look for an answer about there being no food. Continue by saying that the mammals saw a gap in some rocks and clambered through it and after a while they came to a hidden valley. Ask what the animals needed here in order to survive and look for an answer about plants or food. Say that there was food and the animals grazed on it. Ask what else they would need to survive. You may have to coax the children to say 'water'.

Class activities

- Emphasise that animals need air, food and water in order to survive and ask how children care for their pets. Begin with herbivorous mammals such as rabbits and guinea pigs then move onto carnivorous pets such as cats and dogs. Draw out details of the variety of food eaten by each type of pet and the frequency of feeding and water provision. Write the details on the board.
- Having established how pets are fed and watered, ask about other ways in which the animals should be cared for to keep them healthy. Look for answers about exercise, e.g. taking a dog for a walk, having a wheel for a hamster, providing a run for a rabbit or simply letting the cat out.
- Ask each child to select a pet and write instructions on how to care for it.
- Return to the story of the mammals on the island. Say that the mammals were at all different stages in their life cycles. Their life span was only 20 years but 100 years later there were still animals on the island. Ask what had happened and look for an answer about the animals having bred.
- Say that pets breed too and when they do we can find out more about their life cycles. Show the pictures of the baby pets growing up and ask the children to comment on the changes they see.

Plenary

Review the requirements of land animals for survival. Pick out a few children to talk about how they would care for their pet. Ask how you could measure the growth of a pet and look for an answer about weight or length or height. Emphasise care in looking after pets (see Further lesson ideas and activities 2, 3 and 4).

Lesson 3 Keeping healthy

Working scientifically skills: Observing
Scientific enquiry type: Identifying, classifying and grouping

You will need: a picture of a jogger (or arrange for someone who goes jogging to visit the class) and a picture of a plate of food featuring meat, potato, and vegetables.

Getting started
Ask the children what humans need to stay alive and healthy. Look for answers about air (they may even say oxygen), food, and water. Ask what you should do if you had very dirty legs and got a cut on one. Look for an answer about cleaning it up and steer the conversations around to germs in dirt and keeping clean. Show the children the picture of (or introduce) the jogger and discuss why people do this. Look for an answer about exercise. Summarise by saying that people need food, good hygiene and exercise to stay healthy.

Class activities
* Ask the children to call out foods they like and write them on the left side of the whiteboard. Tell the children that, in order to make it easier to study, scientists often put data into groups. Organise the foods into three groups: food to make you grow (meat, fish, eggs); food to give you energy (bread, potatoes, biscuits); food to keep you well (vegetables, fruit). Call out each food group. Ask the children to put their hands up for each food group they eat foods from. Record the data in a bar chart on the whiteboard and discuss it.
* Show the picture of the plate of food and ask what food group it belongs to. Look for an answer that it features all three food groups and conclude that it is a healthy meal. Challenge the children to draw pictures of meals they like. Ask them to label their drawings, putting a G on foods for growth, an E on foods giving energy and a W for foods that keep you well (see Further lesson ideas and activities 5).
* Ask the children what they should do before they have a meal. Look for an answer about washing their hands to remove dirt that might have germs that could make them ill. Ask them about why they should have showers and baths and look for answers relating back to dirt and cuts.
* Give the children a big smile and point to your teeth. Ask how you should keep them clean. Develop a discussion on cleaning teeth and conclude that children should clean their teeth in the morning and at bedtime.
* Stand up and stretch your arms. Demonstrate the muscles in your upper arms moving your lower arms. Say that muscles all over the body provide the power for movement. Point to the elbow and say that the bones in our skeleton have joints. Say that the body needs exercise to keep the muscles and joints strong. Ask about the exercise that children do and make a table with numbers for football, dancing, running, gymnastics, and swimming. Let the children make a bar graph of the results and colour in the bars.

Plenary
Ask the class what advice they would give to a person if they wanted to be healthy (see Further lesson ideas and activities 6).

Further lesson ideas and activities

1. After establishing the concept of a human life cycle and the changes that take place in it, you may like to add other lessons on this theme. The first could be the life cycle of mammals where the children talk about their pets such as cats, dogs and rabbits. The second could be the life cycle of birds. For this you may like to use an incubator to hatch some chicks and rear them a little until you give them to a farmer or smallholder. It is important to feature animals which undergo metamorphosis so you may like to include a lesson on insects (perhaps acquiring some moth pupa from an educational supplier) and a lesson on amphibians (perhaps featuring frogs when frogspawn is available in the early spring). You will need to make the children aware of the correct way to care for any real-life examples of animals you provide and be sure to release them into a suitable environment when appropriate.

2. After establishing that land animals need air, food and water to survive and breed through the story and pet studies, you may like to link this back to habitat studies and see how animals in a habitat acquire their food and water. After this you may like to try idea 3.

3. Say that zoos were originally collections of living animals from around the world that were made for scientists to study (ignore commercial reasons at this level). Today most of them have programmes where they breed animals that are rare or in danger of becoming extinct. In order to do this they must make the enclosures as similar to the natural habitat as possible. Let the children read information about various zoo animals which describe their habitat and food and show pictures of enclosures to see how the animals' needs are met. Alternatively you may like to arrange a trip to the zoo, following school policies, where the children can take part in these activities on site.

4. Air enables animals to inhale oxygen and exhale carbon dioxide. Most aquatic animals have gills (or simply their skin) which they use to take in oxygen and release carbon dioxide. You could establish this with the children by studying goldfish as pets and the early life of tadpoles.

5. The children could complete the task of drawing and labelling their meals 'G', 'E' and 'W' as homework.

6. If appropriate you may like the children to assess their lifestyles regarding healthy eating, keeping clean and taking exercise. They could work out a three-star self-assessment and think of ways to have a healthier lifestyle if necessary.

Cross curricular links

- Work on caring for pets in lesson 1 could be linked with any activities on caring. The work on stages in life cycles could be linked to any conservation work with habitats.
- Lesson 2 contributes background information for activities in conservation.
- Lesson 3 can be built into a whole school health campaign or activity.

Year 2: Uses of everyday materials

What does the curriculum say?

• *Identify and compare the suitability of a variety of everyday materials, including wood, metal, plastic, glass, brick, rock, paper and cardboard for particular uses.*
• *Find out how the shapes of solid objects made from some materials can be changed by squashing, bending, twisting and stretching.*

What do I need to know?

The first humans used stone, bone, antler, wood, skins, sinews from meat for thread, thin woody stems for ropes, powdered rock for pigments and oil, and water and grease for paint. They lived in what is referred to as the Stone Age. Scientific evidence suggests that these people were at least as intelligent as us and their work shows great application in the use of materials as shown for instance in flint knapping for making knives. Some metals such as gold, silver and copper occur in their metallic state naturally and were known to these people but most metals are combined with other chemicals in rocks (called metal ores) and their presence was revealed by chance (perhaps rocks round a campfire becoming roasted and releasing their metal content). Over the centuries metals were discovered, the making of glass from sand was discovered and the making of plastic from various chemicals and then from the chemicals in oil and natural gas. Today, scientists are constantly searching for new materials with new properties which can be used to help us live our lives. The children will learn in Year 4 that materials can be grouped as electrical conductors and insulators but, early in scientific research on electricity, semiconductors were discovered which are used in many devices such as mobile phones and computers.

John Dunlop (1840–1921) was born in Scotland but went to work in Ireland as a veterinary surgeon. He invented the pnuematic (air filled) tyre for his son's tricycle to provide a smoother ride. It was made from a sheet of rubber that had been formed into a tube.

Charles Macintosh (1766–1843) experimented with chemicals and materials. He discovered how to dissolve rubber and make it into a solution and invented a waterproof fabric by using the solution to stick sheets of cloth together. This new material was used to make a type of coat – the mackintosh.

John McAdam (1756–1836) built roads by setting up a base of large stones on which crushed stone and gravel were placed and bound together. Later tar was added to make a smoother water repellent surface which is still known today as tarmac.

Vocabulary

Balsa: a very lightweight, very easily shaped wood obtained from the balsa tree in South America.
Mahogany: a reddish hardwood from the mahogany tree which grows in Central and South America.
Oak: a strong wood produced by oak trees in many parts of the world.
Pine: a lightweight wood which is easy to shape, produced by pine trees that grow in the Northern Hemisphere.

Progression

This topic builds on the foundations laid down in the materials topic in Year 1 by emphasising the study of material properties then linking them to uses. It introduces material change by studying the effects of forces on soft materials. It considers the material used both inside and outside buildings. The properties studied here are revisited in Year 3 when rocks and soils are studied.

Technical tip

Lesson 2 and Further idea 4: Have helpers available to supervise the use of elastic bands. If school policy requires it, issue safety spectacles. For Further idea 4, you may wish to secure each paper to its bowl before giving it to the children so that the children are simply adding weights until they fall through.

Lesson 1 Materials, properties and uses

Working scientifically skills: Observing
Scientific enquiry type: Identifying, classifying and grouping

You will need: a curiosity box containing a plastic block, a piece of metal, a piece of wood, a glass object, a piece of pottery, a piece of paper, two different types of metal, two different types of wood, and two different types of paper. You will also need a pan with a wooden or plastic handle, a bowl of hot water, a metal spoon, a wooden spoon and a plastic spoon (all the same size and quite short), a plastic knife, a tub of butter, and a stop watch.
Preparation: do a test run before the lesson to see how long this experiment will take.

Getting started
Tell the children they are going to carry on the study of materials that they began last year. Take out each of the materials out of the curiosity box. Ask the children to identify each one and say how they recognise it. Mention that they are using the material's properties to help them. Point out that materials are used to make the objects we use every day. Ask if only one material is ever used to make one object. Look for an answer that an object can be made from several materials, each one performing a particular task to make the object useful. Produce the pan and ask about the materials it is made from. Look for an answer about the pan being made from metal and the handle being made of wood or plastic. Ask why the two materials are used and encourage an answer about the metal getting hot to cook the food and the handle staying cool so it can be picked up. Say that you are going to set up an experiment to test the idea.

Class activities
- Show the children the three spoons and let them identify the materials. Say that you are going to put each one in the hot water and put a small lump of butter on the end of each handle. Ask them to predict what will happen and to explain their predictions. Set up the experiment and start the stopwatch. Depending on the time it will take, either let the children gather round to watch then move on to step 2, or place the experiment where everyone can see it and move on to step 3, returning to the experiment when ready.
- Look at the spoon experiment and you should find that the butter on the metal spoon has begun to melt and slide down while the others remain in position. Say that this experiment shows another property of a material: it can be a conductor of heat or a heat insulator. These properties are used in making a pan. The metal conducts the heat from the oven to the food and the handle material does not conduct heat and insulates the hand from the heat of the pan. You may run the experiment longer from the time of melting just to show that heat does not get through the two other materials.
- Return to the curiosity box and take out one of the metal objects, let the children identify the material then take out the other metal objects to establish that there are different types of metal. Repeat this procedure with the woods and papers.

Plenary
Review the investigation about heat conductance and the properties of the materials and let the children draw up a 'property list' for each group – for example, metal: shiny, feels cold, smooth, conducts heat well.

Lesson 2 Changing shapes

Working scientifically skills: Observing closely; performing simple tests
Scientific enquiry type: Comparative tests

You will need: an elastic band, a balloon (not inflated) and a balloon pump. Each group will need a sock, a piece of aluminium foil, and a sponge. Each child will need a ball of modelling clay about 5 cm across.

Getting started
Show the children an elastic band and stretch it. Ask the children what will happen when you stop pulling on it and look for an answer about it going back to its original shape. Check the children's prediction. Show the children the balloon and ask what will happen to the rubber if you blow up the balloon. Look for an answer about the rubber stretching as the balloon fills with air. Inflate the balloon then hold the end and ask what will happen if you let go. Look for an answer about the rubber contracting as the air is released then let the balloon go to check the prediction. Point out that some materials can be stretched but can return to their original shapes.

Class activities
- Give out the socks and ask the children to stretch them and then let them go. Ask them to describe their observations.
- Give out the aluminium foil and ask if they can twist and stretch it. Ask for their observations. Ask if the sock and the foil can be bent and look for positive answers.
- Give out the pieces of sponge and ask the children to stretch (they may tear), twist and squash them. Ask for their observations.
- Give out a piece of modelling clay to each child and ask them to stretch, bend, twist and squash them. Ask for their observations.
- Let the children use their ball of clay to make a model. It could be a model of anything, e.g. a person, an animal, a monster or a space ship.

Plenary
Let the children present their models to the class and explain how they made them using the words 'roll', 'squash', 'twist', 'stretch' and 'bend'. They could then put them on display (see Further lesson ideas and activities 3).

Lesson 3 Materials and their uses

Working scientifically skills: Observing closely; using their observations and ideas to suggest answers to questions
Scientific enquiry type: Identifying, classifying and grouping

You will need: a hammer with a metal head and wooden handle, a piece of wood and a nail, a piece of carpet and access to the school buildings and grounds. You will need a helper with a clipboard and a table with three columns (see below).

Getting started
Show the children the wood, nail and hammer and tap the nail lightly a little way into the wood. Ask why the hammer head is made of metal and look for an answer about it being hard. Ask why it is not made out of jelly. Ask why the handle is made out of wood and not rubber and look for an answer about the wood not bending. Say that we select materials to use because of their properties. Metal is used for hammer heads because it is hard, wood is used for the handle because it does not bend.

Show the children a piece of carpet and ask why it is not used for clothes. Look for an answer about it not being flexible or light in weight. Ask why it is useful on the floor and look for an answer about it not wearing away easily. Remind the children that last year they looked at materials in their classroom and now they are going to look at materials around the school.

Class activities
* Take the children around the school, pausing at appropriate places for the children to identify the materials there and to say why each is being used. These comments should be written in the table by the helper, for example: Place: School entrance; Material: Glass; Use: In the window to let in light.
* You may like to extend your journey outside and look at the school's roof, guttering, walls, paths and play areas.
* Back in the classroom, look at the number of times a material is featured in the table and list the materials from most to least common. At the top of the list, the most common materials are likely to be plastic, metal and wood. Fabrics (clothes, carpets, curtains) and paper may be in the middle, with glass, stone and brick at the bottom.
* Tell the children that some people say we live in a 'plastic age'. Show some pictures of mid Victorian life. Say that in the age of their great, great grandparents plastic had not been invented and the main materials used then were wood and metal.
* Tell the children that 8,000 years ago metals had not been discovered. In those days people used stone, wood and rope made from twine for all the things they needed. This age was known as the Stone Age.
* For homework, let the children find out about the uses of materials inside and outside their homes.

Plenary
Review the link between objects and the properties of the materials from which they are made. Select a few materials and discuss how their properties are useful. Ask the children to report on their homework about the uses of materials inside and outside their homes.

Further lesson ideas and activities

1. The children could shred waste paper and mix it with water to make a pulp. They could put the wet pulp on a metal gauze to let the water escape, put the pulp on a bread board and roll it with a rolling pin to squeeze out more water, then leave the flattened pulp to dry into paper. They could then test the strength of the paper.
2. After making their own paper in idea 1, they could research the work of people who have invented materials such as John Dunlop, John McAdam and Charles Macintosh.
3. You may like the children to make a dough and shape it into a loaf which can then be baked. Follow your school policies on hygiene for this activity.
4. Testing the strength of paper. Each group will need a plastic bowl, an elastic band, pieces of paper (for example, tissue, kitchen roll, newspaper) cut to fit over the bowl and be secured by the elastic band and each piece should have a small tear in the centre, a set of weights (wood or plastic blocks, marbles).

    Say that they are going to compare the strength of different papers. Show the children a piece of paper with a tear in it (to weaken it) and say that they will add weights until the tear increases and the weights fall through. They should then count the number of weights that caused the paper to collapse. Let the children carry out their investigations. They should make tables in which to record their data.

    Ask a spokesperson from each group to read out their results and fill them in on a table on the board. Finish by comparing the results and look for agreement. Where there is disagreement, discuss how the group have explained the anomaly. If children have made predictions, ask them how they compared with the results. Say that the results of the investigation can be used as evidence of paper having different strengths.

Cross curricular links

- You may like to make a survey of materials used in various periods of history that the children are studying.
- You could integrate the topic with design and technology work.

Part 2:
Lower Key Stage 2 (Years 3–4)

What does the curriculum say?

The principal focus of science teaching in Lower Key Stage 2 is to enable pupils to broaden their scientific view of the world around them. They should do this through exploring, talking about, testing and developing ideas about everyday phenomena and the relationships between living things and familiar environments, and by beginning to develop their ideas about functions, relationships and interactions. They should ask their own questions about what they observe and make some decisions about which types of scientific enquiry are likely to be the best ways of answering them, including observing changes over time, noticing patterns, grouping and classifying things, carrying out simple comparative and fair tests and finding things out using secondary sources of information. They should draw simple conclusions and use some scientific language, first, to talk about and, later, to write about what they have found out. 'Working scientifically' is described separately at the beginning of the programme of study, but must always be taught through and clearly related to substantive science content in the programme of study. Throughout the notes and guidance, examples show how scientific methods and skills might be linked to specific elements of the content. Pupils should read and spell scientific vocabulary correctly and with confidence, using their growing word reading and spelling knowledge.

Year 3: Plants

What does the curriculum say?

- *Identify and describe the functions of different parts of flowering plants: roots, stem/trunk, leaves and flowers.*
- *Explore the requirements of plants for life and growth (air, light, water, nutrients from soil, and room to grow) and how they vary from plant to plant.*
- *Investigate the way in which water is transported within plants.*
- *Explore the part that flowers play in the life cycle of flowering plants, including pollination, seed formation and seed dispersal.*

What do I need to know?

Each major part of the plant has one or more functions. The roots collect water and minerals from the soil and hold the plant firmly in the ground. The stem holds up the leaves so they can gather light to make food and holds up the flowers so they can receive pollen and disperse their fruits. It also conducts water and minerals from the roots to all parts of the plants and food made by the leaves to all the other parts of the plant. The trunk of a tree is a stem in which the plant makes wood to give it extra support so it can greatly increase in size. The leaves make food by trapping light and using its energy to construct carbohydrates such as sugar and starch from water and from carbon dioxide taken in from the air. The function of the flower is reproduction. In this process, flowers of the same kind of plant exchange pollen. This leads to fertilisation and a structure called an ovule in the ovary becoming a seed. The ovary then becomes a fruit which helps the seed leave the plant in a process called dispersal.

In the introduction to lesson 1, the children are introduced to a technique used by scientists called a thought experiment. They do not do any practical work but think about what might happen. These thought experiments can be used as the basis for predictions to set up real practical experiments.

Interesting fact

Plants disperse their seeds in many different ways. Ash trees and sycamores have wings to help them fall slowly through the air, dandelions and thistles have parachutes to carry them away, coconuts float away on the sea, berries containing seeds are eaten by birds who carry them away, digest the berry and release the seed unharmed with their droppings. Burdock seeds stick to animals and lupin fruits explode to scatter their seed.

Vocabulary

Extinct: when all the plants or animals of a particular type (species) die out.
Flower: the part of the plant which is concerned with reproduction.
Fruit: a structure made by the ovary which helps disperse the seeds.
Nectar: a sugary liquid that insects drink to give them energy to fly.
Ovary: the part of the plant which contains the ovule and later turns into a fruit.
Ovule: a small part of the ovary which becomes a seed when it receives the contents of a pollen grain.
Petal: a large colourful part of a flower which attracts insects.
Pollen: tiny grains made by the stamen which are needed by ovules in ovaries to make seeds.
Seed: a capsule containing a tiny plant and a food store.
Stigma: a sticky surface in the centre of a flower which holds onto pollen grains.
Style: a piece at the centre of a flower which connects the stigma to the ovary.
Stamen: a part of the flower which produces pollen at its tip.

Progression

This area of study about plants builds on the plant work in Key Stage 1 about factors affecting growth and focuses on the functions of the plant parts. It introduces the details of plant reproduction, which are dealt with in a more general sense when studying habitats and evolution in other parts of the curriculum.

Technical tip

You may wish to invite a gardener into the class to discuss techniques in sowing and raising plants and using fertiliser.

Useful websites

For lesson 3: http://www.saps.org.uk/primary/teaching-resources. Go to page 2 and find 'Investigating if plants grow better with fertilizer.'

Lesson 1 The parts of a plant

Working scientifically skills: Setting up simple practical enquiries; gathering data; recording findings in drawings; using straightforward scientific evidence to answer a question
Scientific enquiry type: Observing over time

You will need: for each group: a white carnation, a beaker of coloured water and a safe, warm place to leave the flowers for 24 hours.

Getting started
Ask the children to name the main parts of a plant (see the first diagram on page 57). Look for root, stem, leaf and flower in the answers. Tell the children that each part has certain tasks to perform in the life of the plant and we can tell what they are in the following way. Think of a plant part and think what would happen to the plant if the part was not there. Tell the children that this way of working is called a 'thought experiment' and challenge them with the thought experiments in the first four activities of this lesson.

Class activities
- Ask what would happen to a plant if you took its roots away. Look for an answer about the plant not being able to get water, falling over and blowing away.
- Ask what would happen to a plant if its leaves were taken away. Look for an answer about it dying because it would be unable to make food using light.
- Ask what would happen to a plant if the stem was taken away. Look for an answer about all the leaves and flowers separating and dying.
- Ask what would happen if all the flowers were taken away. Look for an answer about the plant being unable to make seeds and so the type of plant would die out (become extinct).
- Show the children a white carnation on a stem. Show the children a beaker of coloured water and ask them how they could use it show that water passes up the stem. Look for an answer about putting the lower part of the stem in the water and looking for the water reaching the petals and changing their colour. Tell the children that guessing the outcome of the experiment (that the petals will change colour) is called 'making a prediction'. Set up the experiment and prepare to leave it for the next day. But first, ask the children how they could make the results of the experiment more reliable. Look for an answer about using more than one carnation. Let each group set up a carnation in coloured water and leave it for the following day. They should write up about their investigation as they go along and include a before and after picture of their carnation.

Plenary
Let the children examine their carnations the following day and record how many had changed colour. Ask them how sure they are that the stem conducts water up the plant. Look for an answer that they are very sure as all or almost all flowers have changed colour.

Lesson 2 Flowers

Working scientifically skills: Making systematic and careful observations; recording findings using labelled diagrams
Scientific enquiry type: Identifying, classifying and grouping

You will need: a tulip flower and a buttercup for each group.

Getting started
Ask the children to describe what happens to a plant when it grows out of a seed. Look for answers including the root growing down, the shoot growing up, leaves sprouting from buds on the stem, the plant increasing in size. Ask the children what happens next and look for an answer (prompting if necessary) that the plant produces flowers. Say that these are all parts in the plant's life cycle and that in this lesson and the next they are going to look more closely at flowers and how they complete the life cycle.

Class activities
- Show the children a tulip flower and give one to each group. Ask them to look for the sepals, green leaf like structures at the top of the stalk, and the petals, the colourful structures above the sepal.
- Ask the children to open the flowers and look for the stamens inside the petals. They form a ring of stout rods each with a swollen top called an anther. This may be covered in a yellow powder made of pollen grains that the anther has produced.
- Ask the children to look inside the ring of stamens and find a central structure which has three parts. At the top is the stigma, which receives pollen. Beneath it is a long column called a style and at the base is the ovary.
- When the children can comfortably identify all the parts of the tulip flower, ask them to make a labelled diagram of it.
- Let the children look at a second flower, preferably a buttercup, and identify the sepals, petals and stamens. Point out that the centre of the buttercup has many carpels, each one made from a stigma, style and ovary.
- When the children can comfortably identify all the parts of the buttercup flower, ask them to make a labelled diagram of it. (See Further lesson ideas and activities 1 and 2.)
- Tell the children that flowers with bright petals also produce a scent and the colours and smells attract insects to them. The insects seek out nectar at the bottom of the petals to drink. As they do so, they pick up pollen from the anthers and take it with them to the next flower where it is collected on the sticky stigma. This process is called insect pollination. In some flowers the wind blows the pollen from the stamens of one flower to the stigma of another. (See Further lesson ideas and activities 3 and 4.)

Plenary
Review the children's knowledge of flower structure, insect pollination and wind pollination.

Lesson 3 Seeds and fruit

Working scientifically skills: Setting up simple practical enquiries; making systematic and careful observations; using results to draw simple conclusions
Scientific enquiry type: Comparative and fair tests; observing over time

You will need: some tomato flowers (or a detailed picture or diagram of them), a bunch of tomatoes on a vine; for each group: examples of hooked fruit (e.g. goose grass, burdock, agrimony), winged fruit (e.g. ash, sycamore, lime), and parachute fruit (e.g. dandelion, willow herb), two seed trays of compost, seeds such as radish, access to water and a warm light place to keep the trays.

Getting started
Show the children that tomato plants have yellow flowers and point out all the parts of the flowers that they have seen before in a tulip. Show the children the tomatoes on the vine and say that a little while after pollination a bunch of tomato flowers look like this. Ask the children if they can see the remains of the flowers and encourage them to identify the sepals. Tell them that the centre of the flower is still there but it has changed into a fruit. Ask the children what you will find if you cut open the tomato and look for an answer about seeds. Cut open the tomato to reveal the seeds.

Class activities
- Tell the following story of what happens in a tomato flower after it has been pollinated. Say that the inside of the pollen comes out of the pollen grain and goes down the style into the ovary where it finds a tiny ovary part called an ovule. It joins with the ovule in a process called fertilisation and the ovule turns into a seed.
- Ask the children what a seed contains and look for it containing a tiny plant. Say that when the seed forms, the life cycle of the plant is complete.
- Say that when a flower forms seeds the next task is to get them away from the parent plant so the new tiny plants inside the seeds can grow. This process is called dispersal and plants like the tomato that make brightly coloured, moist, fleshy fruit use animals to disperse them. The animals eat the fruit, the seeds pass through their bodies and come out in droppings far away from the parent plant.
- Show the children hooked fruits such as goose grass, burdock and agrimony and ask them how these may be dispersed by animals. Look for an answer about being carried on fur and feathers. The children may demonstrate by sticking the fruits to their clothes and walking about.
- Show the children a winged fruit such as a sycamore or ash and a parachute fruit such as the fruit of a dandelion or willow herb and ask them how they think they are dispersed. Look for an answer about being blown by the wind. Let them blow the fruits to demonstrate.
- Tell the children that plants take substances called minerals from the soil to help them grow healthily. These are found naturally but farmers and gardeners use fertilisers to increase the mineral content of soil. (See Further lesson ideas and activities 5.)
- Ask four children to pick up two sheets of green paper, hold them out and think of themselves as plants with roots for feet. Ask them to huddle together with leaves overlapping and feet close together. Ask the rest of the class whether you would expect the plants to

grow well and look for answers about the roots competing for water and minerals, the leaves competing for light and having little air between them.

- Ask the children to devise a real experiment to see if plants from seeds placed close together grow less healthily than those that are more spaced apart. The children should have two trays of seeds: one with seeds packed together and one with fewer seeds well spaced. Let the children look after the seed trays, water them, keep them in the light and compare the growth. They should find that the plants with more space grow more healthily.

Plenary
Review the life cycle of a plant, compare seed dispersal methods and describe the factors required by plants for healthy growth (light, air, water, minerals, space).

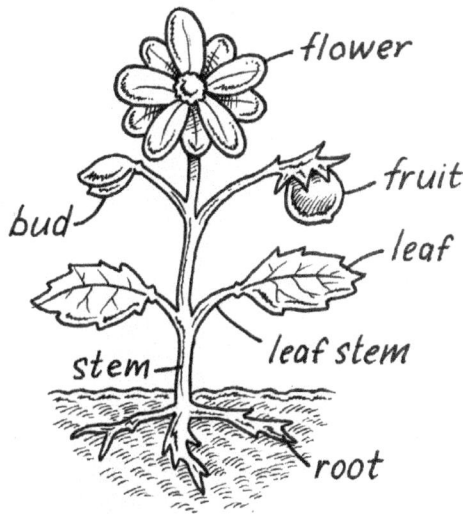

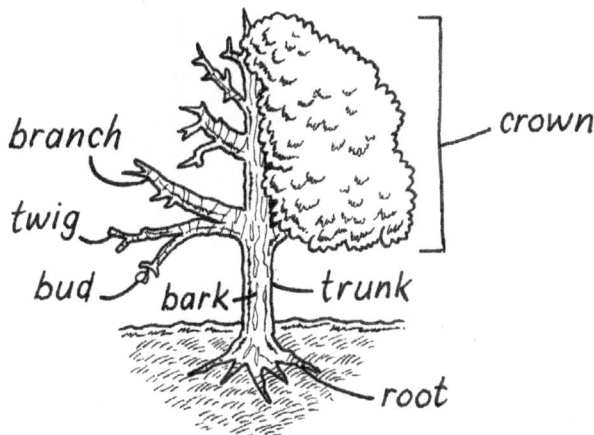

Further lesson ideas and activities

1. After lesson 2, take a gerbera flower (a colourful daisy-like flower usually sold at supermarkets and florists) and challenge the children to find the parts they have seen in the tulip and buttercup. They will not be able to find them because the gerbera is a flower head made of many small flowers called florets grouped together at the top of the stalk. Let the children examine daisies and dandelions and discover that they are both made of flower heads of florets.
2. Let the children look at a selection of house plants, garden plants or wild plants and identify those with single flowers and those with flower heads.
3. Demonstrate insect pollination by asking one child to be an anther on a stamen and hold up three tennis balls (pollen grains). Ask three other children to be stigmas of other flowers and hold out one hand. Ask one child to be a bee and pass the anther and pick up the tennis balls then move around the class giving one each to the stigmas.
4. Demonstrate wind pollination by giving a child two tennis balls (pollen grains) and asking them to throw them to other children who are stigmas in other flowers. Say that as the flowers do not have to attract insects it does not matter how they look or smell. Show them some grass flowers at the top of a stalk or a hazel catkin and compare them in size, colour and smell to the flowers adapted for insect pollination.
5. Use the internet link to saps.org.uk for a downloadable PDF of an investigation into the beneficial effects of fertilisers (growing radishes with different numbers of fertiliser pellets). This activity may take four weeks. Alternatively, ask a gardener to come into school to talk about the use of fertilisers.

Cross curricular links

- Get children completing a nature diary as a writing project and let the children describe the plants they see at different times of the year.
- The children could do a maths project related to the number of plants in flower in a certain area through the seasons.

Year 3: Animals, including humans

What does the curriculum say?

- *Identify that animals, including humans, need the right types and amount of nutrition, and that they cannot make their own food; they get nutrition from what they eat.*
- *Identify that humans and some other animals have skeletons and muscles for support, protection and movement.*

What do I need to know?

Along with fibre and water, there are five groups of nutrients needed for health: proteins, fats, carbohydrates, vitamins and minerals (see vocabulary). The aim of the study of nutrients is to encourage children to have a balanced diet and to help them realise that an unbalanced diet leads to ill health. Lack of a nutrient group can cause ill health. For example, a lack of vitamin D prevents bones forming properly and leads to the disease called rickets. Too much of some foods can also cause ill health. For example, too much sugar leads to tooth decay and if the person is inactive the energy in sugar is stored as fat. The fat in fatty foods such as butter, lard and cheese, is also stored as fat in inactive people. Extra body fat increases the strain on the circulatory system to supply blood to all parts of the body, increasing the risk of a heart attack. The extra weight also increases the strain on joints and growing bones.

Many invertebrate animals such as earthworms and slugs have water held inside them by muscles which acts as a skeleton. Arthropods such as insects and crustaceans have an exoskeleton – a hard covering on the outside of their bodies. Sharks and rays have skeletons made of cartilage. All the skeletons provide a support for the muscles. Muscles are attached to bones by tendons and bones are attached to each other across a joint by ligaments. Muscles can only contract (get shorter) so they must be arranged in any animal so that when one muscle contracts another relaxes and stretches. When this second muscle contracts it stretches the first and restores it to its original length ready for action again. Muscles arranged like this are known as antagonistic pairs.

A water skeleton does not give much protection so snails and clams have developed shells to protect themselves. Exoskeletons give almost complete protection to the body beneath it and parts of a body skeleton such as the skull and rib cage provide protection to the organs they enclose.

The aim of lesson 1 is to promote healthy eating habits but it must be handled with sensitivity as some family budgets may not be large enough to buy the wide range of foods discussed.

Interesting facts

The smallest bones in your body are in your ears and help you hear. The longest bone in your body is the upper leg bone, the femur.

Vocabulary

Arthropod: an animal with an outside skeleton (exoskeleton), e.g. insects, spiders, crabs and lobsters, centipedes and millipedes.

Balanced diet: meals taken over a period of time that include all of and have the correct balance of the nutrients needed for the body to stay healthy.

Carbohydrates: nutrients consisting of carbon, hydrogen and oxygen, which provides energy that the body can release quickly for its activities.

Carnivore: an animal that only eats other animals.

Fats: nutrients which provide a store of energy and build a heat insulating layer under the skin.

Herbivore: an animal that only eats plants.

Invertebrate: an animal without a skeleton of bone or cartilage.

Minerals: substances such as calcium (that aids bone growth) and iron (that helps the blood carry oxygen) that are necessary for processes in the body.

Muscle: a part of the body that brings about movement when it contracts.

Omnivore: an animal that eats both plants and animals.

Protein: nutrients that help the body grow and repair injuries.

Tendons: non-elastic cords that attach muscles to bones.

Unbalanced diet: meals taken over a period of time which have too much of some foods and too little of others which leads to the body not receiving all the nutrients it needs to stay healthy.

Vertebrate: an animal with a skeleton of bone or cartilage and a backbone made up of many small bones called vertebrae.

Vitamins: substances such as vitamin A (which increases resistance to disease) and vitamin B (which prevents digestive disorders) that are needed for general good health.

Progression

This area of study builds on the vertebrate structure studied in Year 1 and invertebrate structure in Year 2 in work on habitats. It also builds on studies of food in Year 2 and forms the foundation for work on digestion in Year 4.

Technical tip

In lesson 2, the paper bones could be about 1 cm in diameter and lengths varying from 2 cm to 10 cm. The bone should be tested until it bends.

Useful websites

Lesson 1: www.sciencekids.co.nz/sciencefacts/humanbody/teeth.html
Lesson 1: www.sciencekids.co.nz/sciencefacts/humanbody/digestivesystem.html
Lesson 2: www.sciencekids.co.nz/sciencefacts/humanbody/skeletonbones.html
Lesson 3: www.sciencekids.co.nz/sciencefacts/humanbody/muscles.html

Lesson 1 Food

Working scientifically skills: Classifying and presenting data in a variety of ways to help in answering questions; identifying changes related to simple scientific ideas and processes
Scientific enquiry type: Identifying, classifying and grouping

You will need: shopping bags with pasta, rice, bread, potatoes, sugar, sweets, butter, cheese, chocolate, biscuits, red meat, chicken, fish, eggs, peas, beans, lentils, oranges, apples, pears, plums, cabbage, cauliflower, carrots, swedes, tomatoes, onions, and a packet of cereal. You will also need three large labels for a desk display reading 'Foods for energy', 'Foods for growth', and 'Foods for health'. You will also need photographs of three meals, two of which are well balanced (e.g. steak, potatoes and salad; chicken, rice and peppers) and one of which is unbalanced (e.g. fish and chips; bread and butter).

Getting started

Remind the children about food chains from their study of habitats and review that while plants can make their own food, animals cannot and must get it from plants or other animals. Ask them to define 'herbivore', 'carnivore' and 'omnivore' and to give examples of each. Ask the children about the types of food they feed their pets and what types of feeders their pets are. Steer the discussion around to humans being omnivores.

Class activities

- Show the children the table of nutrients on the side of the packet of cereal (use a visualiser so all the children can see). Say that foods contain nutrients. These are protein, carbohydrate, fat, vitamins and minerals. Indicate the different nutrient groups, in the table, as you talk about them. Point out that the amounts of nutrients are also shown because the amounts of nutrients in food are important. Show the serving guide on the front of the packet.
- Say that we can think of food more simply as foods which give us energy, foods that help us grow and repair injuries and foods that keep us healthy. Place the large labels on a table, unpack the shopping bags and place the foods in the following groups. Energy: pasta, rice, bread, potatoes, sugar, sweets, butter, cheese, chocolate, biscuits. Growth: meat, chicken, fish, eggs, peas, beans, lentils. Health: fruits and vegetables. (See Further lesson ideas and activities 1.)
- Ask the children which of the foods they eat for energy, growth and health. You could make a table and tally chart to find the most and least consumed foods.
- Remind the children about the significance of amounts of nutrients. Draw a large triangle on the board and divide it into four horizontal sections. Each section indicates how much of a particular food type you should have in your meals. Start at the bottom and say this section represents foods for energy, the next represents food for health, and the next represents food for growth. Pause at the empty, top segment and say we must look more closely at the foods for energy. In the bottom layer are foods the body uses quickly like rice, pasta, potatoes and bread. But some foods like butter, chocolate and biscuits contain large amounts of fat. Fat only releases energy slowly and is stored in the body. Too much stored fat makes the body overweight. Point out that too much sugar damages teeth.
- Show the children the photographs of the plates of food pointing out that two of them have a good balance between foods for energy, growth and health and the last one is unbalanced with just food for energy and growth. Ask the children to think about their favourite meals, draw and label them and assess their balance. (See Further lesson ideas and activities 2.)

Plenary

Review the food groups and the need for balance. Let the children display their meals and talk about how they are healthy or what they could change to give it a better balance. (See Further lesson ideas and activities 3 and 4.)

Lesson 2 Skeletons

Working scientifically skills: Setting up a simple practical enquiry; gathering, recording, and presenting data in a variety of ways; using straightforward scientific evidence to answer questions
Scientific enquiry type: Fair test

You will need: X-ray photographs of a skull, a hand and an arm; a model skeleton; a labelled diagram of a skeleton; and a box with a hinge. Each group will need newspapers, scissors, sticky paper, weights on a hanger or a yoghurt pot 'bucket' and blocks.

Getting started
Ask the children to gently rub their heads and feel the hard structure beneath their skin. Ask them to squeeze their fingers and feel the hard parts in the centres. Ask them to hold out their right arm, grip the lower part above the wrist with their left hand and swivel their right hand. They should feel hard parts in their lower arm swivelling too. Ask them what they have been feeling, look for an answer about bones then show them the X-ray photographs.

Class activities
- Show the children the model skeleton and present the diagram. Make sure the children learn the names of the bones: skull, backbone, shoulder blade (scapula), collarbone (clavicle), humerus, ulna, radius, breastbone (sternum), rib, pelvis, femur, knee cap (patella), tibia, and fibula. You need only point out that the hands and feet are made of many bones.
- Ask the children to draw what a person would look like if they did not have a skeleton of bones. Look for a picture of a collapsed body like a jellyfish with a face at the top. Be prepared for some monsters! Conclude that the skeleton provides support for the rest of the body.
- Ask what other things the parts of the skeleton might do and tap your head. Look for an answer about protecting your brain and move the discussion to protection in general, pointing out that the backbone is hollow and protects the spinal cord which joins the brain to other parts of the body. Beat your chest and say that the rib cage protects the heart and lungs.

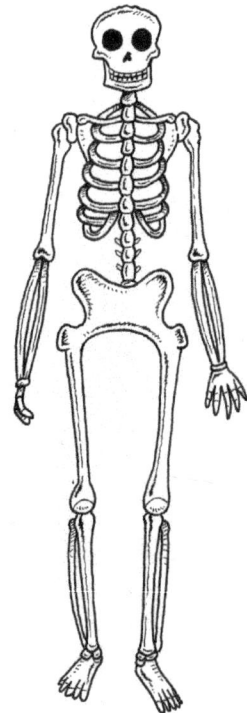

- Ask what else parts of the skeleton might do and wave your arms about. Look for an answer about movement and say that between the bones are joints which help this happen. Move the lower arm up and down and show the position of the elbow joint. Open and close the lid on a box, point to the hinge and say that some joints are hinge joints and move bones in two directions. Move your upper arm in a circular manner and make the model skeleton arm move in the same way. Point to the ball and socket joint, between the humerus, shoulder blade and collarbone. Show the ball and socket joint between the pelvis and the femur.
- Show the children the backbone and point out that it is made of lots of small bones. Say that surely it would be stronger with just one long bone. Say that scientists often use models to test their ideas. Challenge the children to test bone strength: make model bones by rolling up two newspapers to an equal thickness but making them different lengths. Let the children place the paper bones in turn between two chairs and hang weights from them. They should place a box beneath the weights to catch them if they fall when the 'bone' bends. (See Further lesson ideas and activities 5.)

Plenary

Test the children's knowledge of the skeleton by pointing to bones in the model or on their bodies. Ask them to present the results of their bone experiments. They should conclude that shorter bones are stronger. Ask them for another advantage in having a number of smaller bones rather than just one long one and look for an answer about flexibility. (See Further lesson ideas and activities 6.)

Lesson 3 Muscles

Working scientifically skills: Asking relevant questions and using different types of scientific enquiries to answer questions; setting up simple practical enquires; making systematic and careful observations; using results to draw simple conclusions; making predictions; for new values, suggesting improvements and raising further questions
Scientific enquiry types: Fair test; pattern seeking

You will need: a model skeleton, metre and half metre rules or tape measures, a sports tape measure for the 'ten stride' activity.

Getting started

Show the children the model of the skeleton and revise the names of the bones. Point out that a skeleton cannot move on its own even though skeletons may move around in scary stories! Say that the skeleton is covered in muscle. Let the children feel their upper and lower arms and say that under the skin are muscles which move the bones. Ask the children to hold out their right arms and push the fingers of their left hand into the front of the upper arm. They should feel that there is a soft muscle there. Now ask them to raise their forearms and keep feeling with their fingers. They should feel that the soft muscle becomes hard. Explain that the muscle is working to raise the bones in the forearm.

Class activities

- Let the children lower their forearms and ask them to spread out their fingers along the upper arm muscle. Ask them to raise their forearms again and feel for changes with their fingers. They should feel that their fingers come closer together. Explain that when a muscle is working it also gets shorter.

- Keep the children flexing their arms and say that muscles can only work by getting shorter. The muscle that has raised their forearm, the biceps, cannot do anything about lowering it. For the arm to be lowered a second muscle, called the triceps, on the other side of the upper arm, works to pull the bones down. Let the children feel for this muscle and raise and lower their arms.
- Say that muscles are attached to bones by tendons which are like cords. Ask the children to feel inside the elbow of a flexed arm to feel how the biceps connects to bones in the lower arm. Ask the children to feel behind their knees when they are sitting down and find the hamstring tendons which connect the muscles of the upper leg to the lower leg. (See Further lesson ideas and activities 7.)
- Ask the children to think about the bones and muscles in their legs and how they work together to enable walking. Steer the discussion around to trying to find out if people with longer legs take longer strides. With the children, work out an experiment in which the length of the leg is measured from the hip down; a length of stride is measured; this is checked by measuring the distance covered by ten steps and dividing by ten. (See Further lesson ideas and activities 8.)
- Tell the children that exercise is needed to keep the muscles, bones and joints healthy. Write a table on the whiteboard with the column headings: Activity; Hands and arms; Trunk; Feet and legs. Ask the children which parts of the body they use during different activities (e.g. watching television, walking, playing football). List the activities in the table and place ticks or crosses in the column for each body part depending on whether they are used or not. (See Further lesson ideas and activities 9.)

Plenary
Review the action of muscles on bones. Let the children present their findings from their investigation into the correlation between length of leg and length of stride. Work together to produce a healthy exercise regime for the class to do over the course of a week. (See Further lesson ideas and activities 10.)

Further lesson ideas and activities

1. The children categorise the food in their family shopping as food for energy, food for growth and food for health.
2. The children could take photographs of all the meals and snacks they have in a day. They could record the items in a table of the three groups, food for energy, growth and health, as a tally chart and make a bar graph of their results.
3. You could invite a nutritionist to talk to the children about how to make cheap changes to a series of meals to make them healthier.
4. You may want to introduce the words 'protein' (for growth and repair), 'carbohydrate', 'fat' (for energy), 'vitamins' and 'minerals' (for health) in the plenary session.
5. The children can make a full report of the experiment on bone strength by drawing or writing about what they did, constructing a table in which the results are recorded and concluding that the short bones are stronger. You could also ask about which bones in the skeleton could be at most risk of breaking and look for answers about arms, legs and ribs.
6. Remind the children of other animals they have studied. Talk about the vertebrates being divided into five groups and show pictures of their skeletons. Remind the children about the mini beasts they may have studied when looking at habitats and point out that arthropods have outside skeletons of armour and that molluscs and worms have skeletons of water. Fill a balloon with water to show how the water gives support to the balloon. These three boneless groups are part of the larger invertebrate group.
7. Sit the children down with feet flat on the floor. Ask them to feel the muscles in their lower leg with both hands and raise the toe and then the heel. They should feel different muscles becoming harder as they work on these tasks.
8. The children could find out if the length of their stride changes when they run by taking ten running steps, dividing the distance covered by ten and comparing it with their walking stride.
9. The children could assess their activity over a week such as the number of times they played sport, did gymnastics, had dance lessons. If exercise was lacking in their lifestyle they could discuss with others how they could increase it.
10. The children could look at how animals move in a local habitat, a fish tank and describe how their pets move.

Cross curricular links

- Lesson 1 could be integrated into a school based healthy eating project.
- Lessons 2 and 3 could be integrated with appropriate first aid care.
- Lesson 3 could be integrated into a school exercise programme.

Year 3: Rocks

What does the curriculum say?

- *Compare and group together different kinds of rocks on the basis of their appearance and simple physical properties.*
- *Describe in simple terms how fossils are formed when things that have lived are trapped within rock.*
- *Recognise that soils are made from rocks and organic matter.*

What do I need to know?

There are three kinds of rocks. There are: igneous rocks such as granite and basalt that come from molten rock below the Earth's crust; sedimentary rock such as sandstone which forms from weathered fragments of rock sticking together and limestone which forms from the shells of marine creatures which settle on the sea bed; metamorphic rock such as marble and slate which forms when rocks in the Earth's crust get squashed and heated in processes such as mountain building.

Fossils form when a plant or animal dies and is quickly covered with silt or mud so that it cannot be broken up by scavengers or rotted by microbes. In time sediments build and squash the mud, turning it into stone. The materials in the body are replaced by minerals that flow in water through the rock. They settle out in the body and form rock. Besides fossil bodies there can be fossil footprints and even fossil dinosaur droppings.

Soil is made from tiny rocky particles such as sand, silt and clay made when rocks are broken down by the action of the weather. These particles mixed with the decaying matter of dead plants and animals (which form a substance called humus) to form soil. The proportions of these soil substance vary so there can be sandy or clay soils or soils rich in humus which are called loams.

Interesting fact

The Earth can be compared to a hardboiled egg. The shell can represent the rocky crust we live on and, if broken, resembles the plates on the crust. The white can represent the mantle layer and the yolk can represent the core.

Vocabulary

Arthropod: an animal with an outside skeleton and jointed legs, e.g. insects, crustaceans, spiders, millipedes and centipedes.
Humus: the material in soil made from the remains of dead plants and animals.
Igneous rock: molten rocks from inside the Earth, e.g. basalt and granite.
Metamorphic rock: rock that has been changed by heat and pressure when mountains form. Some rock is also changed by being close to hot igneous rocks, e.g. slate and marble.
Sedimentary rock: rock formed from particles that have settled in layers and become joined together, e.g. sandstone and limestone.
Palaeontologist: a scientist who studies fossils.
Weathering: the breaking down of rocks due to the effects of weather such as wind, rain and ice.

Progression

The study of rocks builds on the work on materials in Key Stage 1. It provides details of solids for further consideration in Year 4. The study of fossils provides evidence for evolution, studied in Year 6. The study of soil provides an extension of the study of materials in Key Stage 1 and contributes to the study of plants and habitats in Key Stage 2.

Technical tip

In lesson 2, rehearse the fossil making exercise before the lesson to check the consistency of your plaster of Paris and water mixture. You will need to take photographs of the monsters, upload them to the computer and print them off but keep them secret from all the groups.

In lesson 3, to use a magnifying glass, place it about 8 cm from your eye and about 15 cm from the object you are looking at. Move the glass to and fro to see a magnified view of the object.

Useful websites

www.sciencekids.co.nz/sciencefacts/earth/igneousrocks.html
www.sciencekids.co.nz/sciencefacts/earth/sedimentaryrocks.html
www.sciencekids.co.nz/sciencefacts/earth/metamorphicrocks.html
www.sciencekids.co.nz/sciencefacts/earth/rocksandminerals.html
peterdriley.com/volcanoes-plate-tectonics-and-natural-processes
peterdriley.com/stalagmites-and-stalactites-in-the-postojna-cave-in-slovenia
Lesson 2: peterdriley.com/fossil-hunt-on-the-jurassic-coast

Lesson 1 Rocks

Working scientifically skills: Making systematic and careful observations; using results to draw simple conclusions
Scientific enquiry type: Identifying, classifying and grouping; fair test

You will need: a homemade 'planet,' 'volcano' and erosion demonstration, and a sample of shells, sandstone, limestone and chalk. Children should have access to a white card and small samples of sandstone, limestone, chalk, granite, basalt, slate and marble.
Preparation: make a 'planet'! You will need: 10 small pieces of modelling clay (about 1 cm across), 10 small lumps of modelling clay (about 3 cm across), 10 large lumps of modelling clay (about 5 cm across). Make the volcano! You will need: a clean plastic bottle containing a tablespoon of baking soda, placed in a tray with sand piled around it to make a cone shape. Add a few drops of red food dye to half a cup of vinegar. Use a funnel to pour the vinegar into the bottle quickly when ready. For demonstrating erosion, you will need three pieces of porous rock (e.g. sandstone, pumice stone). Put two rocks in foil dishes, cover them with water and freeze them. Thaw one out before the lesson.

Getting started

You may like to begin by using the information in the background section to explain where the rocks originally came from. You could get the children to help illustrate the later part of the story by giving out a small piece of modelling clay to ten children and asking them to join them together to make a larger lump, giving out the small lumps of modelling clay to another ten children and adding the newly made lump and asking the children to join them together and repeating the procedure with the large lumps so that a 'rocky planet' of modelling clay is made. Say this is the way the Earth formed and they are now going to look at the rocks in more detail.

Class activities

- Remind the children about how the insides of stars are hot and say that the insides of planets are hot too. Say that sometimes the hot rock bursts out onto the plane surface and introduce the volcano model. Add the vinegar quickly to the bottle and move back so the children can see the volcano erupt. Say that in this model you have used two ingredients used in baking to make the eruption and not heat.
- Show the children samples of basalt and granite. Say that basalt forms from rock that erupted on the surface and granite formed from rock that got trapped in the crust and cooled down.
- Say that once the rock is on the planet's surface it is exposed to the weather. Show the children the sandstone in the block of ice and pour off the water from the thawed stone to reveal particles broken off by the action of the ice. Show samples of sandstone and mudstone. (See Further lesson ideas and activities 1.)
- Show the children a collection of shells and say that these can join together to form rock and show them limestone and chalk. Say that rocks formed from collections of rocky particles and shells are called sedimentary rocks.
- Tell children about the movement of the rocky plates and place two flannel facecloths side by side on a table. Push them together to show how they ripple to form 'mountains'. Say that the heat and pressure in making mountains changes the rocks in them. Say these rocks are metamorphic rock and show slate and marble samples. (See Further lesson ideas and activities 2.)

- Ask the children how they could compare the hardness of rocks and look for an answer about rubbing two rocks together over white card and seeing which one produces the most fragments. Issue the card and rocks and let the children carry out their tests. (See Further lesson ideas and activities 3.)

Plenary

Review the three types of rock and how they are formed and let the children present their results. The hardest rocks should be granite and basalt, the weakest should be chalk. There may be some variation in the others depending on the samples. (See Further lesson ideas and activities 4.)

Lesson 2 Fossils

Working scientifically skills: Setting up simple practical enquiries
Scientific enquiry type: Observing over time; grouping and classifying

Your will need: for each group, a sea shell such as a periwinkle, a ball of modelling clay about 4 cm across, a plastic knife. When the moulds are ready you will need to mix plaster of Paris with water in a jug until it forms a runny mixture. You will need pictures or specimens of an ammonite and a trilobite, and a picture of a dinosaur skeleton. Each group will need pipe cleaners, card, scissors, sticky paper. To make monsters, groups will need a tray of sand, a teaspoon and a basting brush. You will need a camera.

Getting started

Ask the children about the animals they see in their local environment. Look for answers about squirrels and different birds. Tell the children that when animals die their bodies are decomposed by mini beasts such as beetles and fly maggots and organisms that live in the soil. Say that this has always taken place but just occasionally a body falls into a place where other things cannot get at it. Ask them to imagine a dinosaur walking along the edge of a river. It is ill and falls into the river, dies and is covered with sand being washed down from weathered rocks of a mountain. In time, the sand layer builds up and turns to stone and the body turns into a fossil.

Class activities

- Tell the children that one way fossils form happens when a body is trapped in rock. The body is then dissolved and washed away by water passing through the rock and the space is filled with other minerals washed in by the water. When the body goes it leaves an impression in the rock which is taken up by the minerals. Tell the children that they are going to make a fossil in a similar way and show them the modelling clay, shell and plastic knife.
- Demonstrate by cutting the clay ball in half, pressing the shell in to one half then enclosing it with the other half so that the shell makes a cavity inside the ball. Open the ball and remove the shell and cut a channel in each half from the top of the ball down to the cavity. (It should be wide enough for the plaster mixture to flow freely.) Close up the ball, pour in the mixture and leave for the plaster to set for about half an hour.
- Issue a clay ball, a shell and a plastic knife to each group and let them make a fossil cavity. When they are ready, mix some more paste, pour it into their moulds and let the children leave them for half an hour.

- Show the children an ammonite and ask what animal group it might belong to. Look for an answer about molluscs. Show the children a trilobite and look for an answer about it being related to insects or crabs and lobsters (it was an arthropod). Show the children a picture of a dinosaur skeleton and say that when skeletons are found they are often broken up and the palaeontologists have to carefully remove them from the ground and work out how the bones are connected together.
- Tell the children that they are going to make model monsters using a variety of materials. Each group must work in secret, photograph their model then take it to bits and put it in a tray of sand.
- Each group swaps trays and, using spoons and basting brushes, they should carefully remove all the pieces of the monster and try to assemble it as they think it might have been.

Plenary

Let the children peel back the modelling clay carefully to find the 'fossil' shell. Let groups present the model monsters they have assembled and let the original groups present the photographs of the monsters they made for comparison. Point out that fossils often need to be assembled so sometimes mistakes are made and later corrected as more fossils are found.

Lesson 3 Soils

Working scientifically skills: Setting up fair tests; taking systematic and careful observations and taking accurate measurements using standard units; recording findings using drawings and labelled diagrams; using results to draw simple conclusions and make predictions for new values
Scientific enquiry type: Identifying, classifying and grouping

You will need: each group will need a soil sample, white card and a magnifying glass, a clear plastic beaker, a teaspoon, a funnel and plastic bottle, a measuring cylinder, a beaker of water, a coffee filter.
Preparation: you can make a funnel and beaker by cutting the top off a plastic bottle and inverting it in the rest of the bottle.

Getting started

Review how rocks are weathered and point out that they make tiny fragments like sand grains. Remind the children that the bodies of most dead animals are broken down into the soil and say that this also happens to all the dead parts of plants. Say that in the autumn, parks and gardens are covered in dead leaves but in spring, even if they have not been swept up, they will have rotted into the soil. Tell the children they are going to look closely at soil and find out what kind of a material it is.

Class activities

- Give each group a soil sample, white card and a magnifying glass. Ask them to spread out some soil and look at it with the magnifying glass. Ask them to describe what they see in words and a picture.

- Give each group a beaker of water, ask the children to pour in the soil and stir it up with a spoon then leave it for five minutes. Ask the children to report on what they see. Look for an answer about the soil separating into layers with the largest pieces at the bottom and the smallest at the top. There may be some even smaller pieces which are floating in the water and making it cloudy. There may be black or brown material floating on the water's surface. This is humus: the remains of mostly dead plants but also some dead animal material. Let the children draw and label their soil.
- Remind the children of when they tested materials for being waterproof or absorbent. Ask them for their ideas and with them construct an experiment to test the absorbency of soil. This should involve putting a coffee filter in a funnel (to stop the soil falling through), placing a certain amount of dry soil in the funnel (until it is half or two thirds full) placing the funnel over a beaker or the top of a measuring cylinder, pouring in a certain amount of water (100 ml) and timing how long it takes the water to pass through. The children should write the method you have devised together, carry out the experiment and record the results. They should discover that the soil drains a certain amount of water and also absorbs a certain amount of water.
- Ask the children how they could compare the drainage of sand with the draining of soil and look for the idea that they could repeat their experiment with dry sand. Ask for predictions with explanations. Good predictions and explanations are that the sand drains faster because it has larger fragments with larger spaces between them or it has less humus to soak up the water.
- Let the children carry out the experiment with sand. (See Further lesson ideas and activities 6.)

Plenary

Ask the children how soil is formed and about its components. Ask each group to report on how much water was absorbed by their soil and how much drained through. Ask them to compare this data with the data from the sand experiment. Look for children explaining how much more water drained through the sand than the soil. If you have made investigations as suggested in Further idea 6, let the children present their results.

Further lesson ideas and activities

1. You may like to extend the study of weathering by saying that water can dissolve some rocks and make pot holes, caves and gorges. Assemble a sugar lump mountain (a cube with sides ten cubes long) in a tray and let the children take turns at pouring teaspoonfuls of water onto the top. In time, pot holes will form, 'streams' will come out of the small 'cave' in the side and the top will collapse to form a 'gorge'.

2. You may like to give the children a selection of rocks and ask them to group them based on their appearance. The children could use magnifying glasses to look at the surfaces of the samples. They may see small crystals in basalt due to rapid cooling of the rock and larger crystals in granite due to a more rapid cooling. They should see sand grains in sandstone and shells in limestone. A powerful microscope is needed to see the shells in chalk as they are made from the shells of tiny sea creatures.

3. Ask the children how they could find out if a rock absorbed water or if it was waterproof. Look for an answer about pouring a teaspoon of water on the top of each rock and leaving for a minute. If the water went into the rock it is absorbent but if it remains on the top it is waterproof.

4. Once the children can identify rock you could take them on a walk to look for rocks in the environment. They may find sandstone and limestone used as building materials or rockeries. They may find granite and marble used in prestigious buildings in a town. Note that garden centres can be a good source for different kinds of rock.

5. Arrange a visit to a local museum to look at their fossil collection. Arrange for the curator to present them to the class.

6. Collect soils from different places which are known not to have been fouled by pets. These could be samples from different gardens, different habitats, commercial seed compost, and in the school sand pit and test them for drainage and water retention.

Cross curricular links

- The ability to recognise different types of rock can be tested on any science or geography based field trip.
- Rocks can also be considered as materials in any building projects.
- A study of minerals can be related to art based projects in the context of jewellery.
- A knowledge of the formation of fossils over time can be used in the topic of evolution in Year 6 when the theory could be debated.
- In lesson 3, the work on comparing the drainage of soils can be used in habitat study to explain why some areas are wetter than others.

Year 3: Light

What does the curriculum say?

- *Recognise that they [the pupils] need light in order to see things and that dark is the absence of light.*
- *Notice that light is reflected from surfaces.*
- *Recognise that light from the Sun can be dangerous and that there are ways to protect their eyes.*
- *Recognise that shadows are formed when light from a light source is blocked by a solid or opaque object.*
- *Find patterns in the way the size of shadows change.*

What do I need to know?

Light sometimes behaves as if it is made from waves and sometimes as if it is made from a stream of particles, which we call photons. The term 'light waves' is often used in everyday conversation along with 'light rays' and 'beams'. It is a term used to explain a laser which is a beam of light in which all the light waves are the same frequency and in phase with each other. The term 'photon' may be used by scientists in television programmes. It may also occur in science fiction films even though it is a real concept.

Light rays and beams travel in straight lines as can be seen in light beams shining down through clouds or through gaps in bedroom curtains in the morning. Optical fibres carry light beams but due to their construction can make the beams bend.

The Sun's light is due to the conversion of hydrogen to helium within its core. During this change, energy is released as light and heat. Light is released when materials such as wood and wax burn. Filament lamps which the children use in their electricity investigations in Years 4 and 6 have a thin wire which gets so hot when electricity passes through it that it gives out light.

We see everything around us that are not light sources by reflected light. Light is made of seven colours that the children will investigate in Year 6. When light strikes an object, some colours are absorbed and some are reflected. It is the reflected light that gives an object its colour.

Interesting fact

Light takes eight minutes to travel from the Sun to the Earth.

Vocabulary

Concave mirror: a mirror which bends inwards.
Convex mirror: a mirror which bends outwards.
Image: the scientific word for the picture of a scene or person seen in a mirror.
Incident ray: the ray shining onto a mirror.
Light beam: a wide, straight line of light (made of many rays).
Light ray: a straight, narrow line of light.
Reflected ray: the ray reflected from a mirror.
Reflection: the everyday word for a picture of a scene or person seen in a mirror.

Progression

This is the first area of study about light and forms the foundation for work in Year 6. The investigations on light here give the children an opportunity to make measurements to answer questions, a science process that can be used in other areas in the following years.

Technical tip

In lesson 1, make a light testing box from a shoe box. Cut a hole about 1 cm in diameter in one end, cut the rim off the lid at this end so that you can slide the lid away from the side with the hole.

Useful websites

www.sciencekids.co.nz/sciencefacts/light.html
optics.synopsys.com/learn/kids/optics-kids-light.html

Lesson 1 Light, dark and reflections

Working scientifically skills: Setting up a simple practical enquiry; making systematic and careful observations; recording findings using simple scientific language and a labelled diagram
Scientific enquiry type: Fair test

You will need: a grey woollen pullover, a pair of shiny shoes, a transparent plastic sheet, a wooden block, some tissue paper, a light testing box (see Technical tip) with a selection of dull and shiny materials of different colours. You will also need two white cards 10x10 cm held upright by modelling clay, a torch, a ruler, shiny wrapping paper and a piece of aluminium foil.

Getting started
Remind the children about the work they have done on materials that relate to light. Show them the pullover and shoes as examples of dull and shiny materials. Show them the plastic sheet, wood block and tissue paper as examples of transparent, opaque and translucent materials respectively. Say that in this topic they are going to study light but first they must all close their eyes and cover them with their hands. Ask what they can see, look for an answer about darkness and say that it is due to an absence of light. Let them open their eyes again and tell them they are going to investigate materials in the dark and in the light.

Class activities
• Show the children the light testing box with a selection of shiny and dull objects inside. Explain that one of them will look through the hole while a friend slowly slides the lid back. They should describe the objects and materials that they can see as the light increases. A third child could note down the objects and colours that the observer calls out.
• While the children wait to take turns using the box they could write up the investigation and include a labelled diagram. Go through the results with the children. The shiny objects should be seen before the dull objects as they reflect more light.
• Point out that all the materials and objects seen in the box reflect light. They do not make it. Say that objects that make light are called light sources and ask the children to identify the light source in the sky in daytime. Warn the children that they should never look directly at the Sun as its light can damage their eyes. Ask about light sources in the night sky. Say that the Moon reflects the Sun's light but the stars are light sources and so are shooting stars. Ask the children about other light sources and look for answers about electric lights, torches, fires and candles.
• Demonstrate the following. Place the two white cards opposite each other about 15 cm apart. Shine a torch onto one card and move the second until you can see it illuminated by reflected light from the first. Move the second slowly backwards until the reflected light cannot be seen and record the distance. Tell the children that this technique can be used to compare how much light different materials reflect. Hold up some shiny wrapping paper and ask if it will reflect more or less than the white card. Stick the wrapping paper on the first card, shine the torch on it and move the second card until it is no longer illuminated with the reflected light. Measure the distance. Repeat with aluminium foil. (See Further lesson ideas and activities 1.)

Plenary
Ask the class to identify light sources and explain how we see objects that are not light resources (by reflected light). Ask them to describe materials that can be seen in dim light and to explain how they could compare the amount of light reflected from different surfaces.

Lesson 2 Mirrors

Working scientifically skills: Setting up a simple practical enquiry; making systematic and careful observations; taking accurate measurements using standard units; using results to draw simple conclusions and make predictions for new values
Scientific enquiry type: Comparative test; pattern seeking

You will need: a piece of white card, a plastic mirror held upright by modelling clay, a torch and a ruler. Each group will need a plastic mirror, a piece of cardboard about 10x10 cm, a pair of scissors, a piece of white card, a torch, a protractor, and large, shiny table spoons.

Getting started
Let two children set up the reflecting test equipment from the previous lesson but replace the first card with a mirror. Ask the class to predict the result then let the children shine the torch on the mirror and draw back the card a long way until it is not illuminated. Ask the children for the conclusion that the mirror is the best reflector.

Class activities
- Ask the children what mirrors are used for and look for an answer about people using them to check their presentation, combing hair, putting on make-up, shaving. Issue the plastic mirrors and let the children look at themselves. Ask them if their image is just like them and look for an answer about it being the other way round: touching the right cheek looks like touching the left cheek in the mirror.
- Let the children further check that the image is reversed by drawing half a picture, placing it next to the mirror and seeing the whole picture, and by writing letters the wrong way round to make words that can be seen correctly in a mirror. (See Further lesson ideas and activities 2.)
- Give the children a torch and cardboard. Ask what will happen when they shine the torch at the cardboard and look for an answer about it being reflected. Ask how you could get light to shine through it and look for an answer about cutting a slit. Let the children cut a slit from one edge up towards the centre of the card. Ask them to stand the cardboard up on the white card and shine the light through it. Ask them to describe what they see and look for a beam or ray of light.
- Ask the children to predict what would happen if they shone the light ray directly at the mirror (at right angles to its surface), from about fifteen centimetres away. Look for an answer about the ray of light coming straight back and how just one line of light would be seen on the paper. Let them try and see that the prediction is confirmed. Say that the light is ray is perpendicular to the surface of the mirror, and ask the children to draw a line along the paper to show where the light ray falls. Now ask them to move the torch a little to the left of the perpendicular line they have drawn, but to shine the light into the mirror at the place where the perpendicular line strikes it. They should find that the light ray strikes the mirror at an angle to the perpendicular line they have drawn, and that it has been reflected by the same angle. Ask the children to draw a lines along where the second ray shines on the paper, and to label the two lines 1a and 1b.
- Show the children how to measure the angle of the ray shining on the mirror (the incident rays) to the perpendicular and the angle of the reflected ray. They should find they are the same value.
- Let the children shine the torch from a range of angles, mark the rays and measure their angles of incidence and reflection. They should find that they always have the same value.

Plenary
Ask the children what they know about mirrors and record their responses in note form on the board. Ask what they might expect to find if they examined curved mirrors. Note their predictions on the board then issue the tablespoons and serving spoons and let the children investigate the images of the inside of the spoon (a concave mirror) and the outside of the spoon (the convex mirror).

Lesson 3 Shadows

Working scientifically skills: Making systematic and careful observations; taking accurate measurements using standard units; reporting on findings from enquiries, including oral and written explanations, displays or presentations of results and conclusions; using straightforward scientific evidence to answer questions; using results to draw simple conclusions and make predictions for new values
Scientific enquiry type: Identifying, classifying and grouping

You will need: an empty plastic bottle, two white cards, one with a piece of modelling clay so that it can stand vertically, a torch, a block of wood. Each group needs two white cards, one with a piece of modelling clay so that it can stand vertically, a torch, a plastic model figure (a dinosaur or wizard from small world play in the foundation year), dominoes, two rulers.

Getting started
Place an empty bottle on a piece of white card. Shine a torch on it and note the light passing though. Ask the children about the property of the material and look for the word 'transparent'. Shine the light slightly down on the bottle and point out that even though it passes light through, the bottle casts a shadow as some of the light is absorbed by the material. The shadow is showing up darker because darkness is an absence of light. Show the children a block of wood and ask them to predict what will happen when you shine a light on it. Look for an answer about a dark shadow because the wood is opaque and confirm the prediction. Place the vertical card a little to one side of the block and say that this is a screen. Shine the torch on the block and show that it casts a shadow on the screen. Say it is time for the children to investigate with torches, cards, screen and objects.

Class activities
- Issue the cards, torches and models and ask the children to investigate shadows cast by the model. Let them shine the torch close to the model, far away, overhead, casting shadows on the horizontal card and on the screen. Ask them to make notes of what they discover as they go along as they may not remember everything.
- Review the children's work. The model should not be a regular shape so that, as the torch shines on different parts, it makes shadows with differing shapes. They should notice that the shadow is always attached to the base of the model, the length of the shadow varies with the height of the torch and the size of the shadow on the screen varies with the distance of the object from the screen.

- Tell the children that sometimes scientists investigate by playing with equipment then test their observations by taking measurements. Say that they also like to simplify experiments so from now on the children will use dominoes instead of models as they have a regular shape.
- Say that you would like to investigate how the length of the shadow changes with the height of the torch and show them how to do it by setting up the domino on the card. Place the torch about 20 cm from the domino and use a ruler to measure the length of the shadow. Place the second ruler vertically and move the torch up by about 5 cm. Shine the torch on the domino again and measure the length of the shadow. Let the children copy you then go on to place the torch at different heights and measure the shadow length.
- Next place the domino 2 cm from the screen and shine the torch from about 3 cm. Measure the width of the shadow on the screen then ask what might happen to the width when the domino is moved further from the screen. Let the children test their prediction by copying you then moving the domino and measuring the shadow.

Plenary

Review the children's activity by restating that scientists sometimes play about with things before they begin their investigations. Say that they also simplify things when they set up an experiment and that they check their observations by making measurements. Different groups of scientists repeat the same experiments and then share their results before stating that something is a science fact. Ask the children to present their results and assert any scientific facts they have discovered. (See Further lesson ideas and activities 3.)

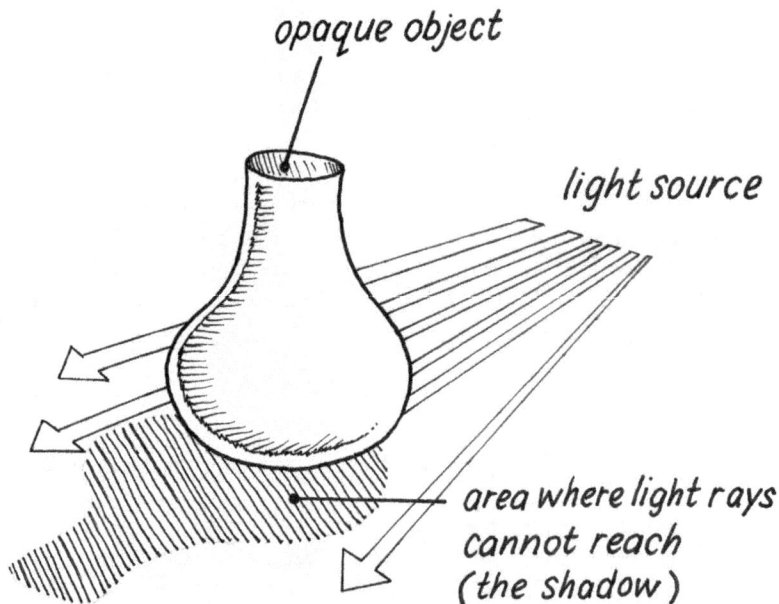

opaque object

light source

area where light rays
cannot reach
(the shadow)

Further lesson ideas and activities

1. You may like the children to try this activity by testing sandpaper, different coloured papers and newspaper.
2. Challenge the children to look in a mirror and write a message on paper in front of it.
3. The children could use their knowledge from Key Stage 1 about the Sun from the weather and seasons studies to see if its changing height in the sky throughout the day affects the lengths of shadows. They could use a pencil held vertically by modelling clay attached to a white card and record the length of the shadow at different times of day. They could also repeat the activity once a month at midday and compare the heights of the shadow through the year. Warn the children never to look at the Sun as it could damage their eyes.

Cross curricular links

- The work on light and shadows can be used when studying paintings and making them.
- Plants need light for making food and some types are restricted to highly illuminated areas or shady places. This information is important in habitat studies in science and growing plants in the school garden.
- The children could find out about the light sources in the periods of history they are studying.
- In artwork the children could use a range of materials which reflect different amounts of light to make a sculpture or picture and shine a light beam on it from different places.

Year 3: Forces and magnets

What does the curriculum say?

- *Compare how things move on different surfaces.*
- *Notice that some forces need contact between two objects, but magnetic forces can act at a distance.*
- *Observe how magnets attract or repel each other and attract some materials and not others.*
- *Compare and group together a variety of everyday materials on the basis of whether they are attracted to a magnet, and identify some magnetic materials.*
- *Describe magnets as having two poles.*
- *Predict whether two magnets will attract or repel each other, depending on which poles are facing.*

What do I need to know?

Three contact forces are: impact forces (when one surface collides into another); frictional forces (occurring when two surfaces are already in contact); and strain forces (generated in elastic materials when they are stretched or squashed). Non contact forces exist between objects not in contact like a planet and something drawn to its surface or a magnetic material and a magnet.

Every object contains an amount of matter called its mass. Gravity pulls on the mass of an object with a force called weight. The Earth and the Moon have different gravitational pulls so the weight of an astronaut varies between the two but the body mass stays the same.

Gravity pulls objects of different weights down to the ground at the same speed. The pulling force is composed of a value for the object's mass multiplied by the acceleration due to gravity. Each object also possesses inertia which can be thought of as a reluctance to move. The larger the mass the greater the inertia so the inertia cancels out the effect of the mass and all objects accelerate at the same rate.

Interesting facts

The unit of force is called a newton. It is named after Isaac Newton who made many discoveries about gravity. One of them was about the Earth's gravity pulling on the Moon. Legend has it that he made this discovery after observing an apple fall from a tree. Curiously the value of one newton is the same as the weight of an average apple and weight is a force caused by the gravitational pull of the Earth on the apple.

Vocabulary

Force: a push or a pull. It cannot be seen but its effects can.

Friction: a force that exists between two surfaces in contact.

Magnetic material: a material that is attracted to a magnet and can be made into a magnet.

Non magnetic material: a material that is not attracted to a magnet, e.g. copper, aluminium, wood, pottery, glass, plastic.

Magnetic north pole: a place at the end of the magnet that points towards the planet's North Pole.

Magnetic south pole: a place at the end of the magnet that points towards the planet's South Pole.

Sliding friction: friction that exists between two surfaces when one is sliding over the other. It pushes against the force pushing the object. When that force is removed, the sliding friction slows and stops the object.

Static friction: friction that exists between two surfaces in contact that are not moving. It pushes in the opposite direction to the force pushing on the object.

Progression

This is the first area of study about forces although the children will have studied their effects in Year 2 when looking at how the shapes of materials can be changed. Gravity is introduced here as children are familiar with the word and it provides a foundation for studying the Earth in space in Year 5. Further studies on friction occur in Year 5 and magnetism provides extra information about the properties of materials explored in Key Stage 1.

Technical tip

In lesson 3, you can make a paper clip hover in the following way. Attach a ruler to the top of a cereal packet so that a few centimetres hang over one end. Attach a strong magnet to the underside of the ruler with sticky tape. Tie a steel paper clip to one end of a thread. Place the other end of the thread directly under the magnet and secure it with modelling clay. Raise the paper clip until it is just underneath the magnet but not touching it. When you remove your fingers the paper clip should hover. You may need to adjust the thread length if necessary.

Useful websites

www.sciencekids.co.nz/sciencefacts/magnets.html
www.first4magnets.com/fun-magnet-facts-for-kids-i77
easyscienceforkids.com/all-about-force-push-and-pull
peterdriley.com/make-a-floating-ghost

Lesson 1 Introducing forces

Working scientifically skills: Recording findings using simple scientific language and labelled diagrams; identifying changes related to simple scientific ideas and processes
Scientific enquiry type: Identifying, classifying and grouping

You will need: a ball, a pair of gloves, two cardboard arrows each 12 cm long, a piece of tissue paper.

Getting started
Move the class into the school hall and sit them in a large circle. Ask two children to stand in the middle and throw a ball to each other. Say that their muscles are generating a force to move the ball but we cannot see it. Forces cannot be seen but they can be described. Ask how the children describe the action of throwing and look for the words 'push': they push the ball into the air. Ask the children to kick the ball to each other. Ask for a description of the force and look for an answer about pushing. Say that forces can get things moving.

Class activities
- Ask two more children to kick the ball to each other then ask one to kick it gently, run after it and kick it a bit harder. Point out that the force can change the speed of a moving object. Ask three more children to join the group. Ask the five of them to form a circle and kick the ball around the circle without the ball stopping. Point out that a force can change the direction of a moving object. Finally, ask a sixth child to stand in the middle, receive the ball from each of the others in turn but trap it and kick it on. Point out that a force is stopping a moving object.
- Return to the classroom and ask the children to draw pictures of children throwing and kicking the ball. Remind them that the forces cannot be seen but scientists use arrows on diagrams to show the direction of the force. Let the children draw arrows on their pieces to show the direction of the force.
- Give a pair of gloves to a child and ask them to put them on. Ask the children to describe the movement and look for the word 'pull'.
- Give another child a piece of tissue paper and ask them to tear it. Ask the children to identify the forces used as pulling forces and hold the arrows above each hand to show the direction of the force. (See Further lesson ideas and activities 1.)
- Let the children open and close books, drawers, and doors and establish when they are pushing and when they are pulling. Ask them to think what their foot does as they walk (it pushes on the ground). Ask them to draw pictures of their activities and add arrows to them to show the direction of the forces. Point out that the forces are in contact with the surface where the push or pull occurs.
- Ask the children to take a small object and throw it up the air and catch it. Ask where the contact force was to send the object up (it was between the hand and the object). Ask what made the object come back, and look for an answer about gravity. Say that it was not in touch with the object so it was a non contact force. It was also a pull. Ask the children about any other non contact force they know about – look for the answer 'magnetic force'.

Plenary
Review the work on forces being pushes and/or pulls. Summarise by explaining that forces can be represented in drawings by arrows and that there are two kinds: contact forces and non contact forces. (See Further lesson ideas and activities 2.)

Lesson 2 Moving over surfaces

Working scientifically skills: Observing
Scientific enquiry type: Identifying, classifying and grouping

You will need: a large book; for each group: a smooth plank about 40 cm long, a ruler, modelling clay to hold the ruler vertically, access to a selection of shoes.

Getting started
Remind the children that contact forces occur when two surfaces touch and talk about kicking and trapping the ball. Say that when scientists want to investigate something they try to make the investigation as simple as possible. Put a large book on a table. Point out that the lower surface of the book is in contact with the upper surface of the table. Say that a pushing force can get something moving and push gently on the book (but not hard enough to move the book). Ask why the book did not move and look for an answer about there being a force stopping the movement. Say that this force is called 'friction' and because it acts when something is not moving it is called 'static friction'. Push a little harder so that the book moves and say the pushing force is stronger than the static friction. Ask whether the book will slide away now (it will not). Tell the children that there is a now a force of sliding friction between the book and the table. Stop pushing the book and note that it stops very quickly because there is only sliding friction pushing on it. The book is once again held in place by static friction.

Class activities
* Say that when you take a step the static friction between your shoe and the ground gives you the support to push on the ground without slipping. Tell the children they are going to test some shoes to see which one has the strongest grip. Explain the experiment by saying that they are going to place a shoe on a flat piece of polished wood, hold a ruler vertically at one end of the piece of wood then raise that end to make a ramp until the shoe starts to slide then note the height of the raised end of the piece of wood.
* Ask about the force that pulls the shoe down the ramp and look for the answer 'gravity'. Say that the force of gravity pulls down on the shoe and the force of static friction pulls the other way to hold the shoe on the ramp. As the height of the ramp is increased, more of the force of gravity pulls on the shoe until it is greater than the static friction. The force of gravity is greater than the sliding friction so the shoe moves down the ramp.
* Issue the plank, ruler and modelling clay and let the children set them up and see how to measure the height. Let the children test a selection of shoes and record their results.
* Let the children write up their investigation, with a labelled diagram, a table of results and a conclusion as to which shoe had the best grip and which had the worst.

Plenary
Test the children's knowledge of static and sliding friction. Then let them report on their investigations, compare their evidence and make a 'league table' of shoe grip starting with the best gripper. (See Further lesson ideas and activities 3.)

Lesson 3 Magnets

Working scientifically skills: Setting up simple practical enquiries
Scientific enquiry type: Identifying, classifying and grouping; fair test

You will need: a compass, a globe, a bar magnet, the magnet/paper clip assembly (see Technical tip). Each group will need a bar magnet (north pole: red, south pole: blue).

Getting started
Remind the children about contact forces and the non contact force, gravity. Ask about another non contact force and look for the answer 'magnetic force'. Ask the children what they know about magnets. Steer them to talk about fridge magnets but tell them that there is also a magnetic strip on the inside of the fridge door that helps to hold it shut (some kitchen cupboards have magnetic catches too). Some children may know about magnetic compass or that the Earth seems to contain a magnet. Write all these ideas on the board for later discussion.

Class activities
- Issue the bar magnets and let the children test the materials in the classroom to see if they stick to them. Make sure the magnets are not brought near any computers or other electrical equipment.
- Say that materials that are attracted to magnets are called magnetic materials and materials that are not attracted to magnets are called non magnetic materials. Put a table with these column headings on the board. Let the children call out the materials and suggest the entry in the table. They should discover that some but not all metals are magnetic.
- Show the children the compass and let it settle to point north and south. Say that the north pole of the magnet points towards the North Pole of the planet and the south pole of the magnet points towards the South Pole of the planet. Tell the children that this happens because the Earth behaves as if it has a large bar magnet inside it and the non contact force it produces makes the compass magnet swing in line.
- Point out that the bar magnets have red north poles and blue south poles. Ask the children to put the magnets together in pairs and tell you what they find. Look for answers that similar poles repel and opposite poles attract.
- Ask the children how they would find out if one pole was stronger than the other. Look for suggestions of hanging paper clips in a line from each pole and see which can hold the longest chain. Look also for placing a piece of card between a magnet and a paper clip observing the paper clip being held in place then adding cards until the paper clip falls off. Say that scientists try to use more than one experiment to investigate an idea and let the children carry out the two experiments. They should write a description of the experiments, present tables of data and conclusions. (see Further lesson ideas and activities 4 and 5.)

Plenary
Let the children present the results of their experiments. Remind the children that both gravity and the magnetic force are non contact forces and say that you would like to see what happens when you put something between the pull of gravity and a magnet. Set up the magnet/paperclip assembly (see Technical tip) and carefully adjust the paper clip so that it hovers in mid air. Be prepared for 'wow!'

Further lesson ideas and activities

1. In Year 2, the children explored how the shape of materials can be changed by squashing, stretching, rolling and twisting. You may like to revisit this work and examine the forces used: squash (push), stretch (pull), roll (push) and twist (push and pull).
2. You could let the children hold two similar sized objects of different weights and ask them to predict what will happen to them when you hold them up and let them go. Expect answers about the heavier one dropping more quickly. Hold the two objects over a metal tray and say that if one falls before the other two sounds will be heard but if they fall together only one sound will be heard. Drop the objects and hear only one sound (see 'What do I need to know?' for explanation).
3. Ask what can cause slippery floors and look for an answer about water. Challenge the children to devise an experiment to investigate the effect of water on the grip of a shoe. Look for an answer where a shoe is tested on a dry ramp, then the ramp is made wet and the shoe is tested again.
4. Try these experiments with a horse shoe magnet and a button magnet.
5. The children could test the strengths of their fridge magnets at home by placing small sheets of newspaper between the magnet and a steel paper clip.

Cross curricular links

- You may like to analyse the pushes and pulls used by the body in walking, running, gymnastics and riding a bicycle.
- In technology the children could use friction to compare the smoothness of surfaces. This could be related to safety with floor coverings.
- The children could try and balance the force of gravity and magnetic force by making something hover for a model theatre production (see the fourth Useful website source to see how a ghost is made to hover).

Year 4: Living things and their habitats

What does the curriculum say?

- *Recognise that living things can be grouped in a variety of ways.*
- *Explore and use classification keys to help group, identify and name a variety of living things in the local and wider environment.*
- *Recognise that environments can change and that this can sometimes pose dangers to living things.*

What do I need to know?

The first two people to build up a scientific database of animals and a scientific database of plants were the Ancient Greeks: Aristotle and Theophrastus, respectively. The study of animals and plants involves looking for similarities and differences between them and groups them into some sort of order. Aristotle and Theophrastus both grouped living things according to their complexity: the order of plants started with simple plants such as mosses and herbaceous plants, while the order of animals started with invertebrates, then vertebrates such as fish, ending with mammals, and humans at the top.

Today, living things are grouped into kingdoms of which plants and animals are two. The others are fungi, and two microbe kingdoms, one containing bacteria and the other containing single celled creatures like *Amoeba*. The kingdoms are then divided into smaller and smaller subgroups. These are phylum, class, order, family, genus and species. All living things are known by the genus and species to which they belong and their names are derived from Latin and Greek (often written in brackets after their common name).

The environment is another name for the surroundings. It is made up of the physical features and the climatic conditions of a place usually in which something lives. The features and conditions are linked. For example the climatic conditions of Great Britain of warm, quite dry summers and cool wet winters favour plant growth that produces woodland. This is why a piece of land such as a field will in time become a woodland and woodland plants and animals will move into it. However, if the climate changes to produce hot dry summers and cold wet winters the plants that produced the woodland may die and be replaced by others which in trun provide a habitat for a different set of plants and animals.

Interesting facts

Many tree frogs in rainforests have poison in their skin to deter predators. They are brightly coloured to warn off attackers. The golden poison dart frog is one of the most poisonous animals in the world. A single frog has enough venom to kill ten adult humans.

Vocabulary

Amphibians: cold blooded vertebrates with a scaleless skin. They lay eggs in water and have a tadpole (aquatic, gill-breathing) stage in the life cycle, followed by a lung-breathing adult stage.

Annelid worms: invertebrates with a long thin body divided into ring-like segments.

Arthropods: invertebrates with an outside skeleton and with jointed legs.

Birds: vertebrates with feathers, scales on their legs, and which lay hard-shelled eggs on land.

Conifers: plants that make wood for support. They usually have needle shaped leaves and reproduce by making cones and seeds.

Echinoderms: invertebrates with a spiny skin and a body divided into five or multiples of five parts.

Ferns: plants with underground stems from which large feathery leaves grow. They reproduce by making spores in small brown structures on the undersides of the leaves.

Fish: vertebrates with scales and fins that lay their eggs in water.

Herbaceous flowering plants: non woody flowering plants that have a stem that dies during the autumn or winter. They reproduce by growing flowers and making seeds.

Invertebrates: animals that have no internal skeleton of bone or cartilage.

Jellyfish: aquatic invertebrates with jelly-like bodies.

Mammals: vertebrates with hairy skin. Nearly all females rear babies inside their bodies and all produce milk to feed their young when they are born.

Molluscs: invertebrates with a soft un-segmented body, often possessing one or two shells.

Mosses: small flowerless plants which grow together with others to make a mat or cushion. They reproduce by sprouting whiskery stalks that release spores.

Ozone: an unstable gas formed from oxygen by electrical discharges or ultraviolet light. A high concentration of ozone high in the atmosphere forms a protective layer around the Earth which absorbs much of the harmful ultraviolet light from the Sun.

Species: a group of living things which have a large number of similarities and are capable of breeding together to produce young.

Vertebrates: animals that have an internal skeleton of bone or cartilage.

Woody flowering plants: plants which make wood for support and do not die back in autumn or winter (although many loose their leaves). They reproduce by growing flowers and making seeds.

Progression

This chapter builds on the foundation work on vertebrates in Year 1 and foundation work on invertebrates and plants in Year 2. It extends the work on habitats in Year 2 and provides a knowledge base for work on habitats in Year 5 and evolution in Year 6.

Technical tip

For lesson 2, familiarise yourself with different butterflies using books or internet sources. Gather unlabelled photographs of butterflies to display on the whiteboard when the children are using the butterfly key. Make a slide presentation of plants and animals from around the world.

Lesson 1 The groups of living things

Working scientifically skills: Gathering and presenting data in a variety of ways: recording findings using simple scientific language, drawings, labelled diagrams and bar charts
Scientific enquiry type: Finding things out using secondary sources of information

You will need: pictures of: fish, amphibians, reptiles, birds, mammals, jellyfish, annelid worms (e.g. fan worm, rag worm), arthropods (e.g. crab, butterfly, spider, centipede), molluscs (e.g. octopus, squid), echinoderms (e.g. starfish, sea urchin). You will need live specimens of: annelid worms (earthworm), arthropods (e.g. woodlouse, beetle, millipede), molluscs (e.g. slug, snail), a goldfish, and a frog (if possible). You will also need pictures and specimens of moss, ferns, herbaceous flowering plants, woody flowering plants, conifers.

Getting started
Ask the children to take a thumb and rub it down the centre of their back. Tell them they can feel the bones in their back and ask them what kind of animal they are. Look for the answer 'vertebrates'. Ask about the name of the other large animal group and look for the answer 'invertebrate'. All the animals form a huge group called the animal kingdom. Ask about other living things they have studied. Ask the children what kingdom these things belong to and look for the answer 'the plant kingdom'.

Class activities
- Tell the children that the vertebrate group can be divided into smaller subgroups by looking at the features of animal bodies and the way they reproduce. In turn, show the children your fish, amphibians, reptiles, birds and mammal pictures and specimens. Describe the characteristics of each group from the vocabulary. (See Further lesson ideas and activities 1.)
- Tell the children that the invertebrate group can be divided into smaller subgroups by looking at the features of animal bodies. In turn, show the children your jellyfish, worm, arthropod, mollusc and echinoderm pictures and specimens. Describe the characteristics of each group from the vocabulary. (See Further lesson ideas and activities 1.)
- Tell the children that the plant kingdom contains the following groups: mosses, ferns, conifers, flowering plants (herbaceous and woody). In turn, show the children your plant pictures and specimens. Describe the characteristics of each group from the vocabulary. (See Further lesson ideas and activities 1.)

- Ask the children to select the group they like best, use secondary sources to find out about a member of the group, draw it and say why it is a member of the group.

Plenary
Let the children present their work. Make a bar graph of the two animal groups and plant group to show the number of children selecting the different subgroups.

Lesson 2 Keys

Working scientifically skills: Making careful observations; recording findings using keys
Scientific enquiry type: Identifying, classifying and grouping

You will need: the keys on page 89, a picture of a bird showing the scales on its legs, a range of vertebrate pictures showing more than one representative of each group, a range of plant pictures showing more than one representative of each group, a slide presentation or picture collection showing plants and animals from different habitats around the world.

Getting started
Ask the children to name the two kingdoms of living things they have studied and the subgroups within them. Say there are millions of different types or species of living thing and when scientists discover a new one or one they are not familiar with they use keys to identify it. The information in the keys is related to what the scientist can see in the body of the living thing.

Class activities
- Show the children the key for identifying vertebrates. Point out that a key is read from the top. In this key the scientist must look for the presence of scales anywhere on the body. If they are found the left arm of the key is read down until the animal group is found. Give an example using a picture of the bird.
- Show the children a range of vertebrate pictures and ask them to use the key to identify them. Ask them to explain how they used the key to identify them.
- Challenge the children to make a simple arthropod key to identify a house fly and a woodlouse. (see Further lesson ideas and activities 2.)
- Show the children the key to identifying the main plant groups. Read the key from the top following the arms to their ends. Present the children with the plant pictures and ask them to identify them. Ask them to explain how they used the key to identify them. (see Further lesson ideas and activities 3.)
- Tell the children that keys are also used to identify species within each group and show them the butterfly key. Display the butterflies on the whiteboard and ask the children to use the key to identify them. (see Further lesson ideas and activities 4.)

Plenary
Let the children use their vertebrate, plant and butterfly keys and any invertebrate keys they have made to identify the living things in your slide presentation or collection of photographs.

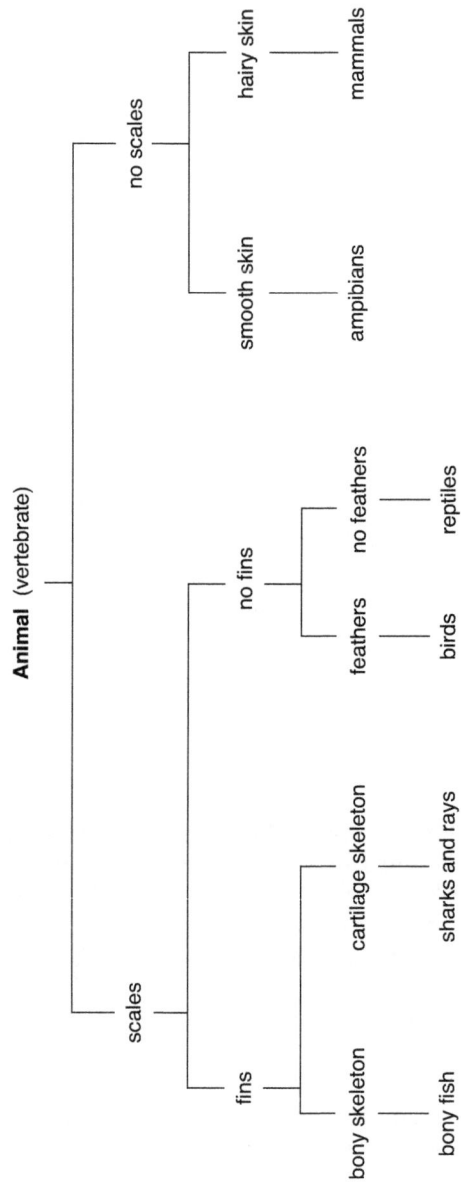

Animal (vertebrate)

scales
- fins
  - bony skeleton — bony fish
  - cartilage skeleton — sharks and rays
- no fins
  - feathers — birds
  - no feathers — reptiles

no scales
- smooth skin — ampibians
- hairy skin — mammals

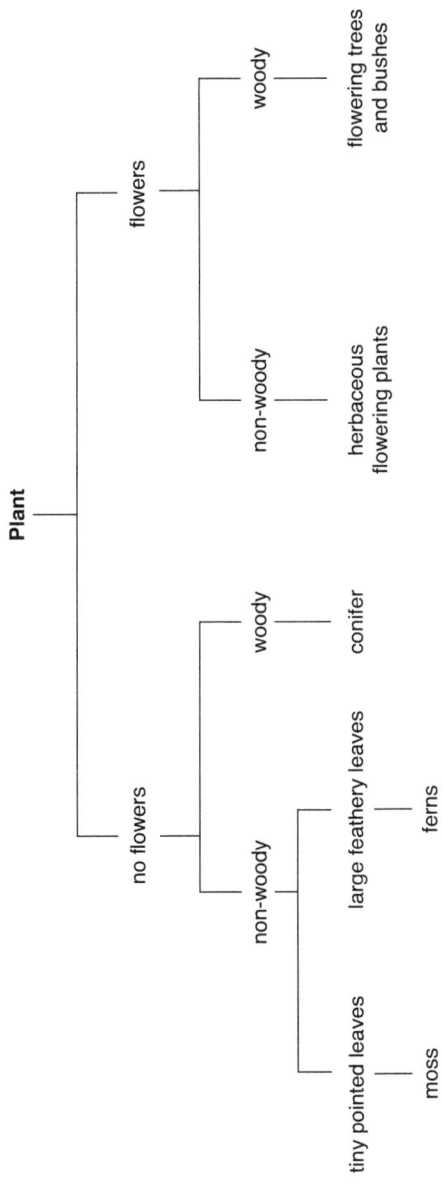

Plant

no flowers
- non-woody
  - tiny pointed leaves → moss
  - large feathery leaves → ferns
- woody → conifer

flowers
- non-woody → herbaceous flowering plants
- woody → flowering trees and bushes

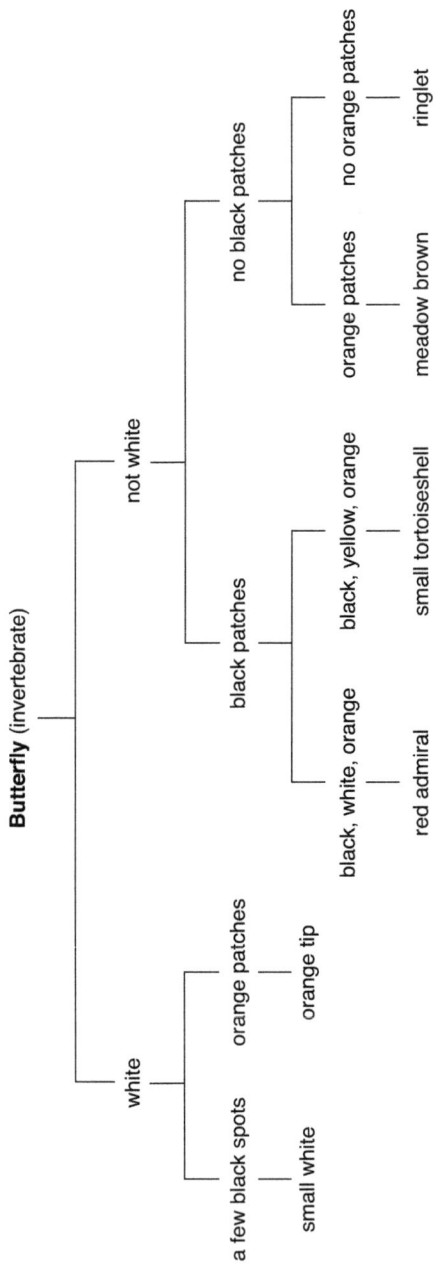

Butterfly (invertebrate)

- white
  - a few black spots
    - small white
  - orange patches
    - orange tip
- not white
  - black patches
    - black, white, orange
      - red admiral
    - black, yellow, orange
      - small tortoiseshell
  - no black patches
    - orange patches
      - meadow brown
    - no orange patches
      - ringlet

Lesson 3 Changes in the environment

Working scientifically skills: Gathering and recording data; identifying changes related to simple scientific ideas and processes; using results to draw simple conclusions, suggest improvements and raise further questions
Scientific enquiry type: Identifying leading to observing over time

You will need: to make a worksheet set out as a checklist all the items mentioned in step 1, leave space for extra examples. You will also need access to the school grounds, a park, woodland or another habitat. You may wish to research internet sites about national parks for Further idea 6.

Getting started
Tell the children they live in a habitat, their home. Ask how many of them are told to tidy their rooms. Ask why they should keep their rooms tidy and look for an answer about not falling over things or standing on things. Emphasise the idea that keeping their habitat tidy is keeping it safe. Say that natural habitats have a natural tidiness. The plants provide food and shelter for animals; the animals are arranged in food chains. Ask the children to name some food chains and identify herbivores and carnivores. Point out that some animals are omnivores so their habitat needs to provide them with a wide range of foods. Say that when there were few people in the world they hunted animals and gathered plants, moving through habitats and causing comparatively little damage. But today, nearly all of the huge number of people on the planet live in a different way and can damage habitats and threaten the lives of plants and animals that live there.

Class activities
- Ask the children how people damage habitats. Look for trampling plants by going off footpaths, riding bicycles off paths, breaking twigs, branches and carving in trees, leaving litter which covers plants and prevents them getting light to make food, broken glass cutting animals, small mammals such as field mice getting trapped in bottles and dying, having fires in undesignated areas, collecting wild flowers.
- Issue the worksheets to the children and go through the checklist then take the children out to survey at least one habitat.
- Back in the classroom let the children share their observations.
- If an area has been found to have been damaged, ask the children how it could be restored. Look for answers about setting up a volunteer group to clear the habitat of rubbish and put up signs about keeping to paths, not dropping litter, lighting fires or picking wild flowers. Ask the children to design posters to help protect habitats.
- Move on to talk about setting up a habitat and say that in many areas around the world woodland habitats develop naturally if they are left alone. Ask the children how they could improve an area of the school grounds to make it develop into a woodland habitat. Look for answers about planting trees and bushes, increasing the number of micro habitats by making piles of logs and stones, letting grass grow long to hide animals and give insects a place to rest. (See Further lesson ideas and activities 5.)

- Tell the children about the ways humans have damaged the environment. The use of CFCs (chlorofluorocarbons) is making a hole in the ozone layer and letting though more harmful rays from the Sun and the burning of fuels is releasing gasses which trap heat in the air and warm the planet. Poisonous substances dumped in the sea and oil spilled in oil tanker accidents is polluting the water. The rainforests are being destroyed for timber, mining metal ores and for use in farming. Balance this by saying that burning fuels could be reduced if everyone switched off electrical equipment when they are not using it. The destruction of habitats to get at metal ores and oil could be reduced by greater efforts at recycling materials. (See Further idea 6.)

Plenary
Review how people can damage habitats and let the children display their posters. Compare them with official posters produced by national parks. Resolve with the class to switch off electrical items when not in use to save energy. Examine ways that the class can improve its contribution to recycling.

Further lesson ideas and activities

1. Arrange for a class visitor to bring in a collection of live animals and talk about them and for a botanist or gardener to bring in live plants and talk about them.
2. If appropriate, challenge the children to make a key to recognise an earthworm, a slug, a snail, an insect and a spider. Look for a key which splits off soft skinned animals, divides them into those with a segmented body and those with an un-segmented body, then divides those with an un-segmented body into those with a shell and those with no shell. The other arm should have those with a hard skinned body, which is divided into those with six legs and those with eight legs (or those with wings and those with no wings).
3. Take the children into the school grounds or park and let them use the key to identify the group to which the various plants belong.
4. On field trips in spring and summer let the children take their butterfly keys and use them to try and identify butterflies they see.
5. You may like to take up some or all of the children's plans and set up a small area of the school grounds as a woodland habitat.
6. Display some information about national parks from around the world to look at how people are working to conserve plants and animals.

Cross curricular links

- In lesson 2, the detailed observation made on living things may be useful in art based activities.
- Lesson 3 could be integrated with a school-based habitat project.
- Lesson 3 could be integrated into any school-based projects on conservation, energy saving and recycling.

Year 4: Animals, including humans

What does the curriculum say?

- *Describe the simple functions of the basic parts of the digestive system in humans.*
- *Identify the different types of teeth in humans and their simple functions.*
- *Construct and interpret a variety of food chains, identifying producers, predators and prey.*

What do I need to know?

The first set of teeth comprises incisors, canines and premolars and the second set also has molars. The first molar appears when a child is about 6 years old with the others following from 11 years onwards. The premolars are replaced at 10–12 years of age. To avoid confusion while introducing teeth you may like to just refer to the premolars as 'molars' as they share the same function. The children replace their first incisors (the two teeth at the front) at 6–8 years of age, their second incisors (the next two out from the centre) are replaced at 7–9 years and their canines at 9–12 years.

When food leaves the stomach it enters the duodenum where it receives bile juice from the gall bladder that breaks down fats and enzymes from the pancreas which digest proteins, fats and carbohydrates. The small intestine also produces enzymes to complete the food digestion. The inner surface of the small intestine is covered in microscopic finger-like projections which increase its surface area for absorbing the digested food.

Scientists trace the path of food through a habitat by making food chains. The food chain begins with organisms called producers. These are the producers of the food. For almost all food chains on Earth the producers are plants. They use some of the energy in sunlight to make food from carbon dioxide in the air and water and minerals in the soil. At the bottom of oceans exist micro-organisms that use energy from chemicals in hot water generated by geothermal activity. They supply food to other organisms in their habitat. All organisms which cannot make food but obtain it from other living things are called consumers. An animal that eats a plant or part of a plant such as a beetle eating a leaf, is called a first order consumer. An animal that then eats it such as a frog eating a beetle is a second order consumer and so on up the food chain. A prey animal is one that is eaten by another. All first order consumers are prey animals but other order consumers are prey too. For example a frog is the prey of the heron. A predator is an animal that feeds on another animal. The frog for example is also a predator because it feeds on the beetle. The heron is a predator because it feeds on the frog. Note that the arrows always go from the food to the feeder to show the path of food.

Interesting fact

Sharks have many sets of teeth in their gums. When they attack they may lose some teeth so new ones grow out of the gums to replace them.

a food chain

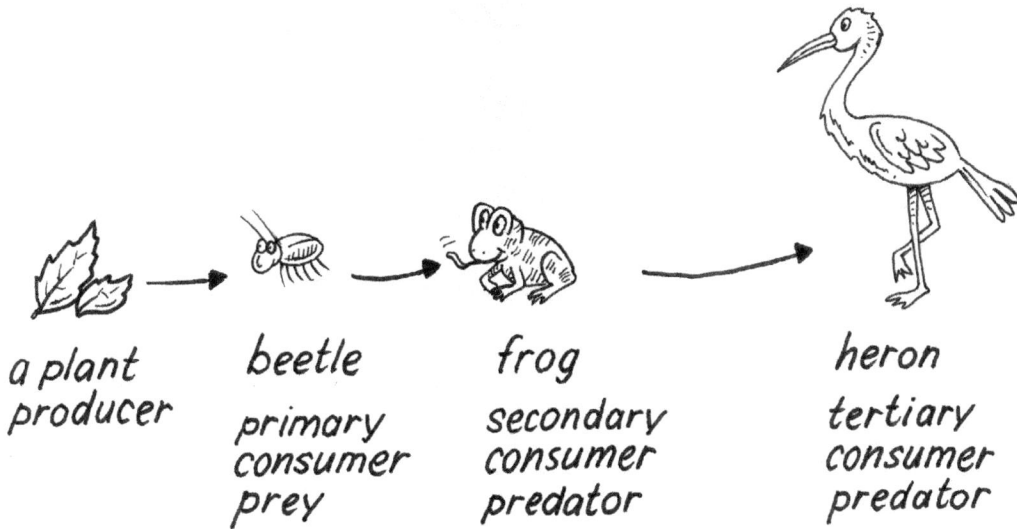

a plant	beetle	frog	heron
producer	primary consumer prey	secondary consumer predator	tertiary consumer predator

Vocabulary

Anus: a muscular valve at the end of the digestive system through which undigested food is passed.

Canines: pointed teeth next to the incisors, used for tearing food.

Digestion: the breaking down of food into very small pieces (molecules) which can be absorbed into the blood and then carried around the body to the parts that need it.

Incisors: front teeth used for cutting food.

Large intestine: also called the 'colon' which removes water from the undigested food.

Molars: teeth right at the back of the jaw used for crushing and grinding food.

Oesophagus: also called the 'gullet' is the tube from the mouth to the stomach.

Predator: an animal that hunts others for food.

Premolars: teeth next to the canines which grind food.

Prey: an animal that is hunted by another for food.

Rectum: a chamber at the end of the small intestine in which the undigested food is stored.

Small intestine: the part of the intestine where digestion is completed.

Stomach: a muscular bag which churns food and begins protein digestion. It also contains acid to kill germs on food.

Tongue: the muscular organ which helps swallow food but also has taste sensors for salt, sweetness, sourness, bitterness and for detecting a savoury taste called 'umami'.

Technical tips

For lesson 1, wash and clean the eggshells for use in the experiment. Break them into similar sized pieces.

For lesson 2, broken sugar lumps are made by putting them in a plastic bag and crushing them with a rolling pin to get some pieces about 7 mm across. Attach one end of a 25 cm clear plastic tube with a minimum internal diameter of 8 mm (obtainable from educational suppliers and some Home Brew shops) to a plastic funnel to make a model mouth and oesophagus. Put the other end in a medium sized clear plastic bag with a zip top and secure it with sticky tape. You should make the dough mix and test step 3 before the lesson.

For Further idea 5 you will need to order owl pellets from the Suffolk Owl Sanctuary (see the second website in the Useful websites section) and it will also help to access to this website for Further idea 4. Prior to this activity, read through the information on 'Pellet Detectives', 'Let's get detecting', and 'Looking at the inside of an owl pellet' and carry out an owl pellet dissection.

Progression

This area of study builds on the human body studies of Year 3 and the work on food chains in earlier years. The work on dentition in various animals can be used as examples of adaptations which is a key feature in the development of the theory of evolution studied in Year 6.

Useful websites

Lesson 1: http://www.bbc.co.uk/bitesize/ks2/science/living_things/teeth_eating/read/1/
Lesson 2: Chris Packham's article, 'The truth about poo', can be found at www.bbc.co.uk/blogs/legacy/natureuk/2010/06/the-truth-about-poo.shtml
Lesson 3: An index of skulls can be found at www.skullsite.co.uk/lists.htm
Further idea 5: peterdriley.com/owl-pellet-dissection

Lesson 1 Teeth

Working scientifically skills: Gathering, recording, classifying and presenting information in a variety of ways; recording findings using labelled diagrams; using results to draw simple conclusions
Scientific enquiry type: Identifying, classifying and grouping; observing over time

You will need: a diagram (to display on the whiteboard) showing the teeth of an adult, a breadboard, a knife, a celery stick, a slice of bread, a nail about 4 cm long, a mortar and pestle, some large sugar crystals, cleaned eggshells (see Technical tip), four beakers, four drinks (water, milk, and two fizzy drinks), graph paper and a camera. Each child will need a plastic mirror.

Getting started
Remind the children about the different kinds of foods that they studied in Year 3 and the food pyramid to guide them into healthy eating. Say that they are going to look at what happens to food as it enters their body and ask them to open their mouths and to look inside each others' mouths. Invite observations about the teeth and the tongue. Ask what the tongue does and look for answers about tasting the food and helping to swallow it. Ask about teeth, record their answers and say that they are going to investigate these ideas about teeth.

Class activities
- Tell the children that people have two sets of teeth as they grow up. The first set are called the milk teeth and there are 20 of them. They begin to be replaced from the age of 6 to 8 years of age. Ask the children to point to gaps in their own teeth where this replacement is taking place.
- Say that there are three basic types of teeth: incisors (make a gnawing motion with your front teeth like a rabbit), canines (point to the fang teeth), and molars (point to your back teeth).
- Tell the children that the incisor teeth are for cutting into food and use a knife to cut up a celery stick on the breadboard. Say that the canines are for tearing up food and use a nail to tear up a slice of bread that you hold on the breadboard. Say the molars grind up the food and place some large sugar crystals in a mortar and grind them with a pestle.
- Once the children can identify the different teeth and their functions, give them a mirror. Let them draw the teeth in their mouth and use the diagram on the board to label them.
- Remind the children about healthy eating and the effect of sugar on teeth. Say that sometimes when scientists want to do an experiment they use a model and for the next experiment you are going to use eggshells instead of teeth. Place each eggshell on graph paper and photograph it then place it in a beaker and pour 100 ml of one of the drinks on it. Leave the eggshells for a few days, but let the children look at them during that time. Then remove the drinks, let the shells dry, and photograph them on graph paper. (See Further lesson ideas and activities 1.)

Plenary
Review the children's knowledge of their teeth. Let them display their labelled drawings of their teeth. Show the children the photographs of the eggshells before and after being immersed in the drinks and look for signs of corrosion. You may also let the children use magnifying glasses to compare clean, unused eggshell to the shells corroded by the drinks to see how the drinks affected the 'teeth'. (See Further lesson ideas and activities 2.)

Lesson 2 The digestive system

Working scientifically skills: Observing; reporting on findings and from enquiry including oral, and written explanations, displays or presentations of results and conclusions
Scientific enquiry type: Identifying; researching using secondary sources

You will need: a model 'mouth' (made from a thick-walled plastic jar with a plastic screw top and six pebbles, a little larger than marbles), broken sugar lumps, bran flakes, a bowl, flour, water, a spoon, cooking oil, a model gullet and stomach (see Technical tip), a ribbon 3 cm wide and 6 m long to represent small intestines, a piece of woolly carpet, a ribbon 6 cm wide and 1.5 m long to represent the large intestine, a poster of the digestive system or diagram from a book under the visualiser, a roll of wallpaper.

Getting started
Remind the children about the model teeth you used in the last lesson and say that you are going to make a model mouth and see what happens when you put food in it. Show the children the 'mouth' and say that the pebbles represent the molars. Mix the bran flakes and broken sugar lumps together and show the children. Put them in the model mouth, screw the top on and shake. Say that this action is similar to the action of the molars. After a minute, pour out the contents of the mouth onto a plate, remove the pebbles and let the children describe what has happened to the food. Look for an answer about how it has been made into smaller pieces. Say that they are going to find out what happens to food in the body.

Class activities
- Ask the children what they feel happening to food when it is in their mouth. Look for answers about it being chewed up and it being moistened. Say that the tongue also makes it into pellets and the moisture helps you swallow it. Point to your neck and say that the food goes down a tube called the 'gullet' or 'oesophagus' then point to your body just below your right ribcage and say that it goes into the stomach. Say you are going to make some more models to show them what happens.
- Put some flour in a bowl and mix it with water to make a sloppy dough. Hold it up on a spoon and let it fall off the edge. It should be about 6 cm to 8 cm long. Add some oil to the dough in the bowl to make it a little slimy. Say that when we chew, our mouth releases saliva which mixes with the food and makes it slippery so that it is easier to swallow.
- Show the children the model oesophagus and stomach and say that the funnel is another model of the mouth. With help from some children, hold up the display, spoon the flour mix into the funnel and show them it flowing into the tube. Squeeze the sides of the tube to push the dough down into the stomach and say that muscles in the oesophagus push the food into the stomach. When the food gets into the stomach, squeeze it about and say that the action of muscles in the stomach wall churn up the food to mix it.
- Tell the children that when the food has been churned up in the stomach, it passes into a tube called the small intestine and attach one end of the ribbon to the side of the plastic bag to represent it.
- Remind the children about the food being broken up into small pieces and that it is moistened with water. Take the bran and sugar mix, pour into a clear plastic beaker, stir it up and leave it. Say that in the mouth, stomach and small intestine substances called enzymes

are added to the food and can break it down or digest it if the food is dissolved. Look at the mixture and show the children that the sugar has dissolved but the bran has not.

- Show the children the piece of carpet and say that this is like a magnified part of the small intestine. The rough surface absorbs all the digested food into the blood.
- Point out that the bran was not dissolved and was undigested and carries on through the large intestine. Attach the second ribbon. Say this undigested food helps the muscles push the food along and in the large intestine most of the water the body has used in digestion is taken back into the blood. The remains are stored in a cavity called the rectum and released from the body through the anus.

Plenary
Ask for a volunteer to have their body outline drawn on the roll of wallpaper. Show the picture of the digestive system and let the children arrange your model inside the body outline. (See Further lesson ideas and activities 3.)

Lesson 3 Food chains

Working scientifically skills: Making careful observations; gathering, recording, classifying and presenting data in a variety of ways to help in answering questions; reporting on findings from enquiries with oral explanations
Scientific enquiry type: Identifying, classifying and grouping; researching using secondary sources

You will need: access to the first website in the Useful websites section (see Technical tip for Further ideas 5 and 6), food chain cards: grass, rabbit, fox; grass antelope, lion; cabbage leaf, caterpillar, shrew, owl; plankton, fish, seal, killer whale.

Getting started
Remind the children about their work on the skeleton in Year 3, tap your head and ask the children to identify the part of the skeleton. Look for the answer 'skull' and look at the human skull on the skulls website and point out how the teeth are arranged in it. Ask the children which feeder type humans are and look for the answer 'omnivore'. Say that the teeth in an animal's skull can be used to identify the type of food it eats.

Class activities
- Tell the children they are going to look at herbivore skulls and show them the rabbit skull on the skulls website. Point out that the skull has well developed incisors for cutting grass and well developed molars for chewing it up. It does not have canines because it does not tear its food. Show the children the sheep skull on the website and point out that the skull has incisors in its lower jaw that cut against a tough pad in the upper jaw like an upside down knife and breadboard to snip off the grass. Point out that, like the rabbit, it does not have canines but has well developed molars for grinding up the grass.

- Tell the children they are going to look at carnivore skulls and show them the tiger skull on the website. Point out that the tiger has huge canines for stabbing prey and tearing meat. Its molars are more pointed than herbivore molars. These are used for holding bones at the back of the mouth so the tiger can apply the full pressure of its strong jaw muscles to crack open the bones and eat the marrow inside. Show the children the wolf skull on the website and point out the prominent canines and molar teeth.
- Show the children the skull of the American black bear on the website but do not say its name. Ask what type of food this animal might eat. Point out the prominent incisors, smaller canines and less well developed molars. Look for the answer 'omnivore' and ask what animal it might be. Steer them towards realising it is a bear skull. (See Further lesson ideas and activities 4, 5 and 6.)
- Remind the children about the structure of a food chain. Say how they start with food producers which are the plants. The food is then eaten by consumers and these are divided into herbivores which eat plants, carnivores which eat animals and omnivores which eat both plants and animals. Explain that in aquatic habitats the plants are microscopic algae which in turn are fed on by microscopic animals and small crustaceans. In the sea, these are joined by the young stages of crabs, molluscs and echinoderms. Discuss the terms 'predators' and 'prey' (see vocabulary).
- Issue the card packs of various groups of organisms mixed up. Ask the children to arrange them into food chains and identify the producers, prey, predators, herbivores and carnivores.

Plenary
Ask the children what types of teeth the antelope and the lion might have. You may like to consider the numbers in each link to show that there need to be more individuals lower down the food chain to sustain smaller numbers at the top. You could link this to conservation work which emphasises that this balance of numbers must be maintained for all the living things to survive.

Further lesson ideas and activities

1. Tell the children that microbes on the teeth feed on sugar and make acids which damage the teeth. Say that vinegar is a common acid and set up an eggshell in vinegar along with the drinks.
2. Let each child chew a disclosing tablet then look at their teeth in a mirror. Let them use their toothbrush to clean their teeth. This could be done as an in-school exercise following school policies or a homework exercise. You may like to follow this up with providing information about the recommended way to brush teeth or with a visit of a dental health care professional.
3. Let the children use appropriate secondary sources to research the digestive system then ask them to write an account of a piece of food as it passes through the body. You may suggest that some children use their information with the model in the outline to explain to the class how the food passes through the body.
4. The children could use secondary sources to find out about how the shape of a bird's beak is related to its food.
5. Tell the children that birds of prey such as owls make pellets of undigested food and regurgitate them. These can be used to find out what the bird eats. Demonstrate an owl pellet dissection after following the procedure in the Resources section.
6. Say that animal droppings or poo can give scientists clues to what animals eat; watch Chris Packham's film on the topic (see the Useful websites box).

Cross curricular links

- Lessons 1 and 2 may be used to support school health programmes.
- Lesson 1 could be used to provide inspiration for an art activity in which the children make models of their own mouths with teeth and gaps using modelling clay.
- The second lesson could be used as inspiration for making and performing a play in an English activity about the passage of a food items such as a sandwich through the digestive system. Pupils could be the sandwich, the teeth, the muscles pushing the food along and the enzymes breaking down the food.
- If the school has a conservation area, the children may like to survey it to find the animals that are living there. They could then use secondary sources to find the food of each animal and use the information to build up food chains. These could then be used as part of a display or information board about the area.

Year 4: States of matter

What does the curriculum say?

- *Compare and group materials together, according to whether they are solids, liquids or gases.*
- *Observe that some materials change state when they are heated or cooled, and measure or research the temperature at which this happens in degrees Celsius (°C).*
- *Identify the part played by evaporation and condensation in the water cycle and associate the rate of evaporation with temperature.*

What do I need to know?

Most things are composed of material in one of the three states of matter. In the past, the changes in materials were explained by the Ancient Greek concept of elements as being earth, fire, water and air, each of which had their properties: earth was cold and dry, fire was hot and dry, water was cold and wet and air was hot and wet. This interpretation of materials was used for many hundreds of years. A few Ancient Greeks also believed that matter was made of particles. Today we know them as atoms and molecules. In the three states the particles are not electrically charged but in a fourth state of matter there are free charged particles called electrons present (see the interesting facts box). There is more on the particulate nature of matter in Year 5.

Below are the melting and boiling points of some common materials:

Material	Melting point (°C)	Boiling point (°C)
Water	0	100
Aluminium	659	1218
Iron	1530	2786
Stainless Steel	1363	2550
Silver	961	1762
Gold	1063	1946

Note that some common materials found in the kitchen are made up from complex mixtures of substances, each with its own melting point, so will melt over a range of temperatures.

The diagram on the next page shows the basic structure of the water cycle. Transpiration is the process in which plants lose water from their leaves as water vapour which then rises to condense and form clouds. Surface run off involves water rushing down streams and rivers and slowing to remain in lakes and ponds for a while. Some water sinks into the ground moving down through porous rocks such as sandstone. When it reaches nonporous rock such as granite it moves along to emerge as a spring at the ground surface.

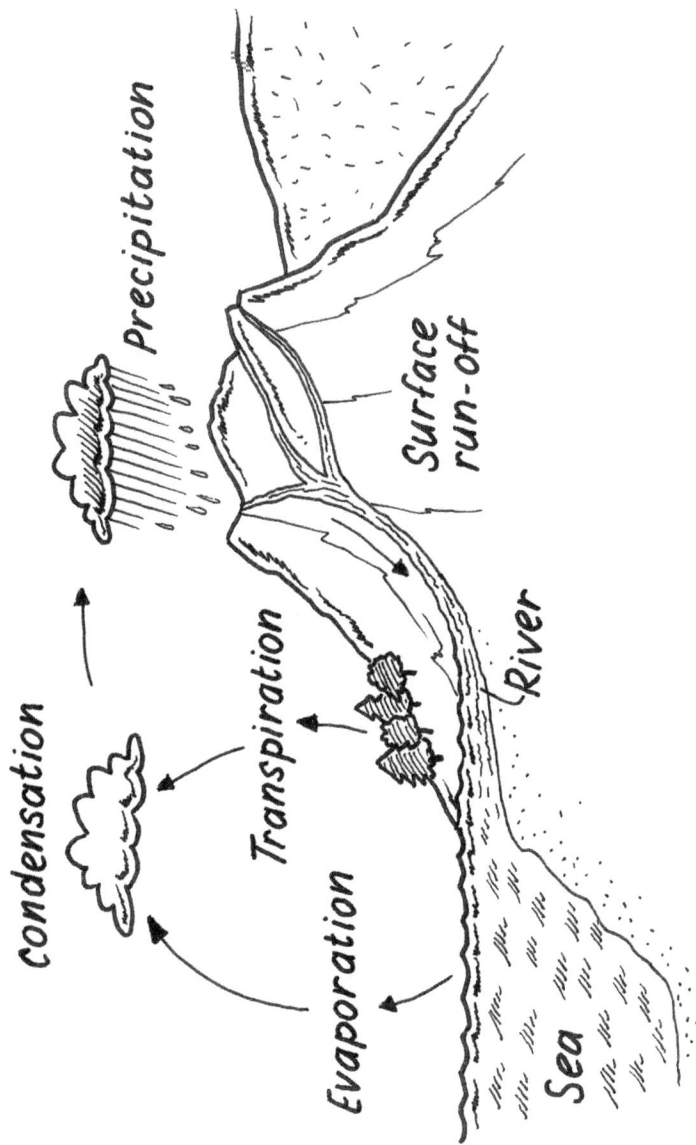

Condensation

Precipitation

Transpiration

Evaporation

Surface run-off

River

Sea

Vocabulary

Condensation: the changing of a gas into a liquid.
Data logger: a device which automatically records and displays changes such as temperature.
Evaporation: the changing of a liquid into a gas at the surface of the liquid.
Freezing point: the temperature at which a liquid changes into a solid.
Gas: a substance without a definite shape or volume.
Liquid: a substance with a definite volume but which takes the shape of its container.
Melting point: the temperature at which a solid changes into a liquid.
Solid: a substance with a definite shape and volume.
Temperature: a measure of the hotness or coldness of something.
Thermometer: an instrument that measures temperature. School thermometers use the Celsius scale, some domestic thermometers may also feature the Fahrenheit scale.
Water cycle: the movement of water between the oceans, land and air due to the processes of melting, freezing, evaporating and condensing.

Progression

This area of study builds on the work on material recognition and properties in Year 1, considering the uses of materials and the effects of forces on them in Year 2. The Year 3 study of rocks and soils sets a geological context for studying materials which can be used to prompt ideas in this area of study which also forms the foundation for further study about changes in materials in Year 5.

Technical tips

In lesson 1, the children may simply weigh their measuring cylinder of water before and after pouring it through the bottles. You may make it more precise by weighing the measuring cylinder without water and then with water and subtracting the difference to find the weight of the water. During the pouring, a little water may be lost and this should be pointed out.

In lesson 2, cool the water to 10°C by putting some ice cubes in it or keeping it in the fridge. During the lesson, check the temperatures as they will move to room temperature (about 20°C). To take the temperature to 25°C and 30°C stir in warm water until the temperature rises the desired amount. Make sure the children keep the bulbs of their thermometers in the water as they read the temperature. You will also need to light a candle and get it to drip over its edges so that the wax flows down the side and refreezes.

Lesson 1 Properties of states of matter

Working scientifically skills: Making observations taking accurate measurements using standard units
Scientific enquiry type: Identifying, classifying and grouping; comparative tests

You will need: a wood block, a plastic block, a transparent plastic bottle of water, a beaker of sand and a bowl, a jug of water and a bowl, a balloon and funnel to pour water in, a bicycle with a deflated tyre and a bicycle pump, a balloon pump and two deflated balloons and coat hanger. Each group will need a ball of modelling clay to make a 2 cm cube, a plastic knife, access to a balance, a jug of water, a measuring cylinder, access to a selection of differently shaped containers.

Getting started
Ask the children to look around them and identify any materials that they can see. Hold up a transparent plastic bottle of water and see if they can identify water as a material. Ask the children how they can tell one material from another. Look for answers about them having different properties and ask the children to give examples. Tell them that scientists have another way of grouping materials, and pass round a wood block and a plastic block. Point out that these both have a fixed shape and you cannot squash them to make them smaller. They are classified as solids. Pour water from a jug into a bowl. Say that this is a liquid. It flows and takes up the shape of its container. Waft your hand around and say that the third group of materials are gases, like those in the air. Say they are about to find out more about these three groups called 'the three states of matter'.

Class activities
- Tell the children that matter is the amount of stuff in something. One way to measure matter is to measure the space that it takes up. This space is called the 'volume'. Issue the balls of modelling clay and ask the children to cut the clay to make a cube with sides 2 cm long. Ask them to multiply the dimension of each side together to find the volume (8 cm^3).
- Say that another way to measure the matter in something is to weigh it. Ask the children to weigh their cubes. Now say that modelling clay is an unusual solid because it can be stretched and squashed and let the children do this to the cube. Now ask them to make the cube again and measure and weigh it. They should find there is no change in weight or volume.
- Issue the water jugs and measuring cylinders. Ask the children to measure out a volume of water, weigh it, pour it into the different containers and make a sketch of how it appears in each one. Ask them to pour the water back into the measuring cylinder and then measure and weigh it again (see Technical tip). (See Further lesson ideas and activities 1.)
- Ask the children if there are any solids that can be poured and look for answers such as sand or a powder. Ask a volunteer to pour out some water and some sand and ask the class to describe what they see. They should see that a poured liquid forms a flat surface and forms drips but a poured solid forms a cone and does not drip.
- Pump some air into a deflated bicycle tyre with a bicycle pump and tell the children that the pump squashes the air into the tyre. As the amount of squashed air increases inside the tyre it makes its walls harder.

- Take two deflated balloons and inflate one with the balloon pump. Tie off the inflated balloon and place it on one end of a coat hanger with the deflated balloon on the other end, and hold up the coat hanger on a pencil. Point out that the inflated balloon goes down on one side of the balance, showing that gas has weight. (See Further lesson ideas and activities 2 and 3.)

Plenary
Ask the children to look around the room and outside through the school windows and classify the things they see into solids, liquids or gases. They could also identify containers which contain liquids and gases (e.g. tyres). Ask them to draw up a list of properties of solids, liquids and gases.

Lesson 2 Heating and cooling

Working scientifically skills: Making systematic and careful observations using a thermometer and data logger; recording findings in tables
Scientific enquiry type: Observing over time; fair test

You will need: four beakers of water labelled 1–4 containing water at 10°C, 20°C, 25°C, and 30°C, a hot water bottle filled with warm water, a sheet of aluminium foil, equal sized samples of butter, margarine, dark chocolate and white chocolate, a beaker of ice cubes, a thermometer or data logger, an unused candle and a melted candle (see Technical tip). Each group will need a thermometer.

Getting started

Ask the children what they know about the word 'temperature' and look for an answer about it being a measure of hotness and coldness. Ask the children how temperature is measured and look for an answer about a thermometer. Ask where the children have used a thermometer before and look for answers about studying the weather. Ask the children if there were any materials that changed as the temperature of the weather changed. Prompt them to talk about water freezing to ice and then melting. Say that this observation is important in studying the states of matter.

Class activities

- Say that the change of water into ice and back to water again means that a material can change from a liquid state to a solid state and back again. It also means that the temperature is important because a change in temperature can bring about a change in the state of a material.
- Tell the children that you are going to check their thermometer reading skills. Ask them to take the air temperature at two places in the room and in the four beakers of water. They should construct a table and fill in the results.
- Ask the children to predict the temperature of a group of ice cubes in a beaker and check their prediction by inserting a thermometer or data logging probe. Ask the children to record the temperature every five minutes in a table with the column headings 'Time' and 'Temperature °C'. Move onto step 4.
- Ask the children about things they know of that melt. Look for answers about butter and chocolate. Ask how they could find out if butter, margarine, dark and white chocolate all melted at the same temperature and show them a hot water bottle. Let the children build up an investigation which features the four foods being placed on a piece of aluminium foil on top of the hot water bottle and seeing how they melt. Set up the experiment and let the children watch the melting. They should conclude that the one that melts most easily is close to its melting point at room temperature and the others that melt more slowly are further from their melting points at room temperature. They should list the foods in order of melting points, lowest to highest. (See Further lesson ideas and activities 4.)
- Show the children a candle that has not been used and ask what will happen when you light it. Show the children the melted candle and ask them to explain why the wax flowing down the side has turned into a solid. Steer the children towards realising that the molten wax moving down the candle cools down until it freezes. Say that all the solids they can see are below their freezing points.

Plenary
Examine the data of the melting ice and point out that the water had started to warm up to the air temperature of the room. Make sure the children understand the melting point and point out that it is exactly the same as the freezing point. (See Further lesson ideas and activities 5.)

Lesson 3 Investigating evaporation

Working scientifically skills: Setting up simple practical enquiries; reporting findings from enquiries including oral and written explanations
Scientific enquiry type: Observing over time

You will need: a damp towel. Each group will need a bowl, a beaker, a measuring cylinder, two more bowls, a warm place and a cold place in which to leave them, a beaker, a foil pie cup, an ice cube, access to warm water.

Getting started
Pass a damp towel around the class. Hang it up and ask what will happen to it over time. Look for an answer about it becoming dry. Ask where the water goes and look beneath the towel for signs of drips. Ask what material around the towel could have taken the water and look for an answer about the air.

Class activities
- Say that when scientists are investigating, they want to keep things as simple as possible so you are not considering the towel but just the water and air. Let the children look at a bowl of water. Say that, given enough time, the water in that bowl would disappear. Ask how the water is escaping from the bowl. It cannot go through the bowl so it must go upwards through the water's surface. Say that if this is so, water with a larger surface will lose water faster than water with a smaller surface.
- Challenge the children to think of a way to test the idea in step 1. Look for taking equal volumes of water, putting one in a wide bowl and the other in a narrow bottle and leaving them for two days then measuring the volume of water remaining in each. Let the children set up the experiment.
- Remind the children about air being made of gases and ask what the water must have become if it is in the air. Look for the answer 'gas' and say that the gas form of water in the air is called 'water vapour'. Say that the process of a liquid turning into a gas is called 'evaporation'. Ask the children how evaporation might be sped up. Remind them how solids are changed into liquids by heating them and look for an answer about heat speeding up evaporation.
- Ask the children how they could see if heat affects evaporation and look for an answer about setting up two bowls with the same amount of water in places of different temperatures and leaving them for two days. Let the children set up the experiment.
- Ask how water vapour can be changed back into liquid water and steer the children towards an answer about cooling the vapour. Show the children the beaker, the foil cup and an ice cube and ask how they could be used to see if evaporated water can be turned back into liquid water. Guide the children towards an answer about putting warm water in the beaker, putting the ice cube in the cup, putting the cup on top of the beaker and looking for water droplets at the top of the beaker or under the cup. Let the children try the experiment.

Plenary
Review the results of the various experiments. Establish that evaporation is the process of liquid water turning into a gas called 'water vapour' and that the changing of this gas back into liquid water is called 'condensation'. Refer to puddles drying up as evidence of evaporation and say that it also occurs in lakes, seas and oceans. Ask where all the water vapour goes and point out that the atmospheric temperature falls with height and lead the children to conclude that water vapour condenses to form clouds (see Further lesson ideas and activities 6).

Further lesson ideas and activities

1. The children could compare the runniness of different liquids by tipping equal volumes of water, oil, honey and syrup onto the top of a ramp made from a metal tray and timing how long it takes each one to flow to the bottom.
2. Help the children appreciate where gases can be found by placing a sponge in water and squeezing it to release bubbles (a sign of a gas in a liquid). Place some dry soil in a transparent beaker. Pour in some water and watch the bubbles of air rise as water pushes air out of the spaces in the soil.
3. You may like to inflate a balloon, measure it, put it in a warm place and then measure it again. The balloon will be larger, demonstrating that heat makes gas expand. Put the balloon in a cold place and then measure it again. You should find that the cold has made the gas contract.
4. Let the children use secondary sources to find the melting points of a range of materials.
5. Make two ice hands by pouring water into rubber gloves and securing them in a freezer. Peel off the gloves and put a thick woolly glove on one of them. Ask which will melt the fastest. They may say the one in the glove but the glove provides insulation which slows down melting so the naked ice hand should melt faster.
6. Let the children use secondary sources to find out about the water cycle. Let them work together to make a class poster about the water cycle featuring melting, freezing, evaporating and condensing.

Cross curricular links

- The changes in state could be related to weather studies.
- The changes from ice to water may be related to conservation/sustainability studies related to the consequences of the melting of the polar ice caps.
- The study of the water cycle may be linked with geography and climate studies in different parts of the world.

Year 4: Sound

What does the curriculum say?

- *Identify how sounds are made, associating some of them with vibrating.*
- *Recognise that vibrations from sounds travel through a medium to the ear.*
- *Find patterns between the pitch of a sound and features of the object that produced it.*
- *Find patterns between the volume of a sound and the strength of the vibrations that produced it.*
- *Recognise that sounds get fainter as the distance from the sound source increases.*

What do I need to know?

Sound is generated when an object vibrates. Some of the energy of the vibrating object is transferred to the air (or other medium around it) and makes its particles move. Sound, then, is a form of energy. The particles vibrate and go backwards and forwards. The movement is better shown as a wave in water at first but in reality it is a longitudinal wave like the one you can make in a slinky. (See Further lesson ideas and activities 6.)

The particles in solids are the most tightly bound and swing backwards and forwards quickly. The particles in liquids are less tightly bound and transfer sound waves more slowly. The particles in liquids are not bound together and so transfer the sound waves even more slowly. In the experiment on listening through the different states this translates as sound being heard more loudly and clearly through solids and less loudly and clearly in gases.

Sound travels at about 340 metres per second through air. Light travels very much faster than sound at 3,000,000,000 metres per second. In a thunderstorm, the lightning flash is perceived almost immediately but the sound waves of thunder take five seconds to cover a mile. Counting the time from the flash to the thunder gives an indication of the distance of the storm.

The pitch is the number of sound waves produced by a vibrating object in a second. If a small number is produced per second the pitch is low like a 'dong' sound. If the number is large the pitch is high like a 'ding sound'.

The volume of the sound depends upon the amount of energy in the sound wave. If the wave contains a great deal of energy the crests of the waves are high and the trough between them are deep and the sound is loud. If the wave contains a small amount of energy the crests and the troughs are much smaller and the sound is quiet.

Interesting fact

Sound waves need particles of a solid, liquid or a gas to move them along. In space there are none of these so sound cannot travel across space. In space films you see and hear explosions. In reality, you would only ever see them.

Vocabulary

Ear protectors: ear muffs with sound insulation to prevent loud sounds reaching the ears and damaging them.

Frequency: the number of waves produced by a vibration in a second.

Fret: a metal strip across the neck of a guitar.

Finger board: the part on the neck of a guitar where the frets are placed and the lengths of the strings are controlled.

Guiro: a musical instrument which is scraped to make a noise.

Percussion instrument: any musical instrument that is struck to make a sound.

Pitch: the highness or lowness of a sound. It is related to the frequency of the sound waves. A high frequency makes a high pitched sound. A low frequency makes a low pitched sound.

Sound wave: the movement of particles in a gas, liquid or solid that transfers the vibrations through it.

Stringed instrument: an instrument which is played by scraping, strumming or picking its strings.

Tines: the two prongs of a tuning fork.

Tuning fork: a metal fork which makes a certain musical note when it vibrates. It is used to tune musical instruments.

Vibration: an up and down or backwards and forwards movement that occurs many times a second.

Wind instrument: an instrument that is played by blowing it.

Progression

This is the only area of study about sound in Key Stage 1 and 2. However, you can draw on what the children have heard in the countryside or in studies on materials to enrich the studies in sound here. It can contribute to the study of animal calls in the study of life cycles in Year 5 and buzzers in electricity in Year 6.

Technical tips

In lesson 1, strike the tuning fork sharply on a piece of wood. If you dip both tines in the water you may splash water over the onlookers!

In lesson 2, the children will need quiet places around the school to carry out their investigations on sound and distance and on sound insulation materials.

For lesson 3, check with your school policies on using elastic bands and, if necessary, ensure the children wear safety spectacles. Make sure the elastic bands are not too tight when put around the box so that they snap. Place the elastic band lengthways around the piece of wood and put a pencil underneath it to raise it a little on one side. Move the pencil right and left to check the elastic band does not snap.

Lesson 1 How are sounds made?

Working scientifically skills: Observing carefully; setting up simple practical enquiries; identifying similarities related to simple scientific processes
Scientific enquiry type: Identifying, classifying and grouping; pattern seeking

You will need: a guiro, a picture of or an actual violin, a guitar, a drum, about 20 rice grains, a drumstick, a tuning fork, a piece of wood, a bowl of water.

Getting started
Ask the children to sit in silence and listen for sounds for two minutes. After this time, ask them to tell you what they heard. Make a list on the board. Ask them to name some other everyday sounds and aim for a list of about 20 items. Remind the children how scientists like to put things into groups for further study. Encourage them to group the sounds they listed as loud sounds, quiet sounds and sounds that are of a medium volume. (See Further lesson ideas and activities 1.)

Class activities
• Say that sounds can be made in different ways and the first way they will be examining is the sound made by striking two surfaces together. Ask the children to make sounds by clapping, slapping a leg, clicking fingers and stamping their feet. Ask what other sounds are made by banging surfaces and look for answers about drums and cymbals. Extend this by looking at bells, jingles and shakers. (See Further lesson ideas and activities 2 and 3.)
• Say that sound can be made by moving air and get the children to whistle. Ask them about musical instruments that produce sound when they are blown and make a list. (See Further lesson ideas and activities 4.)
• Ask the children to rub their hands together and listen to the sound. Demonstrate how a guiro makes a sound when scraped. Show the children a picture of a violin (or show them a real one) and ask how it is played. Look for an answer about scraping the strings with a bow. Some children may say that they are also plucked. Show the children a guitar and ask how that is played. Strum it and pick the strings. Ask the children to look at the strings as you pick them and to describe what they see (it is a blur).
• Say the strings appeared blurred because they were moving backwards and forwards very quickly and this is called 'vibrating'. Show the children a drum and some grains of rice. Ask how the rice could be used to see if the drum skin vibrates. Look for answers about putting the rice on the drum, beating the skin and looking for the rice being flung up in the air. Then try it. (See Further lesson ideas and activities 5.)

Plenary
Review the way sounds are made in different ways and ask how sound reaches the ear. Steer the discussion around to particles in the air. Set a tuning fork vibrating and dangle a table tennis ball on a string close to a vibrating tine. It should swing backwards and forwards as we believe particles in the air do. Set the tuning fork vibrating again and dip one tine in a bowl of water. Let the children see the waves. Say that sound travels through the air as sound waves. (See Further lesson ideas and activities 6.)

Lesson 2 Loudness of sounds

Working scientifically skills: Asking relevant questions and using different types of scientific enquiry to answer them; recording finings in tables and bar charts; identifying changes related to simple scientific ideas and processes
Scientific enquiry type: Fair tests; pattern seeking

You will need: a tuning fork, a phone making a simple repetitive sound, a balloon filled with air, a balloon filled with water, a thick block of wood about 15 cm long (the same size as the inflated balloon for a fair test), rope about 4 m long. Each group will need a sound source, a tape measure or metre rule, a selection of materials such as woollen cloth, bubble wrap, cotton sheet, plastic sheet.

Getting started
Remind the children about the tuning fork. Strike it, hold it up and see if anyone can hear it. Now strike it again but hold the base firmly against the horizontal surface of a wooden board. Everyone should be able to hear the note. Ask how this could happen and look for an answer about the tuning fork making the board vibrate and, as it is bigger, it sends out bigger waves. Say that if sound waves can move though air, a mixture of gases and solids, what else might they move through. Look for an answer about liquids.

Class activities
- Show the children the phone, the piece of wood and the balloon. Ask how they could use this equipment to compare how sound passes through a solid and a gas. Look for an answer about putting the phone next to one side of the wood and an ear at the other side and listening. Then putting the balloon between the ear and the phone and listening again. Ask how they could test a liquid and look for an answer about filling a balloon with water and placing it between the ear and the phone. Set up this equipment and let the children try it individually during the course of the lesson.
- Remind the children about the sound waves and say that scientists sometimes make models to help them study and you are using a piece of rope to represent the air and a hand to represent a vibrating sound-making object. Lay out the rope, ask a child to hold one end and shake it gently. Say this is the model of a quiet sound and note how far the wave travels. Ask the child to shake the rope more strongly. Say this is a model of a loud sound and note that the wave travels further.
- Say that when scientists have used a model they then try an experiment on the 'real thing'. Ask how they could test the idea of the model. Look for an answer about setting up a radio making a quiet sound, moving away until it cannot be heard and measuring the distance, then repeating the process, increasing the loudness of the radio each time. Results could be plotted on a bar graph.
- Say that sound pollution can affect health so materials are used to cover noisy machinery to make them quieter. Also materials are used in ear protectors to reduce the amount of sound reaching the ears from noisy machinery and causing ear damage. Show the children a range of materials and ask them to devise an investigation to find out which one stops sound most effectively.

- The children should plan to set up a sound source and find out how far they must go before it cannot be heard. They should then wrap the sound source in one of the materials, and measure how far they must go before the sound cannot be heard (see Technical tip). This is then repeated with all the materials. The children should record their data in a table and present it as a bar graph.

Plenary
Let the children present their findings for the sound and distance investigation and the sound insulation materials investigation.

Lesson 3 The pitch of sounds

Working scientifically skills: Making comparative test and fair tests; using results to make predictions; using straightforward scientific evidence to answer questions and support their findings
Scientific enquiry type: Comparative and fair tests; pattern seeking; researching using secondary sources

You will need: a guitar, a film of musicians playing or some visiting musicians; each group will need a plastic box with firm sides, three elastic bands of different thicknesses to put around the box, a ruler (see Technical tip), a piece of wood about 8 cm long with an elastic band which a can fit along its length, a pencil (see Technical tip), plastic bottles of different sizes, a straw.

Getting started
Show the children the guitar again. Point out that the strings are of different thicknesses and pluck each one in turn, starting with the thickest. Ask the children how the pitch changed. Look for an answer about it rising as the strings got thinner. Press your finger onto the thick string on one of the frets about midway down the fingerboard. Pluck the string and compare its pitch again (it rises). Repeat with the other strings to establish the idea that shorter vibrating strings make a higher pitch.

Class activities
- Tell the children that they should make a model of the guitar strings by using elastic bands of different lengths; show them how to put them on the box. Ask the children to measure the thicknesses (widths) of the bands before they do so and arrange them so that they will produce sounds that increase or decrease in pitch. They could record their sounds for the plenary.
- Remind the children about the effect on pitch of changing the length of the guitar string and show them how to set up the elastic band, pencil and wood block. Ask them to place the pencil in the middle of the string and predict the pitch of both sides when plucked (they will be the same). Ask them to predict what will happen if they move the pencil a little to one side and then try it. The shorter length has a higher pitch than the longer length.
- Show the children the guitar, pick a string, tighten it and pick again and ask the children how the pitch changes (its rises). Ask what you have done and look for an answer about

stretching the string. Now show the children a drum and ask them which part vibrates to make sound (the drum skin). Ask what would happen if you pushed a little on the skin to stretch it. Look for an answer about raising the pitch then confirm it by beating the drum un-stretched, and then slightly stretched, to hear the raised pitch.

- Remind the children about the wind instruments and give out the plastic bottles. Ask them to blow across the top and describe what they hear: low or high pitched sounds. Ask them to arrange the bottles in order from those producing low pitched sounds to those producing high pitched sounds and to suggest an explanation for their arrangement. Steer them towards an answer that the taller bottles have longer columns of vibrating air than the shorter bottles.
- Ask the children to fill their bottles with water and give them a straw. Ask them how they could test their idea about the length of columns of air. Look for an answer about blowing into the straw and raising and lowering it in the water. Let the children try this.

Plenary

Let the children present the sounds of their 'guitars'. Let them describe what happened when they used the pencil and wood block and the straw in the bottle. Say that when wind instruments like the recorder are played, putting fingers over holes changes the length of the vibrating column of air inside. Show a film of someone playing a guitar or a flute or invite in some musicians to demonstrate their art.

Further lesson ideas and activities

1. You may wish to introduce the idea of pitch which the children will study in lesson three 3. If so, you may say that sounds can be low pitched sounds such as 'pong' or high pitched sounds such as 'ping' or a medium pitch such as 'pang'. The children could then group the sounds on the list according to their pitch.
2. The children could research percussion instruments used in orchestras around the world.
3. The children could make their own shakers or a range of shakers using different containers and objects inside them to produce different sounds. They could experiment in using these shakers together to set up different rhythms.
4. The children could research wind instruments used in the orchestra and around the world. Any children who play a recorder, flute or clarinet could demonstrate how the instrument is played.
5. A wooden ruler could be held over the end of a table and twanged gently to make it vibrate.
6. Say that the particles really move backwards and forwards in a sound wave like those generated in a slinky. Set up a slinky on the floor, push and pull one end to send a wave along it.

Cross curricular links

- The work on shakers in Further idea 3 could be used in the study of music or in the accompaniment of school productions such as plays and pantomimes.
- The work on loudness and pitch can be used in the study of music.
- The study of musical instruments from around the world can be used to enrich geography projects.
- History projects could be enriched by the children researching the musical instruments played in the various periods they are studying.

Year 4: Electricity

What does the curriculum say?

- *Identify common appliances that run on electricity.*
- *Construct a simple series electrical circuit, identifying and naming its basic parts, including cells, wires, bulbs, switches and buzzers.*
- *Identify whether or not a lamp will light in a simple series circuit, based on whether or not the lamp is part of a complete loop with a battery.*
- *Recognise that a switch opens and closes a circuit and associate this with whether or not a lamp lights in a simple series circuit.*
- *Recognise some common conductors and insulators, and associate metals with being good conductors.*

What do I need to know?

The children study current electricity. This is generated by chemical reactions in cells. In early studies, the current was believed to flow from a positive terminal of the cell to a negative cell but later studies showed that the reverse was true. The study on static electricity introduces the concept of charge and, in current electricity, the electrons with their negative charges form the current. The voltage is the push on the electrons so a higher voltage gives a larger push. The metal in all the components of the circuit is packed with free electrons and, when the circuit is switched on, the electrons move around the circuit like people in a queue. For more background information see Year 6, Electricity, page 181.

A simple introduction to electricity is provided in the introduction in lesson 1. This features static electricity, which does not feature in the curriculum but is a familiar phenomenon that the children may know about. If you use this introduction a little background, although not needed for the curriculum but to answer enquiring questions, follows.

The children may already have learned that matter is composed of particles called atoms in chapter 3 (States of matter) and the extra knowledge they need to understand static electricity is that atoms contain even smaller particles called electrons, which possess an electric charge. During the rubbing process, electrons move from one material to another, giving one material more electric charge and the other material less electric charge. Materials charged in this way can generate charges in other materials so that they make a balloon stick to the wall, for instance, or make hair charged so it rises up to a charged bag. Note: it is the material moving due to the charges, not the electrons themselves. Electrons move in a current of electricity.

> ### Interesting fact
>
> The electric eel is a South American fish that can produce powerful electric shocks of 300–650 volts. It uses these shocks in order to stun its prey and as a defence mechanism against attack.

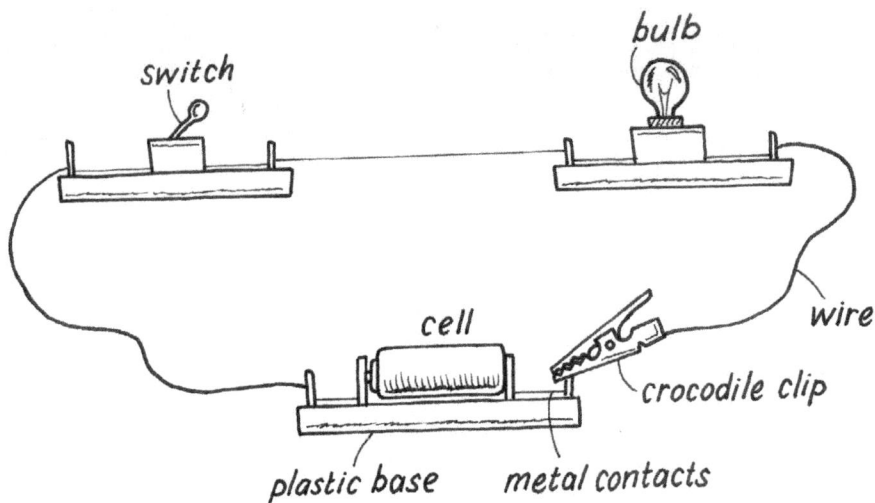

The diagram shows a circuit with labels: switch, bulb, cell, wire, crocodile clip, plastic base, metal contacts.

A safety note

The electricity used in the following activities is weak and not harmful, but mains electricity is much stronger. Tell the children that they must not try any experiments with mains electricity. The children's experience of mains should be restricted to the use of switches – tell them handling switches with wet hands is dangerous, as water can conduct electricity. That is why bathroom light switches have long cords, which keep potentially wet hands away from the switch.

Vocabulary

Atom: the particle from which all things are made. It contains electrons which may be removed in some materials by rubbing.
Battery: a group of cells connected together.
Cell: a container, usually a cylinder, which holds chemicals that generate an electric current when the cell is placed in a circuit and the circuit is switched on.
Circuit: a loop made by wires and other components through which electricity can flow when the circuit is switched on.
Component: a part of a circuit such as a wire, cell, or lamp.
Current electricity: electricity which flows in a circuit.
Negative terminal: the terminal through which electrons flow into a circuit.
Positive terminal: the terminal through which electrons flow from the circuit into the cell.
Static electricity: electricity that stays in one place. It does not flow as a current.
Terminal: the end of a cell through which a current of electricity flows.
Voltage: the power of a cell to produce electricity. This power is measured in units called volts. It is a measure of push of the current not a measure of the size of the current.

Progression

This is the first area of study about electricity. It introduces the concept of a circuit, its components, its maintenance and electrical conductors and insulators. In Year 6 this is further developed by the use of symbols for components in the building of circuits, looking for patterns in the relationship between the number of cells and bulbs in a circuit and the brighness of the bulbs and further investigations on components including the motor.

Technical tip

The power of the cell is shown on the side as a voltage, usually 1.5V. When two cells are placed in series with one negative terminal next to a positive terminal, their voltages combine to give a large voltage such as 1.5V + 1.5V = 3V. If three cells are arranged in series they give a voltage of 4.5. Lamps are designed to work at specific voltages such as 3V or 4.5V. If they receive too high a voltage (e.g. a 3V lamp receiving 4.5V) they burn out. Aim to use lamps with 4.5V tolerance for greater flexibility here and in Year 6.

Useful websites

Lesson 2 and Further idea 4: For Morse code: www.livephysics.com/tools/mathematical-tools/morse-code-conversion-tool/

Lesson 1 Introducing electricity

Working scientifically skills: Recording findings using simple scientific language and drawings
Scientific enquiry type: Comparative test

You will need: a balloon and a dry woollen cloth. Each group will need a plastic pen, some small pieces of paper, a cell, a lamp, a switch, three wires with crocodile clips, a motor and a buzzer.

Getting started
Ask the children to name devices which run on electricity and make a list on the board. Ask them to speculate on what life would be like without electricity and say that electricity only came into common use in the twentieth century. (See Further lesson ideas and activities 1.)

Say that the first investigations on electricity were carried out on a kind of electricity called static electricity. Rub a balloon on a dry woollen cloth and ask the children what will happen if you press it onto a wall. Look for an answer about it sticking. Ask why it does this and be prepared for a few blank faces. Rub the balloon again and place it above the head of someone with long hair and let the children see the hairs rise. Tear up some paper into very tiny pieces. Rub a plastic pen on wool for ten seconds and bring close to the paper. They should see some of the pieces rise and stick to the pen. Say that all these actions are due to static electricity: electricity that, once generated, stays where it is. Say that the children are now going to study electricity on the move.

Class activities
* Issue the children with a cell, three wires, a switch and a lamp and ask them to make the lamp light up. Tell them that to do this they must arrange the components in a loop called a circuit through which the electrons can move. Let the children experiment a little then show them that the circuit should have a wire going from one end of the cell to a switch, another wire from the switch to the lamp and another wire from the lamp to the other end of the cell. (See Further idea 2.) Make sure all the groups set up a circuit in this way and switch on the electricity to make the lamp light up. If the lamp does not light, direct the children to check all the connections to make sure that there are no gaps.
* Remind the children about keeping a record of their activities and ask them to make a labelled drawing of their circuit.
* Take in the lamps and give out the motors. Let the children put the motor into the circuit. Ask them to make a drawing and explain what happens to the motor when the current is switched on. (The motor shaft spins round.)
* Tell the children that inside the cell are chemicals which make a current of electrons flow through a circuit when the circuit is switched on. The electrons flow from one end of the cell, called the 'negative terminal', to the other end of the cell called the 'positive terminal.' (See Further lesson ideas and activities 3.)
* Take in the motors and issue the buzzers. Point out that there is a red wire that must be attached to a wire going to the positive terminal and a black wire attached to part of the circuit connected to the negative terminal. Say that the electrons flow from the negative terminal to the positive terminal and the buzzer is designed to work to this flow of

electrons. Let the children look for the positive (+) and negative (-) symbols on the cell, assemble the circuit with the buzzer, make it work and then make a labelled drawing of it.

Plenary
Review the children's knowledge of current electricity and how they would advise others to set up the three circuits they have made.

Lesson 2 Electrical conductors and insulators

Working scientifically skills: Making systematic and careful observations; using results to draw simple conclusions and suggest improvements
Scientific enquiry type: Comparative or fair test

You will need: a cell, three wires with crocodile clips, a lamp, a switch, a torch. Each group will need a cell, three wires, a lamp, a switch, access to a piece of wood, brick, string, copper wire, cardboard, aluminium foil, a ceramic plate, a plastic plate, an iron nail, a steel spoon.

Getting started
Gather the children round a table and put the components on it. Arrange the cell, wires, lamp and switch in a circle but do not connect them. Point out that they form a loop but that the lamp doesn't light. Ask them why. Look for an answer about the lack of connection and connect each one into the circuit in turn asking why the lamp still does not light and look for the answer that the lamp will not light until all the connections are made and the switch is on. Ask why the electricity did not flow when there were gaps and steer the discussion towards there being air in the gaps. Ask what this tells us about air and look for an answer that it does not let electricity pass through it. Say that materials which let electricity pass through them are called 'electrical conductors' and materials which do not let electricity pass through them are called 'electrical insulators' and they are going to find out more about them. (See Further lesson ideas and activities 4.)

Class activities
- Show the children the range of materials and ask how they could test each one to find out if it was a conductor or an insulator. Look for an answer about setting up the circuit with an extra wire between the lamp and the switch but keeping a gap between the two wires into which the material can be placed.
- Ask how the children will make their test with this arrangement and look for an answer about placing the material in the gap, closing the switch and seeing if the lamp lights. Ask the children to make a table in which to record their results and then follow the plan with each material.
- Ask if any materials did not conduct electricity. Ask how they could make sure they really did not conduct electricity and steer the discussion to increasing the amount of electricity by using more than one cell. Point out that the electrical power of the cells is shown in volts on the side and when adding cells together you add their voltages to find the power you are using.

- Remind the children about how electrons flow around a circuit from the negative terminal to the positive terminal. See if the children can suggest that the cells are set end to end with the negative terminal of one touching the positive terminal of the other. This will make all the electrons flow in the same direction. Ask what would happen if the two negative or positive terminals were put together and look for an answer that the current would not flow because the electrons would be pushing into each other.
- Give the children an extra cell and let them test their theory then let them test the materials again. Ask them to make a drawing of the circuit with two cells in it.

Plenary
Let the children present their results with one cell in the circuit and two cells in the circuit. Say that when two cells are joined together they make a battery. Ask the children about equipment they use that have batteries and how they must note the positive and negative signs on the casing which give guidance on how to place the cells. Pass a torch round and ask them to switch it on. Ask what might be wrong and let them open it to discover that the cells are arranged incorrectly. Let them rearrange the cells so the torch lights up.

Lesson 3 Making switches

Working scientifically skills: Setting up simple practical enquiries; reporting on findings with oral explanations
Scientific enquiry type: Comparative test

You will need: for each group: a cell, three wires with crocodile clips, a lamp, materials to make switches (including cardboard), sticky paper, aluminium foil, a piece of metal, steel paper clips, thin wood sheets, scissors. Introduce a steel ball bearing at step 3.

Getting started
Remind the children of the terms related to switches. When it is switched off, the switch is open, there is air in the gap and, as air is an insulator, electricity cannot flow. When it is switched on, a piece of metal closes the gap and a current of electricity can flow through it because metals are conductors of electricity. Say that a switch is a simple control of the flow of electricity.

Class activities
- Show the children the electrical components for a circuit without a switch and say that they must make a switch to use in it. Talk about the essentials of a switch: it must have some insulating material (the air gap) and a conductor to fit in the gap to close the switch. Suggest they start by using foil, sticky paper and card which they can cut into any shape and bend. The switch should be connected into the circuit in the gap left by leaving out the real switch.
- Let the children try making switches. A simple one may be two pieces of foil on a card with a gap between them. Each is connected to a crocodile clip and a third strip is put across to close the switch. This may be attached to one of the other pieces of foil, or the cardboard. A more complex one is made by bending a card in half, sticking squares of foil to the inside of each half, connecting them to crocodile clips then pressing the two halves together to close the switch.
- Introduce the ball bearing. Say that the switch using a ball bearing is closed by letting the ball roll between the two pieces of foil and touch both at once. The switch is opened by letting the ball roll away from between the two pieces of foil. The children may cut long thin strips of cardboard and stick them to the wood or more card to make a narrow gutter down which the ball bearing can run. They could then add foil to each side of the gutter at one end. When the gutter is tipped one way the ball rolls between the foil contacts and closes the circuit. When the gutter is tipped the other way the ball rolls away and the circuit is opened. The children may work on a device such as a see-saw to help the ball move up and down the gutter.

Plenary
Let the children present their switches and describe how they work. Remind the children that evidence of the current flowing is provided by the lamp that lights up. Keep any unusual switches in a box for use in Year 6, lesson 3.

Further lesson ideas and activities

1. Let the children find out about the electrical appliances in use in the late nineteenth century through the twentieth century and into the twenty-first century.

2. Make out a rectangle on the floor and say that it represents a cell. Line up six children facing one way inside the 'cell'. Lay out a rope from one end of the cell. Add a half metre rule to the end of the rope (this represents a switch). Lay out another rope running from the metre rule to a torch (this represents a lamp). Then lay out another rope from the torch to the other end of the 'cell'. Put the rule across the two ends of the ropes to switch on the circuit and let the children move around it from the negative terminal over the switch. When they get to the torch they switch it on as they pass. The last one switches it off. Switch off the circuit (by moving the metre rule) once they have passed through the positive terminal and back into the cell. Say this introduces the idea of terminals and electron flow but say it is a little more complicated. Ask some more children to stand on the rope and say that electrons are present in the wires and when the circuit is switched on they move too. Let them switch on the torch as they pass and let children leave the cell then switch it off and let them all stop.

3. You may now like to introduce the correct way of talking about a switch. Say that when it is switched off there is a gap in the switch which stops the electricity flowing. A switch in this condition is said to be 'open'. When you turn the switch on, two metal parts in the switch come together. There is no gap, the switch is said to be 'closed' and the current flows. You may like to start using the phrases 'close the switch' and 'open the switch' instead of 'switch on' and 'switch off'.

4. Say that messages have been sent using pulses of electricity generated by turning a switch on and off quickly. Say that the Morse code was invented for this purpose. Challenge the children to make a switch that can make a light flash on and off quickly or a buzzer make long and short buzzes.

Cross curricular links

- The development of electricity can be studied in the context of the Victorians in history.
- The making of switches can be used in the context of design and technology.

Part 3:
Upper Key Stage 2 (Years 5–6)

What does the curriculum say?

The principal focus of science teaching in Upper Key Stage 2 is to enable pupils to develop a deeper understanding of a wide range of scientific ideas. They should do this through exploring and talking about their ideas; asking their own questions about scientific phenomena; and analysing functions, relationships and interactions more systematically. At Upper Key Stage 2, they should encounter more abstract ideas and begin to recognise how these ideas help them to understand and predict how the world operates. They should also begin to recognise that scientific ideas change and develop over time. They should select the most appropriate ways to answer science questions using different types of scientific enquiry, including observing changes over different periods of time, noticing patterns, grouping and classifying things, carrying out comparative and fair tests and finding things out using a wide range of secondary sources of information. Pupils should draw conclusions based on their data and observations, use evidence to justify their ideas, and use their scientific knowledge and understanding to explain their findings. 'Working and thinking scientifically' is described separately at the beginning of the programme of study, but must always be taught through and clearly related to substantive science content in the programme of study. Throughout the notes and guidance, examples show how scientific methods and skills might be linked to specific elements of the content. Pupils should read, spell and pronounce scientific vocabulary correctly.

Year 5: Living things and their habitats

What does the curriculum say?

- *Describe the differences in the life cycles of a mammal, an amphibian, an insect and a bird.*
- *Describe the life process of reproduction in some plants and animals.*

What do I need to know?

The life cycle of a living thing is a series of stages of development, starting with a fertilised egg in animals or a seed or spore in plants. It runs through significant stages of development until the starting stage is reached again.

In a placental mammal (not egg laying or pouched mammals), the fertilised egg develops in the womb and then is born and fed on milk. It is eventually weaned onto the food for which it is adapted then continues to develop to maturity when it can reproduce and the cycle begins again.

In amphibians, the fertilised egg hatches into the tadpole stage. During this stage the tadpole acquires the characteristics of the adult and eventually changes or metamorphoses into the adult form. It then increases in size until it is mature and begins to breed.

There are two kinds of life cycles in insects. In one, a nymph, which is a tiny version of the adult without wings and reproductive organs, hatches out of the egg. It grows and moults several times until at the last moult it acquires the adult's features and is ready to breed. In the second kind, a larva (caterpillar, maggot, beetle grub) hatches from the egg and grows and moults several times before changing into a pupa, from which emerges the adult stage.

Birds hatch from eggs and spend varying amounts of time in the nest being fed by parents, before leaving the nest as fledglings and learning to feed themselves. The following year they are ready for breeding.

You may like to teach these lessons in the spring term when plants and animals are in the reproductive stage of their life cycles. Only the basics of animal reproduction are considered here. You may wish to extend this topic, if appropriate for your children, and it must, of course, be handled with sensitivity. You may wish to read through chapter 2, which considers changes at adolescence, and integrate the two chapters. (See Cross curricular links.) You may also like to read through Year 3, Chapter 1 Plants starting on page 54 before you start this chapter.

Although cells are not featured in the curriculum it is highly likely that the children have met the word. It may be useful to use it in the context of the reproductive stage of the life cycle and link it to the whole body or plants and animals. In flowering plants, the male sex cell is made in the anther and enclosed in the pollen grain. The female sex cell, the egg cell, is made in the ovule. Flowering plants prevent self-fertilisation by releasing pollen before the stigma is ready to receive it. In animals, the egg cells are made in the ovaries and the male sex cells, called sperms, are made in the testes. While most individual flowering plants have both male and female sex organs, individual animals have either male or female sex organs.

In lesson 2, the sperms and eggs are introduced and external and internal fertilisation are described. You may like to extend the brief description of internal fertilisation by saying that the female has ovaries which make eggs and the male has testes which make sperms and these organs have tubes to the outside associated with the tubes which release urine. (In the female there is a separate tube from the vagina to the ovary but in the male the urethra releases both urine and sperms.) These tubes join together to make the transfer.

Interesting fact

The egg case of the dogfish, a type of small shark, washes up on the sea shore and is black with curly edges, which we call a 'mermaid's purse'.

Vocabulary

Anther: the part of a flower which makes pollen.
Cell: a very small structure which joins with millions of others to form the bodies of living things.
External fertilisation: the process in which a sperm cell fuses with an egg cell outside the body.
Embryo: the early stage of development of a living thing enclosed in a seed, fertilised egg or the womb of a mammal. The later stage of development, after all the main features have formed in mammals, is called the 'fetus'. In humans, the fetal stage occurs from the second to the ninth month of pregnancy.
Fruit: the part of a plant which contains seeds.
Internal fertilisation: the process in which a sperm cell fuses with an egg cell inside the body of a female.
Life cycle: the course of development of a living thing from fertilisation until death. It is divided into a number of stages.
Life span: the time between the stage when a living thing germinates, hatches or is born, and its death. An average time is calculated for each type of living thing.
Ovary: the part of a plant which contains ovules; the part of an animal which contains eggs.
Ovule: the part of a plant which turns into a seed after fertilisation of the egg cell it contains.
Placenta: a disc containing the embryo's blood which exchanges materials to let the embryo grow healthily.
Seed: the part of a plant which contains an embryo plant and a food store.
Testes: a part of the body of a male animal that makes sperms.
Womb: a part of a female mammal in which the embryo grows.

Progression

This area of study builds on previous work about the requirements for germination and plant growth and sexual reproduction in plants. The work on reproduction in mammals relates to the human life cycle in chapter 2. The camouflaged egg activity relates to adaptation which is a process related to evolution in Year 6.

Technical tips

For lesson 1, the time from sowing to pod formation of the broad bean takes 16 weeks if sowing is in the spring and 28 weeks if sowing is in the autumn. But the emergence of the flowers and then the pods with the brown beans in them illustrates the complete life cycle and the link between one generation and another really well.

For lesson 2, make the model dividing cells by splitting one ball of modelling clay in half and making two, four and eight smaller balls squashed together. Collect only a small amount of frogspawn and keep it in a tank with some pond weed.

Useful websites

Lesson 1: www.sciencephoto.com/set/1492/pollen-a-closer-look
Lesson 2: www.saburchill.com/chapters/chap0032.html (scroll down to the fourth picture)
ypte.org.uk/factsheets/care-of-frogspawn-and-tadpoles/guide#section
www.topmarks.co.uk/spring/TadpolesDevelop.aspx?age=ks2
www.animalcorner.co.uk/insects/ladybirds/ladybird_lifecycle.html
Lesson 3: www.youtube.com/watch?v=yJXYFaxhq1U

Lesson 1 Reproduction in plants

Working scientifically skills: Recording data using scientific diagrams and labels; planning different types of enquiries including recognising and controlling variables

Scientific enquiry type: Research using secondary sources; comparative test; fair test; observing over time

You will need: access to the school grounds or a park, a spider plant with plantlets, a pot of compost; for each group: a large single flower with separate petals such as a tulip and another large single flower with fused petals like a daffodil or rhododendron, broad bean seeds (sourced from a health food shop so they have not been treated with fungicide – see Technical tips), a plant pot of compost and a detached plantlet.

Getting started
In this session you may like to write answers on the board as the children brainstorm what they know about plants. Ask the children to name the parts of a plant (root, stem, leaf, flower). Ask what plants grow from. Look for the answer 'seeds' (though some may remember about bulbs). Ask about the process in which a plant breaks out of a seed (germination) and the requirements for germination (water and warmth). Ask what plants need to grow (water, warmth and light). Say that when the plant reaches a certain stage of

growth it starts to produce reproductive organs. Ask where the reproductive organs on a plant are and look for an answer about them being in the flowers.

Class activities
- Give the children a large single flower with separate petals and let the children look inside. Ask them to make a drawing of it, label the parts and say they may have to look up information about the parts if they cannot remember them.
- Give the children the second flower (with fused petals) and ask them to make a labelled drawing of it identifying the main parts. Ask them to compare its structure with the first flower.
- Say that the anthers produce pollen which must pass to the stigma of a flower of the same kind of plant for reproduction to take place. Show the pictures of pollen grains (see Useful websites) and ask which they think might be carried on insects' hairy bodies (spiky pollen) or by the wind (smooth pollen). Say that when the pollen grain reaches the stigma it grows a tube and its contents flow into it. The tube connects up with a structure in the ovary called the ovule and when the pollen contents reach it, they fuse with a female sex cell inside it, called the egg. The ovule turns into a seed and the ovary turns into a fruit. (See Further lesson ideas and activities 1.)
- Issue the children with broad bean seeds and say that you would like to investigate the next part of the life cycle of the plant. They must work out a plan to germinate the seed and provide conditions for growth. The children should note the date of germination, the first leaf, the second leaf and so on. They should also measure the length of the bean shoot on Mondays and Fridays. As the plant grows they may decide to plant it outside or in a greenhouse and note the time of flower and fruit formation. (See Further lesson ideas and activities 2.)
- Tell the children that, in reproduction involving pollen, the pollen contains the male sex cell and the ovule contains the female sex cell. When they fuse in the process of fertilisation the first cell of a new plant is formed. This is called sexual reproduction. Show the children a spider plant that has small plantlets on stalks. Ask how this plant is reproducing (it is making copies of itself). Say that no pollen or ovule is involved so this is called asexual reproduction. Ask the children how they could find out if the plantlets would survive if they were separated. Leave some plantlets attached as controls. Detach a few plantlets. Plant all plantlets in compost and let the class monitor them for a few days. Look for signs of root growth. (See Further lesson ideas and activities 3 and 4.)

Plenary
Let the children present their diagrams of flowers, and their reports on the growth of the bean plants and spider plant plantlets.

Lesson 2 Insects and amphibians

Working scientifically skills: Recording data using scientific diagrams and labels; recording data in tables
Scientific enquiry type: Observing over time

You will need: a ball of modelling clay 3 cm across, similar balls but divided into two, four and eight cells (see Technical tips), frogspawn and a tank of clean pond water with some pond weed (see the Useful websites box for a resource for tadpole care), other internet resources. Each group will need modelling clay.

Getting started
Say that the life cycle of a flowering plant starts with a seed. Remind the children that flowers contain the anthers which make pollen that contains the male sex cell and the ovule contains the female sex cell called the egg cell. When the two sex cells meet, fertilisation takes place and the ovule turns into a seed. Say that, while most plants make both male and female sex cells, animals only make either male or female sex cells. An animal that produces male sex cells (sperms) is called a 'male'. An animal that produces female sex cells (egg cells) is called a 'female'. Ask how pollen is moved (by the wind or insects). Say that sperm cells always move in water and have a tail to help them swim and find an egg cell. Show the picture of egg cells and sperms (see Useful websites). When a sperm fuses with an egg, a fertilised egg is produced which starts to divide into more cells and grow to form a new animal. Show the children the model fertilised egg and early cell divisions and say that the fertilised egg divides into more cells and they divide to build up the whole body.

Class activities
- Tell the children that for many animals that live in water, the male releases the sperms into the water and the female releases the eggs. External fertilisation then takes place. If you have collected frogspawn you could set up a rota for the children to make daily observations and fill in a report sheet as the eggs hatch and the tadpoles develop.
- Tell the children that sometimes scientists make models to better understand and observe the focus of their studies. Click onto the third Useful website for this lesson. Issue modelling clay and ask the children to make a model of the newly hatched tadpole, click onto the next frame and ask them to change the model to match the picture (they can make their model a little larger). Continue looking though the pictures and letting the children change their model accordingly until they produce a froglet. The children could write about how a tadpole develops.
- Tell the children that animals living on land start life after internal fertilisation. During this process the male and female join together and the sperms pass from the male to the female. In many animals such as insects the fertilised egg is laid and the embryo develops inside it. When the egg hatches, the young animal emerges and starts to feed. Display the fifth Useful website and show the children the picture of the life cycle of the ladybird. Ask them to make separate models of each stage and write about how the animal changes as it goes through its life cycle.
- Let the children investigate the school ground or park and look for insect eggs and larva on leaves or bushes and trees. They could also dig in exposed soil to look for pupae and larvae such as cranefly larvae and beetle grubs. They could note any flying adults. This could be repeated every two weeks to see if the populations change.

Plenary
The children can report on the development of the tadpoles, and their investigations about insect life cycles in a habitat.

Lesson 3 Birds and mammals

Working scientifically skills: Planning different types of scientific enquiries to answer questions; reporting and presenting findings from enquiries in oral and written forms
Scientific enquiry type: Researching using secondary sources; comparative tests

You will need: Useful website 6, an unfertilised egg broken into a shallow bowl (you may have several so two or three groups could gather round each one with a TA), table tennis balls and modelling clay.

Getting started

Remind the children that birds and mammals are basically land animals, although they may spend their time in the air or in water, and that land animals have internal fertilisation. The life cycles of all animals are matched to the seasons to give their young the best chance of survival. This means that in the spring males and females seek out mates so they can reproduce. In birds, the males seek mates by establishing a territory, an area of land large enough to provide food for the offspring, then singing to attract a mate. Play the dawn chorus (see Useful website 6).

Class activities

- Say that, after mating, internal fertilisation takes place and the female bird adds features to the egg to help it survive outside the female's body. Take an unfertilised hen's egg and crack it into a bowl. Show the children the porous shell which lets air in, the membrane close to it which prevents liquid passing out, the air space at one end that the nearly fully developed chick uses to breathe, the white which provides a 'cushion' around the yolk which is a food store for the developing embryo. Say that in a fertilised egg the embryo develops on this yolk and uses it up to make the chick. Point out the twisted fibres commonly called 'balancers' which help to keep the yolk in place and not to rub up against the shell. (See Further lesson ideas and activities 6.)
- Say that ground nesting birds lay eggs which have camouflaged shells. The patterns on the eggs match their surroundings. Issue table tennis balls to the children. Let them look at the ground around the school and make camouflage patterns to blend in. Let the children work out a way of testing the camouflage by having other children look for the ball from a distance then moving closer until they can see the ball.
- Say that birds that lay eggs on cliff edges lay conical eggs. Ask the children to make a model conical egg with modelling clay, and work out why the eggs are this shape. They should see that the egg rolls around in a circle when touched so would not fall off the ledge. (See Further lesson ideas and activities 7.)
- Say that internal fertilisation takes place in the life cycle of mammals. In the spiny anteater and the duck billed platypus eggs are laid and when the young hatch they feed on their mother's milk. In marsupial mammals the embryos develop for a time in their mother's womb then climb into a pouch and continue their development by feeding on their mother's milk. (See Further lesson ideas and activities 8.)
- Say that in placental mammals such as humans, cats, dogs, horses, mice and rabbits the embryos stay inside their mother's womb, attached to it by a placenta, until it is time to be born. Show the children internet resource 2 and explain that the embryo receives food and oxygen from the mother's blood, via the placenta, and give carbon dioxide and other wastes to the mother's blood. When it is time to be born the baby is pushed out by the muscles of the womb, along the birth canal.

Plenary

Let the children present an assessment of how well they camouflaged their table tennis balls, an explanation about why ledge nesting birds lay conical eggs, a report about egg laying and marsupial mammals and their lists of placental mammals from around the world (if they have made them).

Further lesson ideas and activities

1. Let the children visit the school ground or a park to look for plants in flower. They could draw them attached to the plant, label the drawings and compare them with each other and the ones they have studied in class.

2. Let the children visit the school ground or a park to look for plants germinating and seedlings growing (these do not need to be identified just the evidence that these processes are taking place in the habitat is sufficient). They could look for plants which have flower buds yet to burst open and for fruits forming. The fruits could be divided into succulent fruits and dry fruits such as winged fruits or spiky fruits for animal dispersal. Warn the children not to eat any of the fruits.

3. Give the children some carrot tops and let them put them in saucers of water and draw or photograph the tops regularly over a few weeks. Note that all the parts of the plant will grow except the tap root of the original carrot.

4. Take a geranium and cut off some side branches. Let the children plant them in compost (do not use rooting powder) and see if they can grow into new plants. Alternatively, you could ask a local gardener to come into class to talk about cuttings.

5. Remind the children about bulbs and show them a garlic bulb. Split it into individual cloves, let them plant them and see how many grow into new plants.

6. Show the children a picture of an empty bird's nest from the internet. Point out how the bird made such a strong, egg-holding structure to withstand wet, windy weather. Challenge the children to use craft materials which simulate straw and twigs to build a nest to hold four modelling clay eggs. The children could work out a test to see which nest best resists pushes and pulls as would be experienced on a windy branch.

7. Let the children use secondary sources to find out about the terms 'nestling' and 'fledgling' in the life cycle of a bird. They could then select a bird and describe its life cycle.

8. Let the children use secondary sources to find out about the spiny anteater, platypus and marsupials.

9. Let the children use secondary sources to make a list of 20 placental mammals from around the world.

Cross curricular links

- You may like to integrate this chapter with chapter 2 and work with colleagues to bring religious and citizenship issues into a cross curricular topic on growing up.
- In lesson 2 you may like to use the work on tadpole development in English. The children could imagine they are a tadpole and describe how they change as they grow up.

Year 5: Animals, including humans

What does the curriculum say?

- *Describe the changes as humans develop to old age.*

What do I need to know?

Note that you may wish to refer to your school policies before teaching lesson 3 and bring in a health professional to talk to the children in this lesson.

You may like to integrate this chapter with the previous one as it provides a more detailed look at the stages in the human life cycle. The subject matter of this topic needs to be treated with sensitivity to the various family situations of the children.

The human gestation period is calculated in medicine as being 40 weeks which is the time from the first day of the last menstrual period. During this time the developing human may be variously referred to as the embryo, baby and fetus. 'Baby' is the general name that covers the whole of this development but the embryo stage covers the first eight weeks. During this time the embryo develops from a ball of cells into a small body with the organ systems and a beating heart. After this time the embryo becomes a fotus and continues to grow inside the mother until birth. After the birth the individual is now correctly called the baby. The stages in development vary with different sources. Here is a generalisation. At first the individual is newborn for the first few weeks then becomes an infant for the next one to two years. Childhood then follows and ends when puberty starts (10–13 in girls and 12–14 in boys). This is a period of physical change in which the individual becomes sexually mature and marks the beginning of adolescence which continues until 18 years when the young adult stage is reached. This continues until age 40 when middle age begins and lasts until 70 years of age when old age begins.

> ### Interesting fact
>
> The gas, oxygen, in the air forms a chemical in the red blood called 'oxyhaemoglobin' which travels around the body to where it is needed.

Vocabulary

Anomalous result: a result which does not fit in with a trend or pattern. It may be due to some error in carrying out an investigation or may need further explanation.

Brain: an organ made of billions of nerve cells which co-ordinates the actions of the body as well as storing and processing information.

Gestation period: the period of time from the fertilisation of the egg until birth in the life cycle of a placental mammal.

Hormone: a chemical made by an organ in the body that travels in the blood and causes part of the body to change in some way.

Nerves: cords which transfer information from sense organs to the brain and from the brain to muscles and hormone secreting organs like the adrenals.

Organ: a part of the body that performs a particular task in the survival of the body. For example, the kidneys remove harmful wastes from the blood.

Pores: tiny holes in the skin.

Follicles: tubes in the skin in which hairs develop.

Puberty: the period of time, usually between 12 and 14 years in humans, when the body becomes sexually mature.

Progression

This area of study follows on from the content of the previous chapter and can be integrated with it. It is extended in Year 6 with information about circulation and health issues to provide the children with a strong foundation of knowledge about the working of the body and ways to keep it healthy.

Technical tips

These baby milestones have been simplified by reducing the range so the children can rank them more easily: hold up head: 1 month, smile: 3 months, making sounds: 4 months, sitting up: 5 months, rolling over: 6 months, crawling: 8 months, walking: 10 months, using less than 50 words: 16 months, talking: 36 months. The weights and heights of the baby and children in lesson 2 are approximations to make it easier for the children to develop their graph-making skills.

Useful websites

Lesson 3: www.sciencekids.co.nz/pictures/humanbody/humanorgans.html
www.eschooltoday.com/human-reproduction/the-female-reproductive-organ.html
www.eschooltoday.com/human-reproduction/the-male-reproductive-organ.html

Lesson 1 Gestation period

Working scientifically skills: Recording data in tables and bar graphs; reporting findings from enquiries including causal relationships
Scientific enquiry type: Pattern seeking; researching using secondary sources

You will need: a photograph of a scan of a fetus (at 12 weeks) to put under the visualiser.

Getting started
Remind the children about fertilisation in animals: the fusion of the sperm and egg followed by the division of the fertilised egg into many cells leading to the build up of the body of the embryo and eventually the adult. Remind the children about the role of the placenta in providing food and oxygen from the mother's blood and taking away wastes such as carbon dioxide. Say that the food and oxygen help the embryo to grow and the removal of wastes keep it healthy while it develops in its mother's womb.

Class activities
- Say that the period of time it takes a mammal embryo to grow is called the gestation period and present these gestation periods on the board: cat: 63 days, cow: 280 days, rat: 21 days, sheep: 151 days, guinea pig: 68 days, rabbit: 31 days. Ask the children to record this data in a table. The table should have two columns, 'Mammal' and 'Gestation period (days)'. The children should list the mammals in order starting with the shortest but do not direct them in the first instance and use this as a teaching point to say that scientists organise their data to make it easier to study.
- Say that patterns in numerical data can be easier to see if the data is converted into a graph and ask the children to produce a bar graph. They may need help with choosing a suitable scale. Alternatively they could plot only rat, rabbit, cat and guinea pig gestation periods and you produce a complete graph with the sheep and cow on it.
- After looking at the complete graph ask the children about a pattern they can see. Look for an answer that the larger the animal the longer the gestation period. Ask the children if there are any exceptions to this trend (an anomalous result). The children should see that the guinea pig is smaller than the cat, yet it has a longer gestation period. Ask the children about the condition of newborn kittens (their eyes are not open, they are inactive for many days). Tell them about newborn guinea pigs being able to move around like adults and feed within hours of being born. The reason for their longer gestation period is due to them being in a better state of development when they are born.
- Say that patterns can be used to make predictions and ask them to predict the gestation period of an elephant (624 days).
- Ask the children to use secondary sources to find out about the gestation period of other placental mammals. First they must write down a prediction based on the graph and then look it up. They could research the gestation periods of mice, bats, horses, goats, monkeys, apes, and whales. (See Further lesson ideas and activities 1.)

Plenary
Let the children present their findings about gestation periods and assess their predictions. Remind the children about early cell division. Show them a picture of a ball of cells, most of which form the baby but some of which form the placenta. Say that, in humans, by four

weeks the body is starting to take shape and the heart starts to beat. At the eight week stage all the organs have formed. The embryo is now called a fetus and is 2.5 cm long. Show the children the scan of a fetus and say that the first scan is taken at 12 weeks. At 16 weeks the foetus is 10 cm long and starting to kick. A second scan is taken to check progress between 18 and 21 weeks. At 28 weeks the fetus turns upside down in readiness for being born and by the time of birth is 50 cm long and weighs about three kilograms. The human gestation period is 40 weeks. Ask the children to calculate that in days and compare it with the gestation period of other mammals they have studied.

Lesson 2 Growing up

Working scientifically skills: Recording data using scientific diagrams and labels; recording data as line graphs
Scientific enquiry type: Pattern seeking; observing over time; fair test

You will need: for each group: 'toothy smile' photographs from when the children were about 6 years old, information about the arrangement of teeth in the mouth, plastic mirrors and rulers.

Getting started
Review the development of the fetus in the womb and say that the development continues after birth as the baby grows and develops skills. Say that after birth a baby's early development can be charted in a series of stages called 'milestones'. Present the milestones in any order on the board and the age of development in any order too and ask the children to match them up starting with the first milestone (see 'What do I need to know?' on page 127 for the details and the correct order). Tell the children that babies start to eat solid food in place of milk at about six months old and ask what skills they have acquired by then. Say that these times can vary with different babies.

Class activities
- Tell the children that, as skills are developing, the body is growing and changing too. Let the children examine their photographs and use what they learnt about teeth in Year 4 to identify the teeth that are missing and being replaced. Let them make tooth maps of their mouths now using a mirror and comment on any changes that have taken place.
- Tell the children that the growth of a baby and child is measured by measuring its weight and height. Present children with a table detailing the weight and height of a baby and a child (see page 131). Let the children produce two line graphs from the data and look for the trend that they share (they both increase with time).
- Tell the children that the development of skills is due to the development of co-ordination of the parts of the body and this is brought about by the brain taking information from one part of the body, processing it and sending information to other parts of the body to make it respond. The movement of this information around the body is performed by the nerves as they make very weak electrical currents.

- Show the children how to test their eye and hand co-ordination by working pairs. One person holds up a ruler vertically with the beginning of the scale at the bottom. The second person then holds out their hand beneath the ruler making a gap between their thumb and first finger for the ruler to fall through. The person holding the ruler then lets it go whenever they like and the second person has to catch it by nipping it between their thumb and first finger. A measure of the time to react is made by measuring how much of the scale has fallen between the thumb and finger.
- Ask the children to devise experiments to test which hand has faster reactions. Look for an answer about dropping the ruler between the thumb and fingers of both hands ten times then adding up the scores. The hand that scored the lowest is the faster hand. (See Further lesson ideas and activities 2.)

Plenary
Let the children present their line graphs and the data and conclusion from their co-ordination investigation.

Growth of a child: measuring weight and height

Time in years	Birth	1	2	3	4	5	6	7	8	9	10
Weight (kg)	3	10	12	14	16	18	21	24	27	29	32
Height (cms)	50	75	87	96	103	110	116	123	130	134	139

Tally chart

Life cycle stage (And years)	Number in school
Infant (0–2)	
Child (2–12)	
Adolescent (12–18)	
Young adult (18 – 40)	
Middle age (40–70)	
Old age (70 +)	

Lesson 3 The rest of your life

Working scientifically skills: Recording data using bar graphs
Scientific enquiry type: Identifying, classifying and grouping

You will need: appropriate anatomical charts (see Useful websites), a model skeleton, photographs of people in all the age groups of the life cycle.

Getting started
Ask the children how they feel when they are scared. Look for answers about the sensation of 'butterflies in the tummy', feeling your heart beating faster, breathing faster. Say that this is due to a chemical called a hormone that the body makes to help protect you in scary situations. It prepares your body to defend itself or to help you run away. The hormone is called 'adrenalin' and is made in organs above the kidney. Say that other organs of the body produce hormones and some cause our bodies to change greatly.

Class activities
- Show the children the organs of the body chart (see Useful websites) and point out the position of the kidneys. Say that the adrenals are small organs on the top of the kidneys. Say that there are two sets of organs in the lower part of the body.
- Remind the children that ovaries produce the female sex cell, the egg, and they also produce the female sex hormones which develop the female reproductive system. Show the internet resource 2 and point out the various parts.
- Remind the children that testes produce the male sex cell, the sperm, and they also produce the male sex hormones which develop the male reproductive system. Show the internet resource 3 and point out the various parts.
- Say that both these sex hormones produce some similar effects on both bodies. Show the children the model skeleton and point out the hips. Say that at the front of the hips is a bone called the pubis bone. The hormones make the skin in the area above this bone grow hair known as pubic hair. The time when the body changes is called puberty, which takes place from about 12 to 14 years of age. Say that the hormones also make both sexes grow hair in the arm pits, and make the skin produce more oil which can result in spots.
- Say that the female sex hormones also make the breasts develop to provide milk for any future babies and make the hips wider for carrying the developing baby in the womb. Say the male sex hormone makes hair grow on the face, makes the voice deeper, and makes the testes ready to produce sperm.
- Say that the human life cycle is divided into stages: infant 0–2 years, child 2–12 years, adolescent 12–18 years, young adult 18–40, middle age 40–70, old age 70 onwards. Ask when puberty occurs and look for an answer about early adolescence. Show the children photographs of people in each stage of the human life cycle and ask them to guess the stage. They may struggle to distinguish young adults, middle age and old age so show some more pictures to help them in their recognition.

Plenary
Let the children make a table as shown on the previous page. Ask the children to categorise the people that work or come into the school to help them. They should record each individual as a line in each box to make a tally chart. They may like to include their own class teacher and teaching assistants, office and kitchen staff. They could then transfer this data to a bar chart and compare how much easier it is to read. Let them display their work as a tally chart and bar graph and compare their results. (See Further lesson ideas and activities 3–6.)

Further lesson ideas and activities

1. You may like to remind the children that birds incubate their eggs to keep them warm. Ask them to find out about the incubation periods of various birds, make a bar graph, and compare it with that of mammals. They could try to explain any anomalies they find.
2. The children could design an investigation to see if there is a difference when only the right or left eye is used during the reaction time investigation. This would involve shutting or covering one eye and recording ten drops through each hand then repeating with the other eye covered.
3. The children could make a bar graph of the distribution of the age groups in their families, family friends and neighbourhoods.
4. Distinguish between the terms 'life cycle' and 'life span' and let the children find out about the life span of peoples around the world.
5. The children could find out about the life spans of different animals, researching all the major groups and comparing them to the human life span.
6. The children could find out about the life spans of the oldest plants and compare them with animals and humans.

Cross curricular links

- The content of this topic could be integrated into a school based health topic.
- The research on life spans of people across the world could be used to support school based charity work.

Year 5: Properties and changes of materials

What does the curriculum say?

- *Compare and group together everyday materials on the basis of their properties, including their hardness, solubility, transparency, conductivity (electrical and thermal) and response to magnets.*
- *Know that some materials will dissolve in liquid to form a solution, and describe how to recover a substance from a solution.*
- *Use knowledge of solids, liquids and gases to decide how mixtures might be separated, including through filtering, sieving and evaporating.*
- *Give reasons, based on evidence from comparative and fair tests, for particular uses of everyday materials, including metals, wood and plastic.*
- *Demonstrate that dissolving, mixing and changes of state are reversible changes.*
- *Explain that some changes result in the formation of new materials, and that this kind of change is not usually reversible, including changes associated with burning and the action of acid on bicarbonate of soda.*

What do I need to know?

This topic begins by reviewing the work on properties of matter then allows the children to acquire a foundation for the basic chemistry they will study in Key Stage 3. You may like to point out in lessons 2 and 3 that they are moving over from materials science to chemistry. This change was begun in Year 4, chapter 3, where a simple explanation of early ideas about matter is presented in the introductory section.

Materials are divided into two groups according to how they respond to magnets. Magnetic materials are iron, steel, nickel and cobalt; iron and steel are the two magnetic materials used in school science. All the other materials are not attracted to a magnet so are non-magnetic materials.

Something which dissolves substances is called a solvent. Water is the most common solvent and some everyday items that dissolve (are soluble) in it include sugar, salt and baking powder. Items which do not dissolve (are insoluble in water) include sand, clay, custard powder and flour. Some liquids mix with other liquids, such as concentrated squash and water. They are said to be miscible. Oil and water stirred up do not mix: they are immiscible.

A mixture of water and an insoluble substance can be separated by filtering. Two solids with different sized particles such as sand and clay can be separated by sieving. A substance dissolved in water can be separated from it by letting the water evaporate.

A reversible change is one in which a substance changes but can also change back again. Ice can melt to form liquid water in one change and then the water can freeze to form ice in another change. Melting and freezing are examples of reversible changes.

An irreversible change is one in which the substances taking part cannot change back. In this type of change a chemical reaction takes place which changes the substances. For example, when wood burns it produces ash, smoke and carbon dioxide. These three substances cannot be put together to make wood again, so burning is an irreversible change.

A key theory in chemistry is particle theory, which the children will study in Key Stage 3 but, as they may already be familiar with the words 'atoms' and 'molecules', you may like to clarify two meanings of 'particle' (see Vocabulary, and use the particle theory to explain the behaviour of solids, liquids and gases. (See Further lesson ideas and activities 2 and 3.) One of the confusions in vocabulary that you must look out for is the confusion of melting and dissolving. To a child, a sugar lump seems to melt into the water. It is here that particle theory can help the child visualise the dissolving process. (See Further lesson ideas and activities 3.) The loss of the shape of a solid as it dissolves can also look superficially like melting, and again particle theory models will help.

Interesting facts

Chemistry developed from alchemy. The aim of alchemy was to discover a substance that had the power to transform base metals into gold. It was also hoped that the elixir of life, a drink that could give eternal life to those who drank it, could also be derived from this substance.

Vocabulary

Atom: a particle from which substances are made.
Chemical: a substance made of atoms or molecules. Everything is made of chemicals.
Dissolve: to break up into tiny pieces and spread out in a liquid.
Filter: a paper with small holes in it which lets a liquid pass through but keeps back any solid particles. It separate solids from liquids.
Insoluble: cannot be dissolved in a liquid.
Irreversible change: a change which cannot easily be reversed such as the changes that take place in burning.
Melt: to change from a solid to a liquid when a certain temperature is reached.
Molecule: a particle made from a group of atoms.
Particle: can be used to describe small pieces of material that can be seen such as a grain for sand. It can also be used to describe tiny pieces of matter that cannot be seen without very powerful microscopes.
Reversible change: a change which can be reversed such as turning a solid to a liquid and back.
Sieve: a device with small holes which lets small solid particles pass through and keeps larger particles back. It is used to separate smaller particles from larger particles. Sieves with holes of different sizes are used by ecologists to separate the different sized particles in soil to help understand its structure.
Soluble: dissolves in a liquid.
Solute: a substance that is dissolved in a liquid.
Solution: the mixture of a solute and its solvent. A liquid with something dissolved in it.
Solvent: a liquid that dissolves other substances.

Progression

This study of everyday materials began in Year 1 and was followed in Year 2 by looking at the uses of everyday materials. In Year 3 the children studied materials in the context of geology by looking at rocks and soil. The Year 1 and Year 2 materials topics and the Year 4 work on electrical conductors and insulators are revisited here to consolidate the children's knowledge of materials. The study of reversible changes was begun in Year 4 and is continued here and its relevance to separating materials is investigated. Finally irreversible changes, chemical changes, are also studied. The work done in this chapter will form the foundation work in chemistry at Key Stage 3.

Technical tips

In lesson 1, you may like to let the children do the set of five activities as a carousel. They should keep magnets away from electrical equipment. The activity about thermal conductance has a control, the uncovered beaker, so it is a controlled fair test.

In lesson 2, if you have filter funnels and paper, the paper needs to be folded in half, then half again and one of the enclosed sections widened and spread out inside the funnel. If you are using a funnel made from cutting the top off a clear plastic bottle, turning it upside down and placing it back in the bottle, you could use coffee filter bags.

For lesson 3, you will need to warm the milk either by using an oven in the staff room or placing the milk in beakers in a bowl of hot water before the lesson. Rehearse pouring the carbon dioxide over the lighted candle before the lesson.

Lesson 1 Properties of materials

Working scientifically skills: Planning different types of scientific enquiry; taking measurements; using a range of scientific equipment with increasing accuracy and precision; taking repeat readings when appropriate; reporting and presenting findings
Scientific enquiry type: Identifying, classifying and grouping

You will need: a piece of cloth; for each group: five sets of materials as follows. Set 1: a transparent, hard plastic sheet; a transparent, flexible plastic bag; wood; metal; a torch; a nail. Set 2: a magnet; objects made of steel, iron, plastic, wood, stone, pottery. Set 3: three plastic cups; a thermometer; two fabrics, one thick, one thin; sticky paper, a stopwatch, scissors. Set 4: a cell; a switch; a lamp, four wires, pieces of iron, steel, copper, aluminium, wood, plastic, brick. Set 5 a test beaker; a jug of water; a bowl for used water; sugar; salt; tea leaves; coffee; bath salts; custard powder; flour; washing powder and flakes (hand washing types); sand; modelling clay, a spoon for stirring, paper towels, digital balance (optional).

Getting started

Show the children a piece of cloth. Say it is a material and ask if all materials are pieces of cloth. Look for an answer that materials are all around us and ask the children to point them out (wood, glass, plastic and so on). Query the idea that an object can be made from only one material and look for answers about several materials often being used to make one object. Ask for examples. Challenge the children to explain why objects are made from different materials and steer the discussion towards the materials having different properties. Ask for examples. Tell the children that they are going to perform five sets of experiments. They must make a record of each one with a table of results and present their findings in a scientific seminar at the end.

Class activities

- These tests are for transparency and hardness. Say that you want a material to make a window. Give the children the set 1 materials. Ask the children to perform an experiment to find materials suitable for windows. Say that the window is going to be used in a desert where sandstorms scratch surfaces and ask them to work out which material is best to use. They should scratch the two plastic materials with a nail.
- This is the test for magnetic materials. Let the children use set 2 materials. They should use the magnet to test each material and then group them into magnetic and non magnetic materials.
- This is a test for thermal insulation. Let the children use set 3 materials and equipment. They should draw up a table with the headings as shown in the example on the next page and they should put a thick material around one cup and thin materials around another and leave one uncovered. They should secure the materials to the cups with sticky paper and use scissors if they wish to cut the material to make it fit more closely. They should fill each cup two thirds full with hot water (from the hot water tap) and record the temperature of the water in each cup (it should be the same). They should start the stopwatch and take the temperature of the water in each cup every two minutes for half an hour. And present their results as three line graphs – one for each cup.
- This is a test for electrical conductivity. Let the children use set 4 equipment and materials. They should set up a simple circuit comprising a cell, a switch and a lamp in series. There

should be a gap in the wires connected to the lamp and the cell. The switch is put in the off position, a material is placed across the gap so that it touches the ends of both wires and the switch is put in the on position. The children then record whether the lamp lights (the material is a conductor) or does not (the material is an insulator). They move the switch to the off position and repeat with other materials.

- This is a test for dissolving. Before the children begin, say that we know that sugar dissolves in water but do all materials do so? Let the children use set 5 equipment and materials. They should pour water into the beaker until it is half full. They should set out the materials for testing on a paper towel and aim to set out the same amount of each material. For a more accurate comparison the children could weigh out the same amount of material on a digital balance. A material is then poured into the water in the beaker. The children may decide to observe for a minute for signs of dissolving or begin stirring straight away for a certain time such as one minute then observe the material for signs of dissolving. They should then record in a two column table headed 'Dissolves in water' and 'Does not dissolve in water'. The water in the beaker must be changed after each material has been tested.

Plenary

This is the scientific seminar where each group presents its findings and conclusions. When groups come to discuss the evidence, look for the mention of fair tests. Look for groups having used equal volumes of water in the experiments and suggest the use of a measuring cylinder for greater accuracy if they do not mention it. Records of the experiments could form part of a wall display. (See Further lesson ideas and activities 1.)

Thermal insulation test

Time (mins)	Thick coated cup (temp, °C)	Thin coated cup (temp, °C)	Cup without coat (temp, °C)
0 2 4 – 30 mins			

Lesson 2 Physical processes

Working scientifically skills: Observing
Scientific enquiry type: Identifying, classifying and grouping

You will need: for each group: a beaker of sand, a beaker of small gravel such as aquarium gravel, a spoon, a sieve, filtering equipment (see Technical tips).

Getting started

Ask the children how they can tell a solid from a liquid (solids hold their shape and do not flow or drip, unlike liquids), a liquid from a gas (a liquid does not expand to fill all of a container or spread out everywhere, a gas does) and a solid from a gas (a solid has a definite shape and volume, a gas does not). Ask for examples of solids, liquids and gases from around the classroom. (Solids: wood, plastic, glass, metal. Liquids: water, drinks. Gases: air.) Ask about how a material can change from one state to another and look for an answer about solids melting to liquids, liquids evaporating to gases, gases condensing to liquids and liquids freezing to solids. Point out that they are all reversible changes but there are some processes that allow the composition of materials to be irreversibly changed. (See Further lesson ideas and activities 2.)

Class activities

- Let the children mix some sand and fine gravel together. Ask how they could separate the components of the mixture and lead the discussion to the idea of using a sieve. Let them separate the sand and gravel using this technique. Ask how mixing and sieving are reversible processes.
- Ask the children about materials that do not dissolve. Give them some sand in a beaker. Let them pour in some water, stir it up and leave it for a while. Point out that the sand has formed a sediment. Say that this process takes time and chemists like to speed things up so they use a filter. Let the children stir up the sand and pour it through the filtering equipment (see Technical tips). Ask how mixing and filtering are reversible processes.
- Remind the children about their work on dissolving and their work on changing states of matter and ask how they might separate water from something that is dissolved in it. Steer the discussion to the idea that water evaporates but the solid dissolved in it does not. So, leaving a solution to evaporate would result in the solid being left behind. Let the children set up salt and sugar solutions in a warm place and look daily for signs of the solid. Ask how dissolving and evaporating are reversible processes. (See Further lesson ideas and activities 3.)
- Show the children a tray of sand and then, apparently accidentally, spill a beaker of salt across it. Ask how the salt and sand can be separated and dismiss picking out the salt crystals. Let the children make their plans which involve stirring the sand and salt mixture with water until the salt dissolves, filtering to separate the sand and evaporating to separate the salt.

Plenary

Select one group to present their report to the class of how they separated the sand and the salt. Ask the other groups to add activities of their own that have not been mentioned yet. Let the class make a flow chart for the separation of sand and salt.

Lesson 3 Chemical processes

Working scientifically skills: Recognising and controlling a variable; recording data and results of increasing complexity using scientific diagrams and labels; reporting and presenting findings from enquiries in oral and written forms such as displays and other presentations
Scientific enquiry type: Fair test; observing over time

You will need: some rusty nails (see below), a birthday candle in a sand tray, a jug containing bicarbonate of soda, a beaker of vinegar, a half burnt log. Each group will need an iron nail, a piece of aluminium foil, a piece of copper (e.g. wire), a bowl of water, paper towels, a warm place to leave the wet towels, a beaker of warm milk, a tablespoon, a beaker about a quarter full of vinegar, a sieve, a paper plate, a place to leave the plates; and a small heap of flour and a small heap of bicarbonate of soda on a paper plate, together with a tablespoon.
Preparation: a week before the lesson set up some nails in a wet paper towel and keep them warm so that they form rust.

Getting started

Ask the children what happens when solids are mixed with water. Look for answers about dissolving and not dissolving. Ask how dissolving is a reversible process and look for an answer about using evaporation to regain the dissolved substance. Show the children an iron nail and drop it in a beaker of water. Let them see that it does not dissolve. Say that you wondered if there would be a change if you left iron and water together for a while and show them the wet paper towel. Unfold it to reveal the rusty nails. Say that this is an example of a non reversible change and challenge the children to find out it if takes place with other metals.

Class activities

- Tell the children that you would like them to repeat your experiment to check your results but ask them how they could be sure it was the water that was affecting the metals. Look for an answer about setting up dry towels as a control, then let them gather the metal samples and paper towels and set up their experiment. Tell them that irreversible changes usually take place faster if there is warmth so let them place the towels in a warm place for a few days.
- Ask the children what will happen if water is added to milk. Demonstrate and explain that the water simply dilutes the milk.
- Say that chemists like to experiment with substances around them and show the children a bottle of vinegar. Discuss its use and say that it contains an acid.
- Give out the beakers of warm milk. Give out the beakers containing vinegar and distribute tablespoons. Ask the children to place a tablespoon of vinegar in the milk and stir it. Let them leave it for five minutes, then stir it again. Ask them to pour their mixture through a sieve and use the spoon to empty the contents of the sieve onto a paper plate. This should be examined daily over a few days and any changes noted.
- Ask the children if the vinegar will react with solids and say the best way to test for this is to use powders. Let the children put some flour on a plate and pour a tablespoon of vinegar onto it. Let them repeat the experiment with bicarbonate of soda and see the bubbles.

- Ask what would happen if you used a large amount of bicarbonate of soda and vinegar and show them the jug with the bicarbonate of soda in it (see Technical tips). Pour in the vinegar and let the children see all the bubbles. Explain that a gas is being made and they are going to see what it might do. Light a birthday candle in a sand tray, pour the gas in the jug over the candle and see it go out. Make sure that no liquid escapes from the jug.

Plenary
Review the work with the metals, milk and powders. Ask the children about what happens to the burning candle and look for an answer about it getting smaller. Ask where the matter could have gone and look for an answer about it changing into gases. Explain that the candle wax is made from carbon and hydrogen. When it burns, they both join with oxygen in the air to make carbon dioxide and water vapour. Show the children the log and say that wood contains other substances that do not burn and are left behind as ash. Let the children display the results of their metal and milk experiments.

Further lesson ideas and activities

1. Ask the children to link the properties of the materials they have discovered with their uses in everyday life.
2. If you have discussed matter being made from particles then you could say that scientists use models to show what they believe. Turn a square, metal tin lid upside down and fill it more than half full of marbles or other small balls. Tip the lid slightly so the balls jam together and say that this is the arrangement of particles in a solid. Remove some of the balls and tip the lid to one side so that the balls move over each other. Say that this is how the particles behave when a liquid is poured. Remove most of the balls and move the lid from side to side and up and down so that the balls move in all directions, hit the sides and bounce back. Say that this is how particles behave in a gas.
3. If you have done Further idea 2, you might like to present a model of dissolving by using the liquid model and adding some much smaller balls so that they go between the spaces of the larger ones.

Cross curricular links

- In a food technology topic the children could follow a recipe to make a meal. In the course of this work they should note down when they sieve, mix, dissolve and, if using an oven or heat under supervision, the condition of the material (such as bread dough or cake mix) before and after heating to see evidence of an irreversible change.
- In an art-based topic where a sculpture using different materials is to be made, the children may investigate the properies of a range of materials and aim to provide a sculpture made from as many different materials as possible, each demonstrating a property such as transparency, changing state e.g. an ice cube to water, oil and water not mixing, and a dish containing coloured water left to evaporate which leaves behind rings of colour.

Year 5: Earth and space

What does the curriculum say?

- **Describe the movement of the Earth, and other planets, relative to the Sun in the solar system.**
- **Describe the movement of the Moon relative to the Earth.**
- **Describe the Sun, Earth and Moon as approximately spherical bodies.**
- **Use the idea of the Earth's rotation to explain day and night and the apparent movement of the Sun across the sky.**

What do I need to know?

It was originally believed that the planets, the Sun, the Moon and the stars all moved around the Earth. The work of Copernicus, Kepler and Galileo showed that celestial bodies did not move around the Earth (except the Moon) and the work of Isaac Newton provided the explanation for the movement with his universal theory of gravity.

The solar system is composed of the Sun, eight major planets, moons, asteroid belt, minor planets, and is enclosed in a hollow sphere called the Ort cloud made up of huge lumps of dust and ice. Some of these lumps have left the Ort cloud and formed comets which move in orbits around the Sun.

When the solar system formed it was a rotating disc of dust, rock and gas around the Sun. These substances pulled together under gravity to form the planets which still retained their motion of going around the Sun in an anticlockwise direction as seen from above the Sun.

The Moon is believed to have formed when the Earth collided with another planet no longer in existence as the Solar System developed. The debris from the collision formed a disc of debris around the Earth which eventually became the Moon, again moving in an anticlockwise direction around the Earth as seen from above the North Pole.

The Sun, Moon and Earth, like other celestial bodies, spin on their axis and this motion draws in the material from which they are made to make almost spherical bodies. It takes the Earth 24 hours to spin round once on its axis. During this time places on the Earth face the Sun making it daytime there followed by a period facing away from the Sun when it is night. As places on the Earth spin from the dark to the light the Sun rises over the eastern horizon to a high point in the sky at midday then sinks in the afternoon to the western horizon before disappearing again.

Interesting fact

Halley's comet takes 76 years to orbit the Sun. It was last seen in 1986 and will be seen next in 2061.

Vocabulary

Astronomer: a scientist who studies the objects in space such as stars, moons and planets.

Axis: an imaginary line running between the poles around which the Earth turns.

Constellation: a group of stars which are used to form a picture of an animal, person or object. They are used to map the sky.

Eclipse: an eclipse of the Sun occurs when the Moon blocks light coming from the Sun to Earth. An eclipse of the Moon occurs when the Earth blocks sunlight reaching the Moon.

Element: a substance made in a star. They are made of atoms which may join together to form groups called molecules.

Galaxy: a huge group of stars.

Moon: a natural object (not a space probe) in orbit around a planet.

Orbit: the path of a planet around a star or of a moon around a planet.

Planet: a large object in orbit around a star.

Space probe: a machine carrying instruments to measure the conditions in space and on planets, moons and comets.

Star: a ball of gas made originally from hydrogen and helium which also makes other elements.

Universe: everything in space including us on Earth.

Progression

This area of study provides the explanation of the seasons studied in Key Stage 1. It provides extra information about gravity, studied in Year 4, and supports work carried out this year on forces too. It links the study of materials including rocks in earlier years with the activities on stars.

Technical tips

For lesson 2, make the dowel rods with the 2 mm scale before the lesson. You may like to provide newspaper to put under the bowl to collect flour which flies out when the clay hits the flour. You may want the children to wear safety glasses for this activity.

For lesson 3, you will need a sunny day so check the weather forecasts and plan ahead. If necessary, bring this lesson forward to lesson 1 or let the children set out their plans for the shadow clock investigation to be carried out on the next sunny day.

Useful websites

For a huge range of space photographs: www.nasa.gov/multimedia/imagegallery/index.html

Lesson 1 The Earth in space

Working scientifically skills: Taking measurements with increasing accuracy and precision; reporting and presenting findings from enquiries as displays of other presentations
Scientific enquiry type: Researching using secondary sources

You will need: a cup of cold coffee, a spoon, a small beaker of cream, a balloon, a balloon pump, a bull dog clip to close the neck of the balloon, some black felt-tip pens, rulers or tape measures. Each group will need a cup of cold coffee; a spoon; a small beaker of cream; 10 pieces of modelling clay, 1 cm across; 10 pieces of modelling clay 3 cm across; 10 pieces of modelling clay 5 cm across. The class will need four tennis balls (representing rocky planets), four footballs (representing gas giants) and a larger ball such as a beach ball (to represent the Sun).

Getting started

Tell the children they are going to study the Earth in space but before they do this they are going to learn a little more about space. Say that 13.7 billion years ago a point of light appeared which was smaller than a pinhead. It suddenly expanded rapidly in an explosion which we call the Big Bang and the universe formed. At first there were only two materials in it. They were the gases, hydrogen and helium. They swirled around and the gravity between their atoms and molecules pulled them together into huge balls of gas which became stars. (See Further lesson ideas and activities 1.)

Class activities

• Tell the children that the stars formed into huge groups called galaxies and they are going to make a model of the one we live in. Show the children how to stir up a cup of coffee and mime adding half a teaspoon of cream to it. Now issue the cups of coffee, spoons and beakers of cream and let the children swirl the coffee and drop half a teaspoon of cream into its centre. Ask them to describe what they see. Repeat with a cup of coffee on the visualiser to confirm their results and say that they should form a spiral galaxy.

• Say that astronomers have made observations of galaxies and you are going to make a model based on their observations. Half inflate a balloon and ask volunteers to draw spirals on it with felt tip pens. Ask them to measure the distances between a few of the galaxies then pump up the balloon and ask them to measure again. Ask the children what the astronomers observed and look for an answer about the galaxies moving away from each other.

• Tell the children that inside stars the atoms and molecules of hydrogen and helium join together to make atoms and molecules of other materials such as iron, oxygen, and carbon that we see in charcoal. When a star has used up all its hydrogen and helium it either puffs out all these materials as gases and dust or, if it is a large star, it explodes as a super nova making even more materials and throwing them out into space.

• Say that the dust swirled around with more hydrogen and helium in space and a star formed at the centre with the dust forming a ring around it. Say that gravity started pulling the dust particles together. Give out the 1 cm lumps of modelling clay to the children and let them join them together. Let one child with the combined lump join a group of children with the 3 cm lumps and join them together. Repeat with the 5 cm lump until a small 'planet' has formed.

- Let the children use secondary sources to find out about the eight planets of the solar system, then report back on their findings (see Further lesson ideas and activities 2 and 3). Give out the balls and let the children go outside and make a model of the solar system with the 'planets' moving anticlockwise around the 'Sun'.

Plenary
Review the children's knowledge of star formation, planet formation and the eight planets in the solar system.

Lesson 2 The Sun, Moon and Earth

Working scientifically skills: Planning different types of scientific enquiries to answer questions, including recognising and controlling variables; taking measurements with increasing accuracy and precision and repeating readings; reporting and presenting findings from enquiries, including causal relationships and explanations of and degree of trust in results

Scientific enquiry type: Fair test; pattern seeking

You will need: pictures of Earth from space to display on the whiteboard. Each group will need a table tennis ball and a tennis ball, a model moon made from a ball of modelling clay mounted on a pencil, a torch, moon surface equipment comprised of a bowl of flour 5 cm deep, a dowelling rod with a 2 mm scale (see Technical tips), a ruler measuring in millimetres, lumps of modelling clay 1 cm, 3 cm, 5 cm across, safety spectacles.

Getting started
Say that in the past many people believed that the world was flat. However, when they watched ships sail away over the horizon something happened that suggested it was curved. Place a large sheet of cardboard on a table and let the children look along its edge. Put a model ship with tall masts near them then move it away. Now bend the cardboard into a curve, put the ship on the top of the curve and let the children watch it as you move it further away. Ask how the two views are different and look for an answer about the ship on the flat Earth just gets smaller but on the curved Earth the hull disappeared before the masts.

Class activities
- Say that up until the mid-twentieth century, although people knew the Earth was a sphere because they could travel round it they did not see visual evidence until spacecrafts took pictures from space. Show them pictures on the whiteboard.
- Say that we know the Sun is round but warn the children never to look directly at the Sun as it could permanently damage their eyes. We also know that sometimes the Moon appears to be round but at other times seems to change its shape. When a round Moon passes directly between part of the Earth and the Sun an eclipse of the Sun takes place but astronomers know that the Sun is many times larger than the Moon. Ask how can this be and give the children table tennis balls and tennis balls to demonstrate. Look for them placing the table tennis ball close to the observer and the tennis ball further away.

- Remind the children that the Sun is a light source and the Moon is a reflector. Give each group the model moon and a torch and ask them to find out how different parts of the moon can be illuminated. Look for a demonstration showing a torch shining full on the moon from the front to a small section illuminated as the torch is moved to shine from the side. (See Further lesson ideas and activities 4 and 5.)
- Show the children a picture of the Moon's surface and point out the craters. Remind the children about how the solar system was formed from pieces of rock and the asteroids being pieces of material that did not form planets. Ask how the craters on the Moon were made. Look for an answer about rocks colliding with the surface. Ask them to think how craters of different widths could have been made. Test their ideas using the moon surface equipment.
- Ask the children how the craters could be different depths and set up an investigation to test their ideas.

Plenary
Ask the children to present their results about crater size. Look for 'rocks' being dropped from the same height and the diameter of the craters measured with a ruler. Look for the relationship that the larger the 'rock' the wider the crater. Ask about crater depth. Look for an answer about the same sized 'rock' being dropped from different heights to provide different impact speeds and the dowel being used to measure crater depth. Look for the relationship that the faster the speed the deeper the crater. In both investigations look for evidence of repeating processes to check evidence. (See Further lesson ideas and activities 6.)

Lesson 3 Movement of the Earth

Working scientifically skills: Planning different types of scientific enquiries to answer questions; recording data as bar and line graphs; identifying evidence that has been used to support or refute ideas or arguments
Scientific enquiry type: Observing over time; pattern seeking; researching using secondary sources

You will need: a globe, a large torch, a small model person, modelling clay, a large yellow ball, a diary. Each group will need a shadow stick made from sticking a pencil upright in modelling clay in the middle of a piece of white paper, a ruler.

Getting started
Remind the children about the swirling stars in a galaxy and say that gases and dust swirl around a star to form planets. Say this swirling continues, making the planets spin. Show them the globe and spin it anticlockwise when looking down on the North Pole. Shine a large torch from one side onto the globe so that the children can see one half illuminated and the other in shadow. Stick a small model person on the globe with modelling clay at the place where the torch shines directly overhead. Say that it is midday where the person is and begin to move the globe anticlockwise. Ask what is happening where the person is and look for answers about it being afternoon and the Sun sinking in the sky. Keep turning until the person is about to enter the shady side and ask again. Look for an answer about

it going dark. Move the globe round asking what it is like for the person until it reaches another 'midday.' (See Further lesson ideas and activities 7.)

Class activities

- Ask the children what they know about light and shadows and look for an answer about light shining from a height makes objects cast shorter shadows. Ask how this could be used to measure time and look for an answer that the shadow length could be related to the height of the Sun which in turn is related to the turning of the Earth. Ask how this could be checked and look for an answer about setting up a shadow stick, measuring the length of its shadow every hour and making a bar chart or line graph. (See Technical tip.)
- Remind the children about how planets are made by the crashing together of rocks. Say that at some time in the Earth's early history it was hit by an enormous rock and its axis was knocked from the vertical by 23 degrees. Show the children the globe. Say that the Earth's axis always points in the same direction as it goes in its orbit around the Sun and that the Earth moves in an orbit which is anticlockwise if you looked down on the Sun and Earth. Place a large yellow ball in the middle of a table. Move the globe round it in an anticlockwise direction, always keeping the axis pointing in the same direction, for example, towards one wall. (See Further lesson ideas and activities 8.)
- Point out that the globe can be divided into two halves or 'hemispheres', the north and south, and select an area at about a 50° latitude (e.g. Great Britain). Set up the globe with the axis tilting towards a torch (representing the Sun) and point out the area of light shining on the area. It should be quite bright and intense, and say that in this position it is summer in the area because the Sun is shining from a high position in the sky. Move the globe so that the axis is pointing away from the torch and point out that the light is now less intense as the Sun is shining on it from a lower position in the sky.
- Ask how the movement of the Earth round the sun will affect the shadows cast by the shadow stick. Look for an answer about the shadows being longer in winter than in summer and changing in length as the Earth moves around in its orbit. Let the class work out an investigation to check this using a diary to set up dates for checking their ideas.

Plenary

Let the children report on the data collected by their shadow sticks and sort out teams to test changing shadows at dates through the year.

Place the yellow ball, representing the Sun, in the middle of an open space. Ask a child to move around it anticlockwise with the globe. Ask the children to see if the globe is always pointing in one direction. Give a tennis ball, representing the Moon, to another child and ask them to move anticlockwise around the globe as it moves around the Sun. Say that the Moon goes round the Earth 12 times (once each month) as the Earth goes around the Sun once. Challenge the two children to model this. Let other pairs of children try it. Point out that the movement of objects in space can be complicated but in the last four hundred years scientists have made many great discoveries in space. (See Further lesson ideas and activities 9.)

Further lesson ideas and activities

1. There are white, blue, yellow, orange and red stars. The children could cut out holes in black card, attach coloured cellophane across them and shine a light behind to make a star display. This can be used as a preliminary activity to idea 8.

2. The children will discover that the inner four planets of our solar system are made of rock and the outer four planets are mainly gas. You may wish to reinforce the idea of not being able to land on a gas giant by stirring up some soapy water in a tall beaker and dropping a model space ship into it.

3. You may like to set some children the task of finding out about asteroids and comets.

4. Ask the children to keep a 'Moon diary'. They should try to observe the Moon every night and draw the shape of the illuminated portion. Check with the phases of the Moon on the internet to find when the Moon can be seen, as sometimes it can be seen in the day-time.

5. You could use a globe and a tennis ball to show how the Moon moves in orbit around the Earth. If you shine a torch from one side you can show how the light strikes the Moon as it moves in orbit and link this to the phases of the Moon. Note that the Moon is not in line with the Earth to make an eclipse but moves a little above or below the Sun when on the Sun's side of the Earth and a little above or below the Earth when it is on the side away from the Sun.

6. The children could research the terms 'meteor', 'meteorite' and 'shooting star'.

7. The children could look at a chart showing the time zones around the world. They could then work out the time in various places such as where their family or friends live or places they have visited on holiday.

8. As the Earth moves round in its orbit, different stars appear in the sky. Say that from the earliest times people have looked at the stars and arranged them into groups that looked like animals and people to them. These groups of stars are called constellations. The children could use star charts at home to look for some of them.

9. The children could use secondary sources to find the Earth-centred universe according to Aristotle. They could see how Ptolemy tried to explain the observation that sometimes planets seem to move backwards and Copernicus believed that making the Sun the centre of the Solar System was a better explanation. They could find out about the data collected by Tycho Brahe which was used by Kepler to show that the planets moved in elliptical orbits around the Sun. They could find out that Galileo used his telescope to show that not everything moves around the Earth when he saw the moons of Jupiter and how Newton showed that gravity was the force that provided the movement of the planets and Moon.

Cross curricular links

- The night sky can be used as inspiration in English for poetry or stories.
- The movement of the Earth in its orbit can be linked to religious festivals.
- The movement of the Earth can be used in studies of seasonal change in habitat management in school conservation projects.

Year 5: Forces

What does the curriculum say?

- *Explain that unsupported objects fall towards the Earth because of the force of gravity acting between the Earth and the falling object.*
- *Identify the effects of air resistance, water resistance and friction, that act between moving surfaces.*
- *Recognise that some mechanisms, including levers, pulleys and gears, allow a smaller force to have a greater effect.*

What do I need to know?

In Ancient Greece there were people called 'philosophers'. They developed ideas about everything, argued about them and taught them to their students. One of their ideas was about matter and materials. They thought that everything was made up from four things they called elements: fire, air, water and earth. They used this idea to explain movement by drawing four concentric circles, labelling them, from the centre outwards, earth (land), water (lakes and seas), air (atmosphere) and fire (the Sun and stars). They are argued that the elements in something tried to find their own level: flames rise because of their fire, solid objects fall because of the earth they contain.

The amount of matter in an object is its mass. One of the properties of mass is its inertia (its laziness), its reluctance to move. As the mass increases, so does the inertia which cancels out its effect when things fall so they all fall under the same pull of gravity which makes them fall at the same speed.

A force can be defined in physics as the mass of an object multiplied by its acceleration. In the ramps experiment acceleration is seen which means a force is at work.

Air resistance is the force of the air pushing on an object as the object moves through the air. The air pushes as it moves round the object. A streamlined object such as a rocket has a shape which allows the air to move over it more easily and reduces the push of the air on it. A non-streamlined object such as box has large flat surfaces which the air pushes against strongly and slows it down as it moves.

Water resistance is the pushing force of water on an object moving through it. Fish with streamlined shapes like the tuna can move quickly whereas angelfish with a less streamlined shape move more slowly. Boats have streamlined shapes so they can part the water with their hulls as they move forwards.

Friction is the force between two touching surfaces when one surface is pushed or pulled over the other. A frictional force develops between a book and a desk when you gently push it but it does not move. Static friction is working to stop the movement. If you push more strongly, you overcome the static frictional force and the book begins to move. The book still pushes against your push with a force called sliding friction. The sliding friction force is reduced if the two surfaces in contact are very smooth such as ice and the runner of a skate.

In work on simple machines you may use the term 'load' for the weight and 'effort' for the force applied. A machine is a device that makes work easier. We tend to think of machines being very complicated such as a washing machine but there are some very simple machines such as levers, pulleys and gears. They make work easier by allowing a small force to move a larger load. They do this by applying the small force over a long distance which in turn moves the larger load over a shorter distance.

In the lever a small force applied to the end of the long arm of the lever moves the end of the arm further than the other end where the load is resting. This arrangement lets the load be raised over a smaller distance – enough to get the work done.

When one pulley is used with string it simply reduces friction making the applied force lift the load more easily. When more than one pulley is used the string is pulled a long distance by a small force but this is enough to raise a heavier load a smaller distance to get the work done.

Gears are wheels with teeth which interlock so that when one turns it makes the other turn. A small force applied to a large gear wheel over a long distance will generate a larger force in a smaller gear wheel which acts over a shorter distance but is enough to get things moving. Think of the large gear wheel operated by the pedal of a bicycle connected by a chain to a smaller gear wheel on the axle of the back wheel.

Interesting fact

The force of gravity acts between the Sun and the planets, and between the planets. This holds the planets in their orbits.

Vocabulary

Acceleration: an increase in speed in a particular direction.
Air resistance: the push of the air on an object moving through it.
Element: for the Greeks, these were air, water, fire and earth. For modern scientists, elements are the substances formed in stars which make up all the materials in the universe.
Force meter: an instrument that measures force using a stretched spring.
Gravity: a force between any two objects in the universe.
Newton: a unit used for measuring force.
Sliding friction: friction that exists between two surfaces when one is sliding over the other. It pushes against the force pushing the object. When that force is removed, the sliding friction slows and stops the object.
Static friction: friction that exists between two surfaces that are in contact and that are not moving. It pushes in the opposite direction to the force pushing on the object.
Streamlined: a shape that allows air or water to flow easily over it.
Water resistance: the push of the water on an object moving through it.
Weight: the force with which an object pushes down on a planet due to the planet's gravity.

Progression

This is the last area of study that completes the work on forces which was begun in Year 3.

Lesson 1 Gravity and air resistance

Working scientifically skills: Identifying scientific evidence that has been used to support or refute ideas or arguments; using test results to make predictions to set further comparative and fair tests
Scientific enquiry type: Comparative and fair tests

You will need: a sand pit or garden plot in the school grounds where you can dig a hole about 20–30 cm deep (make sure it is filled in afterwards), a spade or trowel, a tennis ball. Each group will need a ramp, a cylinder such as a cardboard tube, two objects of different weights but similar sizes (e.g. coins), a metal tray, a metre rule, two pieces of paper of the same size, materials to make parachutes such as plastic sheet, thread, sticky paper, modelling clay, a weight, scissors.

Getting started
Ask the children to spread out, stand on one leg, hold out their arms and shut their eyes. They should wobble about and then have to put a foot down. Ask them how they felt and what was making their body behave as it did. Steer the discussion around to gravity pulling on their body and their muscles trying to adjust their bones so they did not fall over.

Say that as people made observations and discoveries about the world they built up ideas to explain them. One example is the Ancient Greeks' idea of what made things go up and down. Tell the children about the Ancient Greek theory of elements using the background information on page 148 to help you. Say that according to the Ancient Greeks, the children wobbled because the earth in their bodies wanted to get back to the ground. Tell them they are going to perform an experiment to prove them wrong.

Class activities

- Ask the children what gives an object its weight. Look for an answer about the amount of earth in it. Ask how the children think the Ancient Greeks explained why one object weighed more than another. Look for an answer about them having different amounts of earth in them. Ask what would happen if objects of different weights were dropped from the same height. Look for an answer about the heavier one falling faster.
- Ask the children to plan an investigation to test this idea. Ask them to consider how they could hear the sounds made on impact. Look for a plan about dropping the objects onto a metal tray or other sonorous object. Let the children try their experiment. Ask them how they could be sure of their result and look for an answer about repeating it three or five times. Ask which is more reliable and let the children make each drop five times. They should find that the two objects fall at the same speed.
- Tell the children there was a scientist called Galileo who wanted to slow down how things fall or move to the ground so he could study the motion in more detail. Ask how he might have done this and steer the discussion around to the use of shallow ramps. Set up a long ramp and roll a cylinder down it. Ask the children to watch the spot. They should see that it moves more frequently as the cylinder rolls along. Say this shows that the cylinder is changing speed and something that makes things change speed is a force, in this case, the force of gravity. (See Further lesson ideas and activities 1 and 2.)
- Give the children two pieces of paper and ask them to scrunch up one of them into a ball. Ask them to predict what will happen if they are dropped from the same height. If they predict different falling speeds, ask for an explanation. You may list them all, or focus in on air resistance. Let the children try the experiment and repeat it four more times for reliability.
- Say that if the difference is due to air resistance, how could this be checked by making parachutes? Look for an answer about making them different sizes and timing or filming their fall. Let the children design and make parachutes of different sizes and drop them from a height of about 1.5 m. (See Technical tips.)

Plenary

Review all the work in this lesson starting with the Ancients Greeks' idea and how it was disproved. Say that scientists today carry out investigations to test ideas and sometimes they also disprove them. It is all part of science. Discuss the reliability of results by repeating experiments then take the children outside, dig a hole and ask a child to kick the ball into the hole. Let the children see it fall in and ask them what it tells them about gravity. Steer the answer to it pulling things to the centre of the Earth.

Lesson 2 Friction and water resistance

Working scientifically skills: Taking measurements using a range of scientific equipment, with increasing accuracy and precision; taking repeat readings when appropriate; using test results to make predictions to set up further comparative and fair tests; reporting findings including explanations and degree of trust in results
Scientific enquiry type: Comparative and fair tests

You will need: a soft toy like a teddy bear, which can sit up and lie down, or an animal that can stand on four feet and be put on its side, a ramp with a shiny surface. Each group will need a smooth plank about 40 cm long, a ruler, modelling clay to hold the ruler vertically, access to a selection of shoes, a weight (about a kilogram).

Getting started
Ask the children what they can remember about friction. Look for answers about friction being a force between two surfaces, a description of static friction and sliding friction, and finding the friction between shoes and surfaces using a ramp.

Tell them that sometimes investigations produce surprising results. Take the soft toy, sit it up or stand it on its feet on a shiny ramp and raise the ramp until it slides. Note the height of the ramp. Ask the children to predict the height of the ramp when you place the toy on its side with more of its surface in contact. They will probably say that you will have to put it higher as there is more surface to grip. Lay the toy on its back or side and raise the ramp again. You will find it slides at the same height because the force of friction does not depend on the area in contact.

Class activities
- Tell the children that although friction does not depend on the areas of the surfaces in contact it does depend on the force pressing down on them. Ask them to think about putting on the brakes on a bicycle. If you need to stop quickly you squeeze the brake handles tightly so the brake blocks can press as hard as they can on the wheel rim.
- Remind them about the shoe investigation from Year 3: Forces and magnets (Lesson 2: Moving over surfaces), and ask how they could make it more accurate. Look for an answer about putting the same weight in each shoe before it is placed on the ramp. Look also for some children suggesting that you repeat the investigation three or five times to check.
- Let the children set out their plan, construct tables to record data and then carry out their investigation.
- If the children have done the activity in Further idea 1, you could ask how else they could test the forces that the shoes exert, and look for an answer about using a force meter. Encourage the children to attach the shoe to the force meter and let them carry out another investigation.
- Remind the children about air resistance and ask what might happen if they dragged a parachute through water. Let them use one of the parachutes in a bowl of water. They should conclude that water also resists movement. (See Further lesson ideas and activities 4.)

Plenary
Let the children present their findings about the shoes and compare the results of the two tests. Say that scientists try to use at least two different experiments in an enquiry and compare their results before making a conclusion. Let the children present their results of their research about air and water resistance and streamlined shapes.

Lesson 3 Machines

Working scientifically skills: Reporting and presenting findings from enquiries including causal relationships
Scientific enquiry type: Pattern seeking

You will need: a wooden rod, a pulley, a two pulley system (see Technical tips). Each group will need a ramp made from easily cut material such as cardboard (see Technical tips), an object attached to a force meter (this could be something in a small plastic bag), a ruler. Some wooden blocks to raise the ramp to 5 cm for the lever, a roll of modelling clay for the fulcrum, a ruler for the lever arms, a wooden block for a weight.

Getting started
Ask the children to give you examples of machines. Look for examples such as washing machines, tumble driers, food processors, cars, lifts. Tell the children that machines are devices which make it easier to do work such as, for example, washing and drying clothes, travelling or going up and down buildings. Say that machines have mechanisms that make them work. Some of the simplest machines have very simple mechanisms but they all do the same thing, they make work easier to do.

Class activities
- Ask the children to hold the rulers vertically, raise the object in the bag 5 cm and note the force used. Ask them to make a ramp to the height of 5 cm, drag the object up to the top of the ramp and measure the force used. Ask them to compare the two forces and suggest a reason for the difference. They may need steering to the idea that the smaller force had to work over a longer distance. Ask them to make a plan to investigate the effect of ramp length on the lifting force used. Look for repeating measurements.
- Say that a slightly more complicated machine is the lever. Show the children that a lever has a pivot, or 'fulcrum', and an arm on each side of it. Issue the lever equipment and ask them how a lever may help lift something. Ask them to devise and carry out a test. Say that they must only use the feel of their push on the lever as the observation.
- Tie a small weight to a string and put the string over the beam. Ask a child to pull the string and ask the class to identify the force between the beam and the string (friction). Now put the string through the pulley and ask the child to pull it again. Ask if it is easier or harder (it will be easier due to the reduction of friction). Note that the distance raised by the weight is the same as the distance moved by the rope on the other side of the pulley. Now show the children the two pulley system and ask the child to pull the weight again. It should feel even easier to pull but point out that more rope is pulled through the system showing that the smaller the force, the longer it must be applied.
- Show the class some gear wheels and ask the children what they are. Show the film about gear wheels (see Useful websites) and use it to simulate making gear wheel combinations using technology equipment. (See Cross curricular links.)

Plenary
Let the children present their results. They should find that the longer the ramp, the smaller the force needed to lift but the greater the distance over which the force must be applied. They should find that the longer the lever arm, the smaller the force needed to raise the weight but the greater the distance travelled by the end of the lever.

Further lesson ideas and activities

1. Discuss the use of units called 'newtons' to measure a force as outlined in the interesting facts section. Show the children a force meter and say that this was invented following the discovery of another scientist called Robert Hooke who found that a spring could be used to measure the pull of a force. Let the children observe the scale on the force meter then attach a plastic bag to its hook. Estimate the weight of an object, put it in the bag and test the prediction.
2. The weight of an object is due to the pull of gravity on it. In idea 1, the weights are a measure of the pull of gravity so if an object weighs 5N the pull of gravity on the object is 5N. The Moon's gravity is six times weaker than the Earth's gravity and the gravity on Mars is three times weaker. Challenge the children to find out the weight of the objects they have measured on the Moon and Mars.
3. Let the children find out how high they can jump and then calculate how high they could jump on Mars and the Moon where the pull of gravity is three and six times weaker respectively.
4. Let the children use secondary sources to find out about streamlined shapes, streamlined vehicles, and streamlined boats.

Cross curricular links

- Lesson 1 could be used in a topic on space.
- In lesson 2, the research on steamlined shapes may be linked to a technology project.
- Lesson 3 can be linked to a design and technology project in which pulleys and gears are used.
- You may like to use the lesson activities 3 and 4 to provide a seamless link into a technology project.

Year 6: Living things and their habitats

What does the curriculum say?

- *Describe how living things are classified into broad groups according to common observable characteristics and based on similarities and differences, including micro-organisms, plants and animals.*
- *Give reasons for classifying plants and animals based on specific characteristics.*

What do I need to know?

Algae have been studied in years 1 and 4 as one of the groups in the plant kingdom. Here, in Year 6, micro-organisms that have bodies made from a single cell are studied, and there is some debate among scientists as to the grouping of algae. Some say they should be placed in the Protista (also known as the Protoctista) group, since many algae have single-celled bodies; but some algae cells form plant-like structures (such as the seaweeds), so here they are grouped with plants.

When discussing germs (disease-causing bacteria), the topic of viruses may be raised. Viruses are not considered to be living things. They can be stored in bottles for years like crystals and only reproduce (one of the signs of life) when they enter cells, make copies of themselves from the materials available, and destroy the cells and cause disease.

There are more groups of invertebrates than are mentioned in lesson 3. Two more groups they will encounter in Key Stage 3 are flatworms (sometimes seen as black almost tealeaf-like bodies on the surface of ponds) and round worms (some small ones can sometimes be seen making thrashing movements in pond water).

It is important to establish the concept of the species here as it is used extensively in the development of the theory of evolution in chapter 3. In the Scientific Revolution of the 15th–18th centuries people moved away from explaining phenomena in terms of magic and supernatural occurrences and looked at the world more critically. In order to do this they needed to sort out the things they were studying into groups for easier reference as their investigations began and they tried to explain the world more rationally. During this time sailing ships were exploring the planet and bringing back samples of living things never seen before by the emerging scientists in Europe. The task was to fit in these new discoveries with plants and animals that were already known so it was decided to arrange them into groups based on the features or characteristics of their bodies. First living things were grouped on one or major features that their bodies possessed – such as bones. This, for example, made it easier to classify a new animal if it had bones. It could be put in the vertebrates. Other features it possessed would then put it in the mammal group and so on. Over time a system of classification was developed world wide in which individual species are identified by names made mainly from the Latin and Greek languages which are understood by scientists everywhere rather than using local names which vary from place to place.

Vocabulary

Antennae: flexible limbs growing out of the head which have sensory organs for touch, smell and taste. They are commonly called 'feelers'.
Arachnid: an arthropod with eight legs and no antennae or wings.
Arthropod: an invertebrate with a hard, external skeleton and with jointed limbs.
Crustacean: an arthropod with two pairs of antennae (e.g. woodlice, shrimp).
Insect: an arthropod with six legs which can be wingless or have up to two pairs of wings.
Myriapod: an arthropod with a long, flat body (centipede), or a cylindrical body (millipede) with one pair of antennae and many legs.
Species: a group of living things which have a large number of similarities and few differences and the males and females are able to breed and produce offspring that can also breed.

Progression

This area of study builds on the work on classification in Key Stage 1 and in Year 4. It can be used in Year 6 chapter 3 when considering evolution.

Lesson 1 Making keys

Working scientifically skills: Identifying evidence that has been used to support or refute ideas or arguments
Scientific enquiry type: Identifying, classifying and grouping

You will need: 'animal' pictures (see Preparation) on the whiteboard; printed pictures of an orb spider, a harvestman, a fly, a butterfly and a leech for each group, and live specimens of an earthworm, a slug, a snail, and a woodlouse for each group (see Technical tips).
Preparation: On the whiteboard, before the lesson, you will need to show pictures of three animals with circular bodies: the first has short antennae sticking out of the top, the second has long antennae and the third has curly antennae. Also show three animals with the same variation in antennae but with oval bodies. Mix the pictures up on the screen.

Getting started
Ask how you can tell a dog from a cat. Look for answers about body size and shape, use of the tail, sounds, etc. Say that the children have been using differences to separate the two. Scientists use this technique when they are sorting living things into groups. Ask why a lion and a tiger are called 'big cats' and look for an answer about having the same head shape, teeth arrangement and retractable claws as domestic cats. Say that this time the children were looking for similarities, which is another observation skill scientists use.

Class activities
- Present the screen full of the mixed up animal pictures you have prepared, and ask the children to sort them into groups. Ask them to label their groups A (circular body/short antennae), B (circular body/long antennae), C (circular body/curly antennae), D (oval body/ short antennae), E (oval body/long antennae), and F (oval body/curly antennae).
- Remind the children that in their observations they looked for similarities and differences. This would take time when identifying animals in their habitats, so keys are made to help speed up identification. The children will have made keys in Year 4 so give them a few minutes to see if they can make their own for these animals, then show them the 'Animal' key on page 170. Demonstrate how quickly an animal can be identified using the key.
- Challenge each group to make an animal assortment like yours but they can add more shapes and features to increase complexity if they wish. When the picture of the animal assortment has been made, ask the children to swap their pictures, arrange the animals into groups and then make a key to identify them.
- Issue the pictures and live specimens of animals and ask the children to make a key. Their keys should look something like the following. Look for the initial division into hard and soft bodies, then winged and non-winged hard-bodied animals, segmented and un-segmented soft-bodied animals and finally sorting by wing number (fly or butterfly); sucker/no sucker (leech or earthworm); shell/no shell (snail or slug). (See the 'Body' key on page 169).
- Point out that in the 'Animal key', the major types of animals are separated and then subdivided further. Say that when the organisms at the end of the key cannot be further subdivided, these organisms are identified as a species. The butterfly key studied in Year 4 is another example of this. (See Further lesson ideas and activities 1.)

Plenary
Let the groups swap animal pictures and keys, assess how easy each key is to use and report to the class. Show the picture of the mudpuppy (see Useful websites). Ask the children to identify the animal group to which it belongs and give reasons (e.g. amphibian: no scales, hair or feathers, gills like a tadpole).

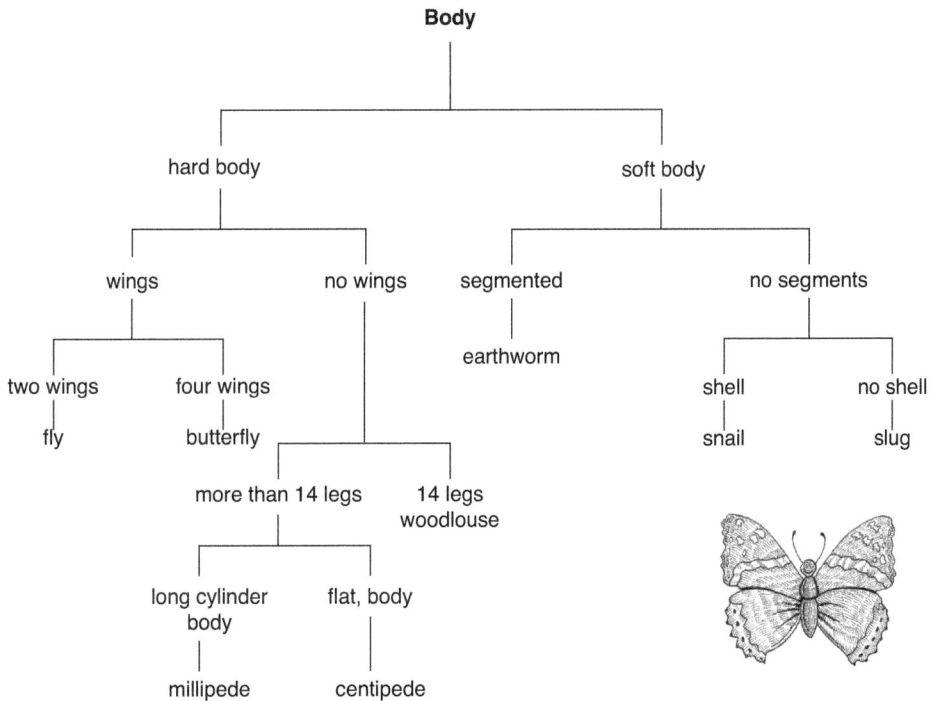

Body

hard body — soft body

hard body: wings — no wings

wings: two wings — four wings

two wings: fly

four wings: butterfly

no wings: more than 14 legs — 14 legs woodlouse

more than 14 legs: long cylinder body — flat, body

long cylinder body: millipede

flat, body: centipede

soft body: segmented — no segments

segmented: earthworm

no segments: shell — no shell

shell: snail

no shell: slug

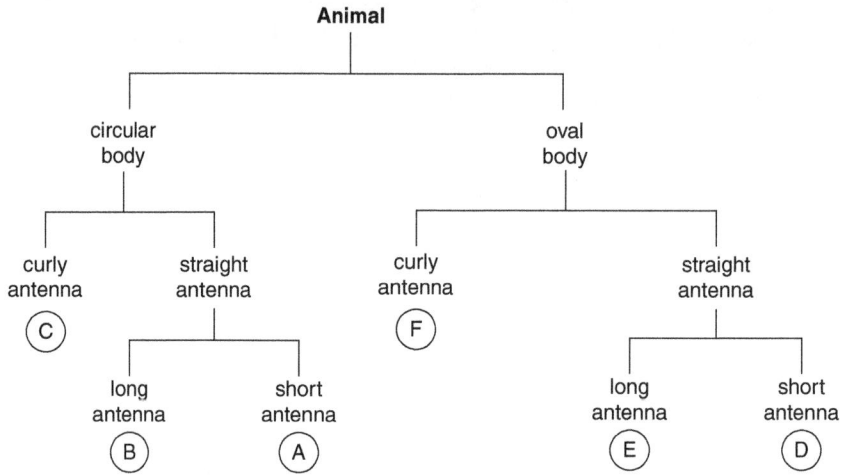

Animal

- circular body
  - curly antenna (C)
  - straight antenna
    - long antenna (B)
    - short antenna (A)
- oval body
  - curly antenna (F)
  - straight antenna
    - long antenna (E)
    - short antenna (D)

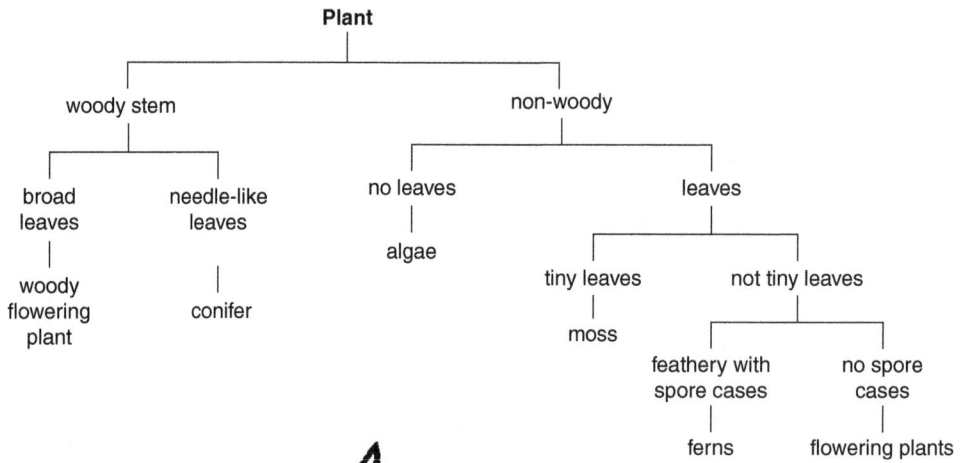

Plant

- woody stem
  - broad leaves
    - woody flowering plant
  - needle-like leaves
    - conifer
- non-woody
  - no leaves
    - algae
  - leaves
    - tiny leaves
      - moss
    - not tiny leaves
      - feathery with spore cases
        - ferns
      - no spore cases
        - flowering plants

Lesson 2 Kingdoms of living things

Working scientifically skills: Planning different types of scientific enquiries to answer questions, including recognising and controlling variables where necessary; taking measurements using a range of scientific equipment, with increasing accuracy and precision; taking repeated readings where appropriate; recording data using classification keys
Scientific enquiry type: Observing over time; pattern seeking; Identifying, classifying and grouping

You will need: a large, open mushroom cap set up, gills-side down, on a white card (set this up the day before the lesson). Each group will need an open mushroom cap, white paper and a shelf, slime in a closed container (from a pond or from a stone), a piece of moss, a fern in a pot, a non woody flowering plant in a pot, a twig of a broadleaved tree in leaf, a twig of a conifer with leaves.

Getting started
Tell the children that living things can be grouped into five kingdoms – Monera, Protista, Fungi, Plant and Animal. Say that in this lesson they are going to consider the first four kingdoms. The first three kingdoms can be put in a group called micro-organisms as most of these have microscopic bodies.

Class activities
- Say that in the Monera group are organisms called 'blue-green algae'. They live on the surface of ponds and, in large numbers, make the surface look oily and give it a blue/green sheen. Say that bacteria are also in this group. Many live in soil and break down dead plants and animals but some live in people and cause disease. We call these bacteria 'germs'. Say that a bacterium can double its numbers every 20 minutes. Say that one bacterium has floated into your mouth and landed at the back of your throat. Ask how many there will be in 20 minutes (two). Ask the children to work out how many there will be in an hour (eight) and every hour afterwards for ten hours. Say that as the numbers build up, the effects of the poisons they make cause disease.
- Say that the Protista group is made up of single celled organisms like the amoeba and the ciliates. Show the pictures of the amoeba and ciliates (see Useful websites 2 and 3). You may like to point out that, even though the ciliates are only made from one cell, they are complicated organisms.
- Show the children some mushrooms and say that they are fungi and it might seem surprising that they can be considered as micro-organisms. Present the mushroom cap and ask a child to lift it up. Point out that a pattern of the gills has been made on the card by spores, which are the micro-organism stage in their life cycle. In Further idea 2, the children can try this experiment for themselves. Say that many fungi really are microscopic and show them the picture of yeast cells (see Useful website 3). Show them some dried yeast and ask how they could see if it was alive, look for an answer about providing water and food (in the form of sugar) and let them set up an experiment (see Technical tips). Ask how they could check if temperature could affect the yeast and let them try again with water at different temperatures checked by a thermometer. They may measure the height of the froth against temperature.
- Say that from the fifteenth century onwards adventurers brought back specimens that biologists had to sort out and make identification keys for. Give each group the selection of plant specimens (or access to them online) and ask them to produce a key to identify each type. (See Further lesson ideas and activities 3.)

Plenary
Let the children present their keys and compare them with the one on page 159. Ask them about their knowledge and thoughts on micro-organisms.

Lesson 3 The animal kingdom

Working scientifically skills: Reporting and presenting findings from enquiries in oral and written forms such as displays and other presentations
Scientific enquiry type: Identifying, classifying and grouping; researching using secondary sources

You will need: the internet resource listed for this chapter in the Useful websites section. Each group will need access to secondary sources to find out about invertebrates and vertebrates in different parts of the world such as oceans, sea shores, rainforests, mangrove swamps, deserts, grasslands, tundra.

Getting started
Remind the children about the mudpuppy they studied at the end of lesson 1 and perhaps show it again. Remind them also of looking for differences and similarities in their observations of the bodies of living things to help classify them. Say that this approach to making observations allows living things to be divided into kingdoms. Then, within a kingdom, more groups can be separated out to help with identification.

Class activities
- Ask the children what invertebrates are (animals without a backbone) and to name the major groups (jellyfish, annelid worms, arthropods, molluscs, and echinoderms). Write these groups on the board. Say that within each group, more subgroups can be made. Ask the children to say what distinguishes arthropods (they have an external skeleton and jointed legs) and suggest how the group can be further subdivided (insects, arachnids, crustaceans and myriapods).
- Say that these groups can be divided further and explain that the arachnids can be divided up into groups such as mites, spiders and scorpions. Explain that there is a system of grouping after Kingdom. So, we have a scorpion in the phylum *Arthropoda*, the class *Arachnida*, the order *scorpiones*. Then there are further groupings of scorpions into families and then families into smaller groups, each one called a 'genus' and finally separated into a type called a 'species'. Show the picture of the Emperor Scorpion and point out its scientific name which is built up from its genus name, *Pandinus*, and its species name, *imperator*. These names are made for the Latin and Greek languages which scientists first used because they could be widely understood.
- Challenge the children to find out about three invertebrates from different parts of the world. They should aim to give each their common name, their scientific name and details of each invertebrate's habitat.
- Ask the children what vertebrates are (animals with a backbone) and to name the major groups (fish, amphibians, reptiles, birds and mammals). Point out that these big groups are further subdivided. For example, fish are divided into cartilaginous fish and bony fish and reptiles are divided into snakes, lizards, crocodiles and turtles. All living things have a generic name and a species name which is used to identify them.
- Challenge the children to find out about three vertebrates from different parts of the world. They should aim to give each their common name, their scientific name and details of each vertebrate's habitat.

Plenary
Let the children present their research on invertebrates and vertebrates from around the world. (See Further lesson ideas and activities 4.)

Further lesson ideas and activities

1. The children could use secondary sources to find out about the work of Carl Linnaeus.
2. Give each group an open mushroom cap and white paper. Ask them to put the cap gills down on the paper and leave it on a shelf over night. They should confirm the result of your demonstration in lesson 2. The children might also like to try this experiment at home. Encourage them to use magnifying glasses to study the spores in detail.
3. The children could use their key in a habitat to check the key's suitability for identifying the major types of animals there. The children could also use it to work out the frequency of the different types of animals in a habitat and draw up a league table. You could challenge them about which is the most dominant and/or influential animal in a habitat. In a field, grass keeps the numbers of other similar sized plants very low. But in a wood, the presence of trees provides shade which prevents large numbers of grass plants from growing.
4. The children could extend this study to plants around the world, looking at different habitats such as the desert, rainforest, tundra, or swamp and selecting a plant from each environment to find its scientific names and details of its life.

Cross curricular links

- If the children have a school conservation area they could survey it, identify the plants and animals, photograph them and label with common and scientific names, then make a display board to be erected near the area.
- If the children are making a study of a country or continent they could enrich it by producing a species list of 20 plants and animals with common and scientific names. They could also find out the largest animal, bird etc. in the area they are studying.
- On a week-long activity week at a residential centre they could spend some time identifying and classifying the plants and animals in the grounds.

Year 6: Animals, including humans

What does the curriculum say?

- *Identify and name the main parts of the human circulatory system, and describe the functions of the heart, blood vessels and blood.*
- *Recognise the impact of diet, exercise, drugs and lifestyle on the way their bodies function.*
- *Describe the ways in which nutrients and water are transported within animals, including humans.*

What do I need to know?

Note that lesson 3 should be handled with sensitivity due to the various family circumstances of the children.

The amoeba lives in ponds. It has a central command centre called the nucleus which co-ordinates all its activities. It feeds by flowing projections called pseudopodia around food and trapping it in a bubble of water, called a vacuole, where digestion takes place. The undigested food is released when the bubble reaches its surface and pops it out. Water passes into the body through its surface and the amoeba prevents being diluted and swollen up by having a special bubble, called a contractile vacuole, which collects the water and pops it out.

Sea anemones have two layers of cells, stinging tentacles which catch prey and push it into the digestive cavity. Undigested food is vomited back out of the mouth. The jellyfish, a relation of the sea anemone, has a similar feeding strategy but also has a system of tubes which distribute materials (a very simple circulatory system). Other animals including earthworms and insects have simple circulatory systems while vertebrates have one based on a single pumping heart. The purpose of a circulatory system is to deliver food and oxygen to all the cells of the body and take away their wastes such as carbon dioxide.

The diet is the variety and quantity of food eaten regularly over a period of a week or a month. It should provide all the nutrients in the correct quantities for health. If any of the nutrients are missing or in short supply (such as iron deficiency causing anaemia) or are present in excess of needs (such as sugar damaging teeth and being converted to fat for storage) the health of the body will be affected.

Our bodies are designed for an active life so we need to take plenty of exercise. It helps to strengthen muscles, heart muscle, ligaments which attach bones together at joints, improve circulation of the blood, and breathing.

There are two kinds of drugs: 1) medicinal drugs which are taken to alleviate suffering and improve recovery from illness and injury. They are taken in the form of a course of medication which should be followed to aid recovery; 2) recreational drugs which are taken to achieve altered mental states which may result in ill health. There is no course of medication, just the user's choice, which can result in overdosing leading to death or the build up of body damage due to the large amounts of harmful chemicals consumed. These drugs are also addictive. Alcohol and nicotine are included in this group.

Vocabulary

Artery: a blood vessel which carries blood away from the heart. It has a thick wall to stand up to the pressure generated by the pumping action of the heart.

Breathing rate: the number of breaths (one inspiration and one expiration) per minute.

Capillary: a tiny blood vessel which connects an artery to a vein. It has a very thin wall so substances like food and oxygen can move quickly from the blood to the cells.

Circulatory system: a collection of interconnecting tubes which move a fluid around the body of an animal.

Liver: an organ of the body that destroys poisons such as alcohol that may be taken into the blood. It also has many functions in keeping the body alive.

Pulse rate: the number of pulse beats per minute.

Vein: a blood vessel which carries blood to the heart. It has thinner walls than the artery because the blood is at lower pressure, due to its passage through the capillaries, and has valves which stop the blood flowing backwards.

Progression

This area of study builds on the work in Year 5 on life cycles and the development of the body. You may like the children to study this biology topic first in Year 6 as it follows on by looking more closely at life processes and body maintenance. It provides information that children can use to develop healthy life styles into the future.

Technical tips

In lesson 2, make sure the exercise is only moderate such as walking for two minutes and running for two minutes. There should be no element of competition and stairs should not be used. The exercise may not be suitable for some children. The heart beat cannot be controlled at will but the mind has greater control over the breathing rate. The children should just breathe naturally at all times and not attempt to hold their breath to modify results.

Take the pulse by holding out the right hand palm uppermost. Put the first two fingers of the left hand on top of the skin on the wrist towards the side of the thumb and feel around to find the pulse.

Useful websites

Lesson 1: www.microscopy-uk.org.uk/mag/wimsmall/sundr.html
fineartamerica.com/featured/a-beautiful-sea-anemone-in-shades-george-grall.html
www.askdrmarisela.com/wp-content/uploads/2013/05/jellyfish.jpg

Lesson 1 The circulatory system

Working scientifically skills: Planning different types of scientific enquiries to answer questions; taking measurements; using a range of scientific equipment, with increasing accuracy and precision; taking repeating readings where appropriate
Scientific enquiry type: Observing over time; pattern seeking; fair test

You will need: a picture of the human digestive system, a balloon pump and balloon; for each group: an earthworm in a dish, a magnifying glass, a stopwatch.

Getting started
Remind the children about their work on bodies being made of cells last year. Say that there are some living things which have a body of only one cell. They are microscopic and scientists have studied them as they are the simplest forms of life. Show them the picture of an amoeba (see Useful website 1) and use the background information to talk about it. Say that most other animals have bodies made of many cells. One of the simplest of this type are sea anemones. Show them the picture of a sea anemone (Useful websites, resource 2) and use the background material to talk about it. Say the jellyfish is like an upside down, free swimming sea anemone, and that it also has a very simple circulatory system. Say that other animals have more complicated ways of moving food and liquids in their bodies.

Class activities
• Issue the earthworms and magnifying glasses and let the children look for evidence of the moving of food or the moving of blood. They should do this by looking closely at the skin – they should see movements of the food along the food canal. Point out the movement of blood moving in a circulatory system.
• Remind the children about their work on digestion and show them a picture of the human digestive system on the visualiser. Revise the work they did on this topic in Year 4.
• Let the children look at the underside of their forearms for blood carrying tubes which provides evidence of a circulatory system.
• Use a balloon pump to partially inflate a balloon and explain how the pump works by taking in air, stopping it flowing back out and pushing it forwards into the balloon. Clench your fist, place it in the middle of your chest and say that the human circulatory system has a pump called the heart which is roughly the size of your fist. Let the children copy you then say that, as it beats, it pushes blood around the body. Slightly unclench and clench your fist to illustrate the pumping action of the heart. Let the children do the same.
• Say that the action of the heart produces a vibration called a pulse in the blood vessels, called arteries. Point out that one artery can be found on the underside of the wrist. Show the children how the take the pulse (see Technical tips) then issue stopwatches and let them see if it changes when the body is lying flat or standing upright. Say that the pulse is measured in beats per minute, but they can take the pulse for 15 seconds and multiply by four if they wish.

Plenary
Let the children present their results from their enquiry. Look for repeating measurements and that the pulse is slightly raised when standing up. Ask for an explanation and look for an answer that the body is doing more work against gravity and so the cells need more food being delivered to provide energy to do it.

Lesson 2 Exercise

Working scientifically skills: Planning different types of scientific enquiries to answer questions; taking measurements; using a range of scientific equipment, with increasing accuracy and precision; taking repeating readings where appropriate
Scientific enquiry type: Observing over time; pattern seeking; fair test

You will need: Each group will need a stopwatch, a safe area in which to walk and run (i.e. without obstructions).

Getting started
Remind the children about their work on muscles and bones in Year 3. Let them feel their biceps and triceps as they move their forearm up and down and say that the muscles need energy from the food to make them work. Say that the heart pumps the blood in one direction along the blood vessels. Arteries take the blood away from the heart. They divide up into tiny blood vessels, called capillaries, in organs like the muscles. Then the capillaries join together again and deliver blood into the veins which take blood back to the heart. (See Further lesson ideas and activities 1 and 2.)

Class activities
*   Remind the children about the pulse activity in the last lesson and ask them how they think the pulse will beat during activity and to explain their reason. Look for an answer that it will increase because the muscle cells need more food for energy. Let the children plan an investigation to test their ideas. It should have the pulse at rest, after walking, after running (see Technical tips).
*   Say that the body needs oxygen to release energy from food. Discuss where the oxygen comes from (the air) and how it gets into the body (through breathing) and where it goes in the body. For this you need to show the children the position of the lungs in the chest. Refer to the pulmonary vein bringing oxygenated blood to the heart to pump out through the aorta to go round the body. Say the veins bring deoxygenated blood back to the heart to be pumped through the pulmonary artery back to the lungs. Mention the need to get rid of carbon dioxide as it is a poison produced when food is broken up to release energy.
*   Using their knowledge from step 2, ask the children to describe how they think the breathing rate might change during exercise and to explain their reason. Look for answers about the breathing rate increasing due to the need for more oxygen to release energy and the need to get rid of the extra carbon dioxide produced as the food is broken up to release energy.
*   Ask the children to plan an investigation about how exercise may affect breathing rate (see Technical tips). Check their plans and if you approve let them carry them out.

Plenary
Let the children present the results of the exercise investigations into pulse rate and exercise and breathing rate and exercise. They should find that both rates increase with exercise. (See Further lesson ideas and activities 3.)

Lesson 3 Keeping healthy

Working scientifically skills: Presenting findings from enquiries in oral and written forms such as displays or other presentations
Scientific enquiry type: Researching using secondary sources

You will need: a shopping bag with the following items: pasta, rice, bread, potatoes, sugar, sweets, butter, cheese, chocolate, biscuits, meat, chicken, fish, eggs, peas, beans, lentils, oranges, apples, pears, plums, cabbage, cauliflower, carrots, swedes, tomatoes, onions. Each group will need appropriate information resources on diet, exercise and drugs.

Getting started
Say that in the last lesson the energy in food was mentioned but food is needed for other reasons. Remind the children that they studied food in Year 3 and here you are going to see how much they remember. Ask them why food is needed and look for the answers 'energy', 'growth' and 'health'. Empty the bag of food and work with the children to put the food into appropriate groups.

Class activities
- Ask if it is good to eat as much of any of the foods as you like and look for an answer about it being unhealthy to eat too much of some foods. Ask why you should not eat too much sugar (it damages teeth and, stored as fat, increases weight which puts strain on bones, joints and the circulatory system). Ask why too much fat should not be eaten (it increases weight which puts strain on bones, joints and the circulatory system). (See Further lesson ideas and activities 4.)
- Say that exercise helps to keep the body healthy. It strengthens the muscles, including heart muscle, helps circulation, and strengthens bones and joints. Ask the children to think about the exercise they take. This should include walking to school, playing in the school yard, playing games, swimming, dancing or going on hikes.
- If the children have already done Further idea 3 about smoking, you could remind them of it now. If not, you could say that smoke stops the windpipe working properly and makes it difficult to clear dust from the lungs so smokers have to cough. This can lead to bronchitis, emphysema and throat and lung cancer. Add that cigarette smoke also contains nicotine which is a drug that makes people want more.
- Say that alcohol is also a drug and makes people uncoordinated and accident prone which can lead to injury. Long term use of alcohol over years can cause fatal liver damage. Say that some substances called recreational drugs, such as cannabis and heroin, cause sleepiness, confusion and brain damage. (See Further lesson ideas and activities 5.)
- Let the children research appropriate resources on diet, exercise and drugs and work out a healthy life style. They could then compare that with their own in terms of diet and exercise and think of ways they could make a healthier life style if necessary.

Plenary
Ask the children to present persuasive arguments to stop people eating unbalanced diets, taking no exercise, smoking, drinking alcohol and taking drugs.

Further lesson ideas and activities

1. Let the children research the circulatory system and see how the blood vessels are arranged in the human body. They should find that almost all arteries are coloured red because they carry oxygenated blood (except the pulmonary artery) and veins are coloured blue because they carry deoxygenated blood (except the pulmonary vein).
2. Let the children research William Harvey and his discovery about the circulation of the blood.
3. Show the children a piece of sponge and say that it is a little like the structure of the lungs. It must be kept healthy so that it can take in all the oxygen needed and get rid of the carbon dioxide. Ask how the lungs might be damaged and look for an answer about smoking. Issue leaflets appropriate to the children's age and read through them together. You could invite in a health professional to talk about the dangers of smoking.
4. You may like to show pictures of various plates of food or menus and let the children assess them for balance.
5. You may like to invite a health professional in to talk about drug abuse and let the children read leaflets appropriate for their age.

Cross curricular links

- Lesson 2 can be integrated with work in PE and games.
- Lesson 3 can be integrated with a school based keeping healthy project.

Year 6: Evolution and inheritance

What does the curriculum say?

- **Recognise that living things have changed over time and that fossils provide information about living things that inhabited the Earth millions of years ago.**
- **Recognise that living things produce offspring of the same kind, but normally offspring vary and are not identical to their parents.**
- **Identify how animals and plants are adapted to suit their environment in different ways and that adaptation may lead to evolution.**

What do I need to know?

You will need to be sensitive to the circumstances and beliefs of the children when considering variation and heredity in humans and evolution.

Darwin studied many organisms to develop the theory of evolution but his finches are particularly famous. It is believed a species of finch reached the Galapagos Islands, bred, spread out and then the individuals began to explore different food sources. The variation among them allowed some groups to start feeding on insects and others on seeds and, over time, these groups feeding and breeding together formed distinct species. They had developed from the variations in the original species by adapting to different food sources in order to survive.

The bird's beak experiment in lesson 3 gives the children a sense of what it must have been like to be a successful competitor and an unsuccessful competitor in picking up food. The children should put cress seeds in a bowl. The children should use the tweezers as a beak (pecking down not putting them down sideways like chopsticks) for one or two minutes to see how many they can transfer to the second bowl representing the bird's stomach. The pecking should be done first with a blunt pair of tweezers and then with a fine pair of tweezers. The task should be carried out by the same person so that dexterity is not a variable, although all members of the group should take a turn. The data should be recorded in a table.

The key points of the theory of evolution by natural selection are:

- Living things usually produce large numbers of offspring. The numbers of offspring usually greatly outnumber the number of parents.
- Populations in undisturbed habitats remain the same despite the great influx of new individuals.
- As the population remains the same there must be great competition for survival.
- The offspring of a species show variation in a number of features.
- The offspring which survive are those which possess the variations which are best adapted to the conditions in the habitat.

Interesting fact

The earliest fossil record for the camel shows that it lived about 40–45 million years ago and was about the size of a rabbit. By 35 million years ago it had increased to the size of a goat and by 15 million years ago it was almost the size of a llama before evolving into the animals we see today.

Vocabulary

Adaptation: a feature of a living thing which makes it particularly well suited to surviving in a particular habitat.

Artificial selection: this is carried out by farmers and other animal and plant breeders. They select individuals with the variations they wish to breed into a type or variety and let them breed and prevent others from doing so.

Natural selection: the way in which a species within a habitat evolves into another species. It is as if the conditions in the habitat select the individuals with the most suitable adaptations to survive.

Progression

This area of study is the culmination of work on habitats and life cycles in the curriculum. It forms a foundation for further studies in Key Stage 3.

Technical tips

For lesson 1, make a fossil bucket by collecting plastic models of a fish, a frog, a reptile, a bird and a mammal. You may like to paint them all grey to make them look more like fossils. On the outside of the bucket, mark the position of five layers in felt-tip pen. Fill the bucket with sand to the top of the first layer and bury the fish in it. Repeat this process with the frog, reptile, bird and mammal models, until all five 'fossils' are buried in their separate layers. Photocopy two dinosaur skeletons onto card and cut them up into the different bones. Mix them up and put them in a bag for each group.

Useful websites

Lesson 1: www.shutterstock.com/s/rock+strata/search.html
www.skullsite.co.uk/Gila/gila.htm
www.skullsite.co.uk/Cat/cat_lat.htm
Lesson 2: www.fanpop.com/clubs/kittens/quiz/show/426517/litter-kittens-usually-consists
www.hollyireland.com/wp-content/uploads/2013/08/SanDiego-LargeFamily-photography.jpg
Lesson 3: www.worldwildlife.org/habitats/deserts
www.flickr.com/photos/29287337@NO2/5688768704
http://fohn.net/camel-pictures-facts/

Lesson 1 Fossil evidence

Working scientifically skills: Identifying scientific evidence that has been used to support or refute ideas and arguments
Scientific enquiry type: Identifying, classifying and grouping; comparative test

You will need: a piece of basalt, a piece of sandstone, a fossil in a sedimentary rock, a 'fossil bucket' (see Technical tips), a tablespoon, a tray for removed sand, a worksheet with the five layers drawn on to match the layers in the bucket. Each group will need a bag containing the dinosaur skeletons (see Technical tips).

Getting started

Remind the children about how the Earth was made from rock during the formation of the solar system. Remind them of the action of volcanoes spreading rock out onto the planet's surface and show them some basalt. Explain how the action of wind and water broke up the rock and the particles formed sediments which eventually turned to stone. Show them the sandstone. Say that when people looked at rocks in earlier times they found things they could not explain, and show them a fossil embedded in a sedimentary rock. Fossils were thought to be stones that just looked like animals or were made by thunderbolts.

Class activities

- Further studies on rocks showed that they formed layers (see Useful website 1). This led scientists to believe that each layer was set down at a certain time, with the one at the top being the youngest and the one at the bottom being the oldest. They had found a way of comparing time in the past and this gave them a new way of looking at fossils.
- Show the children the fossil bucket. Say that this represents five layers of rock and the class are going to investigate the contents of the 'rock' by digging into it, from the top down. Ask the children to come out in turn and take a few spoonfuls of sand out of the bucket. Eventually one of them will expose a model and should take it out and place it on the appropriate layer of the worksheet. Continue until all five 'fossils' have been found.
- Ask the children what this fossil record shows and look for an answer that the fish lived before the frog and so on. Next to the frog on the sheet, draw some fish; next to the reptile, draw some fish and frogs; next to the bird, draw some reptiles, frogs and fish. Say that this is a more realistic representation of what would be found in each layer as animal types from earlier times continued to live on. Ask for suggestions of what it might mean. Look for an answer about some of the fish becoming frogs, some frogs becoming reptiles and some reptiles becoming birds. (See Further lesson ideas and activities 1 and 2.)

- Ask how accurate the model fossils in the bucket are and look for an answer about them not being accurate because only the bones would be left. Say that when the fossils are dug up, the bones may have spread out and mixed with skeletons of other animals. Issue the bags of dinosaur bones and challenge the children to assemble dinosaur skeletons.

Plenary
Let the children present their dinosaur skeletons. Say that sometimes in the past these were not correctly assembled. This led to incorrect ideas about animals that did not exist. Point out that they have yet to consider the mammals from the fossil bucket and ask them to consider which animal group they may have developed from. Steer them through considering the skulls of reptiles and mammals (see Useful websites). Help them to draw the conclusion that some reptiles changed to produce mammals.

Lesson 2 Variation

Working scientifically skills: Taking measurements with increasing accuracy and precision, recording data using bar graphs
Scientific enquiry type: Identifying, classifying and grouping

You will need: the internet resources listed in the Useful websites section, metre rules for measuring height. Each group will need 30 sunflower seeds, a ruler with a millimetre scale.

Getting started
Remind the children that different species cannot interbreed and produce offspring that can breed. Remind them also that they have seen there is fossil evidence that suggests that, over long periods of time, some living things can develop into new kinds of living things. These were questions that scientists thought about and tried to answer. Here is something they considered: when an animal like a cat has a litter of kittens, are they all alike? Expect some anecdotal evidence then display the picture of kittens (see Useful website 4). Describe how they vary, noting fur colour and pattern and the shapes of their heads.

Class activities
- Say that we can look at variation in our own species and show them the picture of a family (see Useful website 5). Ask them to look for similarities and differences between the family members. This implies that some of the features we have are inherited or passed down from previous generations.
- Say that we can look for how humans vary in groups that are not related. Ask the children to group themselves by their hair colour and count the numbers in each group. Ask them to group themselves by eye colour. Then ask them to group themselves according to whether they have ear lobes or not and record their numbers.
- Ask them to group themselves according to height and watch as they arrange themselves in a line of increasing height. Point out that this seems to be causing more of a problem than the other variations. In the first three there was a clear difference (e.g. brown or black) but in the last feature there is only a very small difference, perhaps only a couple of centimetres,

between people. Say that when these features are being studied, size groups are made to record the data. Put the size groups on the board: 130–134, 135–139, 140–144, 145–149, 150–155 (or as appropriate). Let the children make a tally chart and then a bar graph of the numbers of people in the class in each size group. (See Further lesson ideas and activities 4.)

- Say that we have seen how variation occurs in animals so we should check with plants too. Issue 30 sunflower seeds to each group. Ask them to look for differences in colour and markings and to group them accordingly. They should then measure seed length and produce size groups using millimetres as the units. They should then produce a bar graph of their findings.

Plenary

Let the children present their bar graphs and details of sunflower seed variation. Conclude with them that these studies show that variation occurs widely in living things. Return to the idea of variations being passed on and say that farmers breed animals together to produce more meat, more milk and more wool. This means that people can control the variation in their domestic animals and produce animals that help provide more food and material for clothing to help the farmers and the people they supply survive (and profit). Say that in the next lesson they are going to see if the same process occurs among living things in the wild.

Lesson 3 Adaptation and evolution

Working scientifically skills: Recording data; presenting findings from enquiries including conclusions; identifying evidence that has been used to support or refute ideas or arguments
Scientific enquiry type: Fair test

You will need: the internet resources listed in the Useful websites section. Each group will need two bowls, a pair of blunt tweezers, a pair of fine tweezers, a stopwatch, at least 50 seeds.

Getting started

Remind the children about the fossil evidence that shows that living things change. Also remind them of the evidence from variation studies showing that the features of the individuals in a species can vary and can be passed to future generations. Say that when scientists make discoveries that seem to be linked they look for ways to prove the link and to understand it better. It was found that the way to link these ideas together was to look at living things in their habitats and see how it was that they could survive there.

Class activities

- One way of doing this is to look at a habitat with extreme weather conditions and see how plants and animals survive there. Show the image of a desert (see Useful website 7) to set the scene then show children the image of the pebble plant (see Useful website 8). Ask the children, if it has come from a typical plant, how has it changed so it can survive in the desert? Look for answers that it has a stem hidden underground, it has wide round leaves with a thick skin to keep water in, it has grown just far enough from the ground to catch sunlight for making food.

They may also point out that the leaves look camouflaged to stop them being eaten. Say that all these changes from the basic plant types they have studied are called 'adaptations'.

- Show the children the picture of the camel (see Useful website 9) and talk about how a camel has features to help it survive in the desert. Point out that it is adapted to surviving sandstorms by having muscles to close its nostrils and eyelids to keep sand from its eyes. It has strong teeth for feeding on tough desert plants and a fatty hump which stores energy from food for use when it cannot find any. It can drink up to 100 litres of water in only ten minutes and travel over 100 km without drinking again. It has wide webbed feet to stop it sinking in the sand and thick foot pads to insulate it from the hot sand. The long legs also keep its body high above the hot sand to prevent overheating. Say that fossil evidence shows that its ancestors were rabbit shaped and rabbit sized and ask what changes must have taken place as the camel adapted to desert life.

- Say that not only must living things be adapted to the weather conditions of their habitat they must also be adapted to survive and compete with other living things for food. Say that they are going to model this with the following experiment. They will use two dishes, blunt tweezers (to replicate a blunt beak), fine tweezers (to replicate a pointed beak), and a stopwatch to test the efficiency of the beaks in picking up the seeds (see the background information on page 180).

Plenary

Let the children present their beak experiment results. They should show that the blunt beaks are better at picking up seeds. This means that the bird with the fine beak must seek another food source or it will die and its kind would become extinct. The fine beak is particularly adapted for inserting into cracks in bark to find insects so the bird and its kind survive and in time the two kinds of birds evolve into two different species. (See Further lesson ideas and activities 5.)

Further lesson ideas and activities

1. Ask the children to look at a picture of a fish and a newt (which is related to a frog) and describe how they are similar (they are the same basic shape and their limbs and fins are in similar positions). Ask how they are different (the newt has not got scales). Ask how the fish could turn into a newt (its fins became legs and it lost its scales).
2. Ask the children to look at a picture of a lizard and a bird such as a hen and describe how they are similar (they both have scales on their legs and two pairs of limbs). Ask how they are different (the bird has feathers on most of its body and one pair of limbs are wings). Ask how a reptile could have changed into a bird (most of its scales turned into feathers and the front legs turned into wings).
3. Tell the children that small stones were found in the rib cage of some herbivorous dinosaurs. Ask the children to suggest why they were there. Steer the conversation around to them being in the stomach and that they helped to grind the food down. Say that scientists make models when they cannot investigate directly, so how could the idea be investigated? Steer the discussion towards the idea of having two screw top plastic containers to represent dinosaur stomachs, putting a ripped-up lettuce leaf in each, putting some small stones in one container, securing the tops and shaking both for two minutes. They should find that the stones mash the lettuce and support the idea that the stones in dinosaur's stomachs helped grind food.
4. The graphs for heights should show a wide variation with a peak in the centre. You could say that a similar one could be produced for weights. Say that it is perfectly normal for variation to be like this which may reassure individuals who are at either end of the variation range.
5. The children should use secondary resources to find out about Charles Darwin and Alfred Russell Wallace. They should know the key features of the theory of evolution through natural selection (see the background information on page 180).

Cross curricular links

- Geography field trips could provide an opportunity for fossil hunting following local rules and regulations.
- A study of the Victorians in history could provide an opportunity to look more generally at the lives of Charles Darwin and Alfred Russell Wallace.
- In a creative sculpture session or the making of a monster for a school play an animal could be devised with adaptations to a certain life style of the children's choosing.
- This topic may be integrated with work in religious studies.

Year 6: Light

What does the curriculum say?

- *Recognise that light appears to travel in straight lines.*
- *Use the idea that light travels in straight lines to explain that objects are seen because they give out or reflect light into the eye.*
- *Explain that we see things because light travels from light sources to our eyes or from light sources to objects and then to our eyes.*
- *Use the idea that light travels in straight lines to explain why shadows have the same shape as the objects that cast them.*

What do I need to know?

You may like to look at the background to the chapter on light in Year 3 on page 73.

Evidence for light appearing to travel in straight lines can be found by looking at a beam of light shining through a gap in the curtains into a darkened room. It can also be seen by placing a comb across a torch on a table and switching on to see the lines shine out across the table surface.

If an object is put in front of a light source such as a torch, you cannot see it because the light rays cannot bend around the object. They travel in straight lines and are stopped by the object. We see almost all objects around us by reflected light. The light travels in a straight line from a light source to an object and light is reflected also in a straight line. If the line of light is directed towards the eye we will see the object reflecting the light.

When light travels from one medium to another, such as from air to water or a transparent solid to air, the light rays change direction in a process called refraction. This is sometimes called 'bending light' but the phrase must be used with caution as the rays change direction once as they move between media. This change is due to the speed of light in the different media. The change in speed produces the change in direction. In a prism the refraction at both surfaces makes the light spread out to produce a spectrum as each colour of light has its own speed.

Sometimes a shadow with a grey fuzzy edge is seen. This happens because some light rays from the source shine at an angle onto the object and some passing the edge of the object go into the dark area. For example, if a light source is large, like a desk lamp, and an opaque object like a pen is some distance from it, then on the desk top you will see a clear dark shadow. This happens because all the light rays from the lamp are stopped by the pen. If you move the pen towards the lamp a grey shadow appears around the edge of the dark shadow. This happens because some of the light rays from the outer part of the light source pass behind the pen at an angle into the dark area and make it lighter. The dark part of the shadow is called the 'umbra' and the lighter part is called the 'penumbra'.

Vocabulary

Angle of incidence: the angle made by a light ray as it strikes a mirror. It is measured from a line running out from the mirror at right angles to its surface.

Angle of reflection: the angle made by a light ray as it is reflected from a mirror. It is measured from a line running out from the mirror at right angles to its surface.

Light source: something which produces light such as the Sun, a flame, a star or an electric lamp.

Opaque: the property of a material which prevents light rays passing through it.

Reflection: the everyday word for a picture of a scene or person seen in a mirror. In science it is the change in direction of a light after striking a surface. It moves back out into the medium such as air through which it was travelling.

Refraction: the changing of direction of light as it passes from one medium such as air into a transparent medium such as glass.

Spectrum: the colours in white light which spread out after passing through a prism.

Translucent: the property of a material which scatters light rays as light passes through.

Transparent: the property of a material which allows light rays to pass straight through it without scattering.

Progression

This area of study builds on the foundation study of light in Year 3 and prepares the children for work on light in Key Stage 3.

Technical tips

For lesson 1, cut out all the slits for making a periscope (see Useful websites) so that the children have to insert the mirrors to make them work.

For lesson 2, use a protractor to draw lines radiating from a point at angles of 30°, 40°, 50°, 60°, 70°, 80° and 90° on a sheet of paper. Stick the paper to the side of a cereal packet so that the lines radiate from the bottom right hand corner up and across the side. This can be done by the children or by you before the lesson.

In lesson 3, filters of red, blue, green and yellow can be made from transparent plastic or cellophane.

Useful websites

Lesson 1: www.exploratorium.edu/science_explorer/periscope.html

Lesson 3: www.youtube.com/watch?v=9eEyTw4wylkanordinary-life.blogspot.co.uk/2012/07/science-project-splitting-light.html

Lesson 1 Investigating lines of light

Working scientifically skills: Planning different types of scientific enquiry to answer questions; reporting and presenting findings from enquiries including oral and written forms such as displays and other presentations
Scientific enquiry type: Comparative tests

You will need: a torch, an object that is simple to draw such as a football; for each group: a card with a slit in it, a torch, a sheet of white paper to display the light ray, four cards (three with holes about 0.5 cm across), modelling clay, a plastic mirror, a ruler, a protractor, a second plastic mirror, a carton with a slit for receiving the mirrors (see Useful websites and Technical tips).

Getting started
Ask the children what they know about light sources. Look for answers about giving out light and for examples such as the Sun, stars, candles and light bulbs. Ask about what happens to light when it strikes a material that is transparent (most passes through), translucent (it passes through but scatters), opaque (it does not pass through). Ask what happens to light that does not pass through a material (it is reflected). Say that they are going to look more closely at light but you will be asking them to use some of this previous knowledge as they carry out investigations to find out more.

Class activities
- Ask about the form in which light leaves a light source and steer the discussion towards light rays. Ask them to say how they could show this and look for an answer about shining a light through a slit. Let the children do this. Issue the four cards (three of which have holes in) and modelling clay and ask them to set up a further demonstration of light travelling in a straight line. They should set up the cards vertically in lumps of modelling clay, line up the three with holes and shine the torch so the light passes through all the holes and makes a spot on the last one, the screen. (See Further lesson ideas and activities 1.)
- Ask how we see things that are not light sources and look for an answer about the light being reflected. Set up a torch shining on an object and ask the children to look at it. Ask them to use a drawing to explain how they could see the object. Look for a light ray (arrow) going from the torch to the object and an arrow going from the object to a person or eye. (See ideas 2 and 3.)
- Ask what the most reflective object is. Look for an answer about a mirror and ask them to show how light is reflected from a mirror. Issue the mirror, ruler, and protractor to go with the torch and let them show how the angle of incidence is the same as the angle of reflection. Ask them if reflected light from one mirror can be reflected by a second and issue a second mirror. Let them discover that this is so. Issue a small toy and ask the children if it is possible to use two mirrors to see an object that is hidden from view. They should make a horizontal version of a periscope.
- Issue the children with the milk cartons you prepared earlier and let them insert the mirrors to make a periscope and then use it. Ask how they could make the periscope taller and look for an answer about joining two or more cartons together and putting mirrors in the top and bottom. Let them try their suggestions.

Plenary
Let the children display their pinhole cameras and periscopes and explain how they work. Let them present reports of their researches on the eye, telescope and microscope.

Lesson 2 Investigating shadows

Working scientifically skills: Planning different types of scientific enquiries to answer questions; recording data and results using tables, bar graphs and line graphs; reporting findings from enquiries including causal relationships
Scientific enquiry type: Comparative tests; pattern seeking

You will need: for each group: a card with a slit in it, a torch, a piece of white paper, a small wooden block, the angle scale (see Technical tips), a domino, a ruler, a torch.

Getting started
Ask the children what they know about shadows. Look for answers about shadows being dark, not having features such as a face, having the shape of the object that cast them, being formed when an opaque object stops light passing, and being produced by an absence of light.

Class activities
- Ask the children to find out about the edge of a shadow by shining light through a slit to make a beam and shining half the beam on a small wooden block. They should see that the shadow has a sharp edge due to light travelling in a straight line. If it didn't the edge would be wavy or blurred (however, see the background information on page 187).
- Let the children shine a torch on a range of objects and compare the shadows of the objects with the object's shape. They can turn the object to make further comparisons. They should make notes in the form of drawings when the shapes are similar or different. For example, they may find the shadow of a cup different from the cup itself if the handle does not cast a shadow. (See Further lesson ideas and activities 4.)
- Tell the children that sometimes scientists make preliminary investigations just to test ideas and then make more detailed investigations using measurements. Ask them about the relationship between the height of a light source and shadow lengths cast by objects. Look for an answer about the higher the light source, the shorter the shadow. Issue the boxes, torches, dominoes and rulers with the angle lines on them. Ask the children to use these to find out a relationship between the angle the light shines onto an object and the length of the shadow produced. Make sure the children record their results in a table. They could also use the data to make a bar or line graph.
- Ask the children to find out if the distance of an object from a light source and a screen affects the size of the shadow. Look for the children setting up a torch shining along the table at an object and the other side of the cereal packet being used as a screen. Let the children record their findings. You may find some produce a written statement and other produce measurements to back up their statements. (See Further lesson ideas and activities 5.)

Plenary
Let the children present the data and conclusions from the investigations. Look for repetition of measurements and ask the children to assess the accuracy of written conclusions against those backed up with measurements.

Lesson 3 Colour

Working scientifically skills: Recording data using tables; using test results to make predictions to set up further comparative tests
Scientific enquiry type: Comparative tests

You will need: the film of the prism (see Useful websites), a red filter, white paper; for each group: a plastic beaker with straight sides, cards, scissors, paper, a pencil, a pair of compasses, a pair of scissors, a set of coloured pens or pencils, access to a camera; coloured filters (see Technical tips).

Getting started
Ask the children to name some colours. Ask them to name the colours of the rainbow. Show the children the film of the white light passing through a prism and producing a spectrum. Say that this works with natural white light from the Sun or the special white light bulb used in the experiment. Tell the children that there is a way to produce a spectrum without a prism and that they are going to try and do it if it is sunny (or leave until a sunny day).

Class activities
- If it is sunny, show the children the film about white light through a prism (see Useful websites). Issue plastic beakers, a card, scissors and paper. Let the children make a slit in the card, fill the beaker with water and place it on a sunny windowsill with the slit close to the beaker on the sunny side. They may have to move the equipment around a little to spot the small spectrum. (See Further lesson ideas and activities 6 and 7.)
- Having established that white light can be split into colours, challenge the children to use a card, a pencil, a pair of compasses, a pair of scissors and a set of coloured pens or pencils to show that the colours can be mixed to make a white light. The children should make a circle on the card using the compasses, divide the circle into sections and colour them in with the colours of the rainbow. You should make a hole in the centre for them, let them insert the pencil and spin it round. This exercise can be filmed.
- Tell the children that when light strikes an object some colours are absorbed and some are reflected. For example, a red sock absorbs all the colours of the spectrum except red which it reflects. Ask why a blue sock appears blue (all colours except blue are absorbed). Ask why a white sock appears white (it reflects all colours). Ask why a black sock appears black (it absorbs all colours).
- Hold up a white sheet of paper. Ask the children about the light being reflected from it (all the colours). Now hold a red filter in front of it and ask what is happening (the filter stops all light coming through except red).
- Issue red filters to the children and let them look at objects around the room. Note their discoveries for later. Let them investigate with blue, yellow and green filters. They may practise predicting what they will see before they make their observations.

Plenary
Let the children present their colour wheels or films of them spinning their colour wheels. Let them report on their investigations into colour filters. Ask a child to make a drawing with red ink and hold it up. Ask the children to predict what they will see when the red filter is put in front of it. They will find the drawing cannot be seen because all the colours are stopped except red and the red light from the picture passes through with it so it cannot be distinguished.

Further lesson ideas and activities

1. Using a pinhole camera applies the knowledge that light travels in straight lines. The children could use a small, long box such as one used for cracker biscuits. They should cut the flaps off each end, stick a piece of tin foil to one end and make a pin prick in it. They should stick greaseproof paper to the other. Hold up the pinhole towards a light source (not the Sun) or a well lit view and look for an image on the greaseproof paper. They should find that it is upside down.

2. Let the children put a plastic straw into a clear plastic beaker of water and look down on it. They should notice that the straw appears to bend when looked at from above and, when looked at from the side, appears to be magnified. Point out that when light passes between transparent materials such as air and water the light rays change direction in a process called 'refraction'. Explain that the curved surface further refracts the light and produces a magnified view of objects. Point out that a magnifying glass works in this way.

3. Let the children use secondary sources to find out how the eye, a telescope and a microscope work.

4. The children should show that the shadow is attached to the object but challenge them to consider whether this is always the case. Steer them towards the idea of clouds casting shadows and let them test the idea when there are clouds in a sunny sky.

5. Let the children make cards in the shapes of figures and faces (with holes for eyes, nose and mouth), mount them on lolly sticks with sticky paper and present a play in a shadow theatre.

6. You may carefully demonstrate that a cut glass vase has prisms in it and when placed in a sunny window can cast spectra in places around the room.

7. Let the children examine a CD in sunlight to find a spectrum. Let them blow soap bubbles and look for spectra in the bubble skins.

Cross curricular links

- The work on periscopes and pinhole cameras may be integrated with work in design and technology.
- The work on shadows and colour can be used in studies in art.
- The work on the shadow theatre can be used to stimulate writing plays in English.

Year 6: Electricity

What does the curriculum say?

- *Associate the brightness of a lamp or the volume of a buzzer with the number and voltage of cells used in a circuit.*
- *Compare and give reasons for variations in how components function, including the brightness of bulbs, the loudness of buzzers and the on/off position of switches.*
- *Use recognised symbols when representing a simple circuit diagram.*

What does the curriculum say?

The first studies on electricity were made on static electricity (see the background information for Year 4 on page 112). Later investigations made by Luigo Galvani (1737–1798) on static electricity and muscles lead to the idea that muscles contained electricity. Alessandro Volta (1745–1827) used Galvani's work as a basis for his own investigations which led to the building of the first battery of cells which generated electricity through chemical reactions. These have been further developed into all the cells we use today.

Once a steady current of electricity could be made, other scientists began to study its effects. In one investigation it was noticed that a wire carrying an electric current make a compass needle move. The relationship between electricity and magnetism was studied by Michael Faraday (1791–1867) and his work led to the development of the electrical generators used in power stations today and the electric motors which are used throughout the world. In a generator, a free spinning magnet is enclosed in a casing of wire. As the magnet spins it generates electricity in the wires which is drawn away and sent through cables underground, or on pylons, to towns and cities where it is needed. The current is sent at a very high voltage for efficiency and then converted to a lower voltage at local substations which carry warnings about danger.

> ### Interesting fact
>
> Lightning is a flow of electricity travelling at 21,000 km per hour between two clouds or a cloud and the ground. It heats the air around it to 30,000°C – 300 times hotter than a boiling kettle – but only lasts for about a second.

Vocabulary

Atom: the particle from which all things are made.
Battery: a group of cells connected together.
Cell: a container, usually a cylinder, which holds chemicals that generate an electric current when the cell is placed in a circuit and the circuit is switched on.
Circuit: a loop made by wires and other components through which electricity can flow when the circuit is switched on.

Component: a part of a circuit such as a wire, cell, or lamp.

Current electricity: electricity which flows in a circuit.

Electron: a particle which forms part of an atom and carries a negative electrical charge.

Negative terminal: the terminal through which electrons flow into a circuit.

Positive terminal: the terminal through which electrons flow from the circuit into the cell.

Series circuit: a circuit in which all the components are arranged in a line.

Parallel circuit: a circuit in which some components such as lamps are arranged side by side.

Resistance: the property of a material to resist the flow of a current of electricity. A high resistance wire only allows a small current to flow. A low resistance wire allows a large current to flow.

Terminal: the end of a cell through which a current of electricity flows.

Voltage: the power of a cell to produce electricity. This power is measured in units called volts. It is a measure of the push of the current not a measure of the size of the current.

Progression

This area of study builds on the foundations established in Year 4. It, in turn, forms foundation work for Key Stage 3.

Technical tips

Some curious children may experiment by arranging lamps side by side to make a parallel circuit. If they do, the lamps will shine with the same brightness because their resistances do not add together to make them dimmer. Parallel circuits are not featured in the National Curriculum until Key Stage 3.

In lesson 2, give out the lamps, cells and wires as they are needed for each activity. Giving them all out at once can lead to unofficial experimentation which will detract from the aims of the lesson.

In lesson 3, make sure the children do not link the motor, the buzzer and the lamp into one circuit. The motor and buzzer must be kept in circuits on their own.

Useful websites

Lesson 1: www.bbc.co.uk/bitesize/ks2/science/physical_processes/electrical_circuits/read/1/

Lesson 1 Circuit diagrams

Working scientifically skills: Using scientific diagrams

Scientific enquiry type: Comparative tests; pattern seeking

You will need: the internet resources listed in the Useful websites section, cards with each electrical symbol drawn on them. Each group will need a cell, three wires, a switch, a lamp, a motor, a buzzer, an extra cell.

Getting started

Ask the children what they know about electricity. First see what they can remember of static electricity then the movement of electrons in an electric current. Ask about the components of a circuit and the care that is needed in joining them up. Ask them about conductors and insulators and about the switches they made in Year 4.

Class activities

- Issue the components for a simple circuit and ask the children to assemble them and make the lamp light. Remind the children of how they made drawings of the circuits they made in Year 4 but now they are going use to symbols to represent each of the components. Show the children the electrical symbols (see internet resources). Show them how the symbols are linked together to make a circuit diagram. Ask them to make a circuit diagram of the circuit they have just made.
- Take in the lamps and replace them with motors. Ask the children to make a circuit with a motor in it, make it spin and then draw the circuit diagram. (See Further lesson ideas and activities 1.)
- Take in the motors and issue the buzzers. Tell the children that the red wire must go towards the positive terminal and the black wire must go towards the negative terminal. Ask the children to make the circuit, make the buzzer sound and draw the circuit diagram.
- Give the children an extra cell and ask them to add it to the circuit. It should be next to the first cell with its positive terminal next to the negative terminal of the first cell. They should be in line. Say that when similar components are arranged in line they are referred to as being 'arranged in series'. Ask the children to predict the change in the sound made by the buzzer (it gets louder) then close the switch. Ask the children to make a circuit diagram. Note that when cells are in series, the symbol for a cell is drawn twice, one after the other.

Plenary

Ask the children how well they can recognise the symbols, flash the cards and ask them to call out what they are. Ask for volunteers to come out and draw circuits they have made on the board. The class could challenge volunteers to draw the circuits they choose. (See Further lesson ideas and activities 2.)

Ask the children how the voltage of the circuit changed when two cells were used. Look for the answer that it was increased or, more accurately, increased from 1.5V to 3V. (See Further lesson ideas and activities 3.)

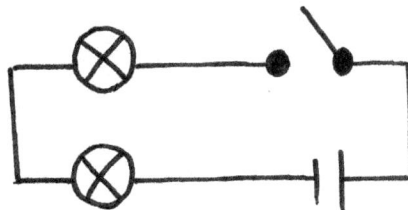

Lesson 2 Changing components

Working scientifically skills: Planning different types of scientific enquiries to answer questions; using scientific diagrams; reporting findings from enquiries including causal relationships
Scientific enquiry type: Comparative tests; pattern seeking

You will need: a diagram of a circuit on the board featuring two cells, a motor, a switch, and associated wires. You will also need the full selection of components set out on a tray. Each group will need three cells, three lamps, a switch, seven wires to connect three cells in series and three lamps in series (see Technical tips).

Getting stared
Show the children the circuit diagram on the board and ask for a volunteer to come out. Select items from the tray, assemble the circuit and show the motor spinning. On your diagram, replace the motor with the buzzer. Ask for another volunteer to come out and assemble the circuit and make the buzzer sound. Ask what would happen if one cell is taken away (less sound is made). Ask why this happens (there is less power in the circuit). Say they have investigated adding cells. Ask the children what happens when the number of lamps is increased. Tell the children they are going to investigate this.

Class activities
- Tell the children that the wire in a lamp has a property called 'electrical resistance'. It resists or tries to oppose the flow of electrons. As the electrons move against this resistance they lose energy as light and heat and this makes the lamp shine and become warm. Ask what might happen when two lamps are arranged in series and the current has to flow through to regions of resistance.
- Ask the children to make a plan to test their prediction and think about how they could record what they see. They might say that a bright lamp has a certain number of light rays coming from it and a dimmer lamp is represented with fewer rays. Or they may suggest photographing the single lamp and the pair of lamps. Some children could suggest that they put a reflecting surface behind the lamp to make its brightness stand out more for the photograph.
- Let the children carry out their enquiry, draw circuit diagrams, present data and draw a conclusion.
- Ask them to predict what will happen when a third lamp is added and then test their prediction, draw a circuit diagram, present their data and draw a conclusion.
- Let the children predict what will happen if the number of cells is increased to two and then three, and then if the number of lamps is decreased from three to one. Let the children carry out their investigations, record their data and draw conclusions.

Plenary
Let the groups of children present their findings to the class in the form of a presentation, perhaps as a demonstration, a slide presentation or a wall display.

Make sure that they realise that increasing the number of lamps increases the resistance of the circuit and makes the lamps shine less brightly; that increasing the number of cells increases the power of electricity in the circuit and makes the lamps shine more brightly; and that decreasing the number of lamps makes the lamp shine even more brightly.

Lesson 3 The electric head

Working scientifically skills: Presenting the findings from enquiries in a novel presentation; using scientific diagrams
Scientific enquiry type: Comparative test

You will need: a collection of switches, space to exhibit the models. Each group will need materials for making the head: a cardboard box, scissors to cut eye holes, coloured paper for different eyes, any material for making hair or hats or scales, sticky paper, modelling clay to hold components (like a motor, buzzer or lamps), wires, switches, lamps, motors (one per circuit), buzzers (one per circuit).

Getting started
Test the children's knowledge of circuits by asking groups to come out to the board and draw a circuit with (1) with a cell, a switch and two lamps; (2) a cell, a switch and a motor; and (3) a cell, a switch and a buzzer. Say that they are going to use these circuits, or modifications of them, in making a model head. The head must have a moving part provided by the motor, a noisy part provided by one or more circuits containing a buzzer and eyes that light up using circuits containing the lamps. Say that a circuit must not have mixtures of components such as a buzzer, motor and lamp, each type of component must be in its own circuit.

Class activities
- Let the children draw pictures of the head they will make and the position of the circuits in the model. They may have a motor to make a bow tie spin in the neck or a motor on top of the head to spin a crown. They may have one to three lamps to make eyes which could be any place on the head. They could have a circuit with a buzzer and a switch that is pressed down when the head is patted or is clicked when the nose or ear is tweaked. Two buzzer circuits could be set up, one for each ear but one with a different number of cells so the head makes a louder 'cry' when one ear is tweaked.
- Let the children make their heads and assemble their circuits and test them. They should make circuit diagrams of the circuits they have made and put them in front of the heads when the heads are put on display.

Plenary
Let the children present their heads and talk positively about each one discussing its appearance (monstrous or cute), the securing of the components and the accuracy of the circuit diagrams. This display could be made available to the whole school.

Further lesson ideas and activities

1. A motor could be used to turn a roundabout made out of cardboard and paper. An almost used up cell may provide a weak current to move the motor slowly.
2. Show the children a picture or actual circuit board from an electrical appliance such as a washing machine to see the complexity of the circuit and the diversity and number of components.
3. You could take the opportunity here to introduce the mains supply saying that it is generated by a spinning magnet surrounded by wire (see the background information on page 193). You could show them a picture showing how electricity reaches homes and schools (see Useful websites). This could lead to considering energy saving strategies.

Cross curricular links

- Work in this topic can be used in school projects on energy saving and on work in design and technology.
- The children could research the work of Galvani, Volta, Faraday, Edison and Marconi as part of a history project.